bake!

bake!

ESSENTIAL TECHNIQUES
FOR PERFECT BAKING

Nick Malgieri

Photographs by

Quentin Bacon

KYLE BOOKS

Published in 2010 by Kyle Books
an imprint of Kyle Cathie Limited
www.kylebooks.com

Distributed by National Book Network
4501 Forbes Blvd., Suite 200
Lanham, MD 20706
Phone: (800) 462-6420
Fax: (301) 429-5746
custserv@nbnbooks.com

Text © 2010 by Nick Malgieri
Photographs © 2010 by Quentin Bacon
Book design © 2010 by Kyle Cathie Ltd

Project editor Anja Schmidt
Designer Dirk Kaufman
Photographer Quentin Bacon
Food Styling Liz Duffy
Prop Styling Roy Finamore
Copyeditor Janet McDonald
Production Lisa Pinnell and
Gemma Jordan

A cataloging-in-publication record
for this title is available from the
Library of Congress

Color reproduction by Sang Choy
Printed and bound in Hong Kong
by C & C Joint Printing Co.

contents

introduction

BAKE! is the book I've always wanted to write. More than 30 years of teaching people how to bake have clearly shown me that the easiest way to learn is to start with a basic recipe or technique and then prepare variations on it. And that's exactly what BAKE! is all about.

Each chapter starts with an Essential Technique—such as brioche dough, high-ratio cake batter, or puff pastry—and the way to prepare that master recipe is shown in step-by-step photographs. Then you can use the master recipe in a variety of ways later in the chapter.

The 20 chapters cover all the main techniques of fine baking, starting with simple pastry dough and moving through puff pastry and Danish pastry, all sorts of breads, quick breads, cakes, and cookies.

Learning "techniques" sounds a little dry and academic, like playing endless scales and other exercises in a music lesson. Nothing could be farther from the truth: once you learn a baking technique (and most of them are really easy to do and easy to master), you'll also reap the benefit of having made something wonderful to enjoy.

Please don't buy into the fallacy that "baking is a science": You'll only wind up intimidating yourself. Hundreds of everyday processes that people often use are also science; driving a car, using a telephone, even grilling a steak can be explained according to strict scientific principles. But we take all those processes for granted and we certainly aren't afraid of them.

Baking needn't be any more difficult than making a phone call; you just need to know what to do in order to do it successfully every time.

And remember, I'm never really too far away if you have a question or want to see a video about one of the techniques. Visit my website, www.nickmalgieri.com, where you'll also find some new recipes based on the techniques in BAKE!

Enjoy, and above all, bake something!

Nick Malgieri

Nick Malgieri
New York City, 2010

ingredients

FLOURS, OTHER GRAINS, STARCHES, AND GELATIN

Flour: Unbleached all-purpose flour is fine for general use, but for the bread recipes, bread flour is preferred. If either may be used, it is stated in the recipe.

Cornmeal: I prefer stone-ground yellow cornmeal for its chewier texture.

Oats: Rolled oats are regular oatmeal, not instant or steel-cut.

Cornstarch: Plain cornstarch is available in the supermarket.

Gelatin: I prefer the powdered gelatin that comes in an envelope since it's the form most widely available.

SUGARS AND SWEETENERS

Sugar: I use plain granulated sugar in all my recipes, never superfine sugar.

Brown Sugar: I call for light and dark brown sugars in this book. The difference between them is the amount of molasses added back to the sugar after it's refined.

Confectioners' Sugar: Confectioners' sugar is finely pulverized granulated sugar. In the United States it has 3% cornstarch added by weight, which is why I never use it in whipped cream.

Corn Syrup: Light corn syrup is used to retain moisture and also impart smoothness in some preparations, such as ganache.

Honey: I buy dark, full-flavored honey but not always one with a fancy pedigree.

Molasses: I use unsulfured molasses, which is milder in flavor than the other type available, which is usually marked "robust flavor." Sometimes the mild type is labeled "light" molasses but this does not refer to its nutritional content.

LEAVENERS

Baking Powder: I use double-acting baking powder, the type sold in most supermarkets. Always check the expiration date on the container.

Baking Soda: Plain bicarbonate of soda—always crush lumps before using.

FLAVORINGS

Salt: I usually use fine sea salt for both baking and seasoning food.

Extracts: Always buy 100% pure extracts.

Whole Bean Vanilla: Look for the best-quality vanilla beans you can find from a reliable source such as Nielsen-Massey (www.nielsenmassey.com).

Ginger: Fresh, crystallized, and ground gingers are used in this book. Don't be tempted to substitute one for another. Each has a unique flavor and texture.

Liquors: A lesser-quality liquor or liqueur can instantly ruin a fine dessert. Here's my advice: If a large bottle of imported rum or other liquor or liqueur is expensive, buy a smaller bottle, rather than buying a lesser brand.

Chocolate: A range of chocolates is used here, including unsweetened, bittersweet, semisweet, and milk chocolates. Remember that a chocolate dessert will only taste as good as the chocolate used to prepare it.

Cocoa Powder: I use alkalized (Dutch process) cocoa exclusively and most supermarkets carry it.

Coffee: Brew triple-strength espresso (3 tablespoons coffee and 3/4 cup boiling water) or use instant espresso.

Jam: Your favorite jam or preserves will work just fine.

NUTS AND NUT PRODUCTS

Nutmeats with the skin on are generally referred to as natural or unblanched. Those with the skins removed are referred to as blanched or skinless. Almonds, pistachios, and hazelnuts (also called filberts) are available both natural and blanched. Pecans and walnuts are not blanched but the skins are so thin that they don't need to be removed.

Store nuts in a plastic bag in the freezer. If you need to grind nuts in a food processor, bring them to room temperature before grinding. Cold nutmeats will clump up and never grind finely enough. Warm ones will turn almost immediately to nut butter.

EGGS

All the eggs called for here are large eggs, 24 ounces (680 grams) per dozen.

DAIRY PRODUCTS

Butter: I use unsalted butter in the recipes here. I never use so-called European or extra-anything butters. All the recipes were tested with plain butter available at the supermarket. If you substitute butter with a higher fat content, you might get different results, especially in cookie batters and pastry doughs. They will have a tendency to spread more and be highly fragile after baking. Butter is probably the most important ingredient in fine baking, so it needs to be fresh to be good. Unwrap a stick of butter and scratch the surface with the point of a table knife. If the butter is lighter colored on the inside than on the outside, it has oxidized and become stale. Such butter won't impart anything but a stale flavor to whatever you bake with it. If you stock up on butter during a sale, by all means store it in the freezer. If you intend to keep it for more than a month or so, wrap the packages in plastic wrap and foil to keep them as airtight as possible.

Milk: When I call for milk, I mean whole or full-fat milk, unless an alternative is indicated.

Buttermilk: Naturally low in fat yet rich in texture, buttermilk lends moisture and tenderness.

Cream: Heavy whipping cream has a fat content of 36%, which is why it whips to a silky and luxurious consistency. When half-and-half is called for, it is traditional half-and-half (about 18% butterfat).

Sour Cream: When I call for sour cream, I mean the full-fat version. Nonfat will not work in some baked goods.

Cheese: Freshly made ricotta and mozzarella taste better and have a better texture than their industrially made counterparts. True Parmigiano-Reggiano knows no substitute.

OILS

Vegetable Oils: When vegetable oil is called for, safflower, peanut, and canola oils will all work fine. Look for "cold-pressed" oil, with the caveat that while in Europe, the term "cold-pressed" is regulated, whereas U.S. manufacturers may label oil as they wish, so the term has less meaning. You will also see oils labeled "expeller-pressed," which means they have been expressed without the use of chemical agents; but this does not necessarily mean the oil has not reached a high temperature during processing, which can destroy its flavor. (It can also make the oil resistant to high heat, desirable at times for cooking but rarely for baking.) Your best bet is to find a brand that you think smells and tastes good and stick with that.

equipment

BAKING PANS

Layer pans: These are round cake pans. Layer pans may be 1½ to 2 inches deep and are always 9 inches in diameter.

A 9-inch layer pan that's 3 inches deep may be used for the baked cheesecake recipe, but a springform pan is also good.

Rectangular Pans: For baking cookies, Danish, or different kinds of large or individual pastries, you can use a cookie sheet or a rectangular jelly-roll pan. These come in a variety of sizes, including 10 x 15-inch and 11 x 17-inch sizes (domestic sizes) and 12 x 17½-inch commercial half-sheet pans. Thin, flexible cookie sheets without sides are useful for moving dough and cake layers and for chilling pieces of dough, in addition to baking cookies. Insulated cookie sheets are worth the expense if your oven has a tendency to burn things on the bottom. Only use them in the bottom of the oven, though. You can also get the same effect by stacking two pans together for baking in the bottom of the oven. A 9 x 13 x 2-inch rectangular pan is called for in some recipes.

Tube Pans: This can be a 1- or 2-piece 16-cup (10-inch) tube pan, or what's commonly referred to as a Bundt pan, also 16-cup capacity.

Loaf Pans: I use 9 x 5 x 3-inch loaf pans, which have a capacity of 7 cups.

Springform pans: A springform pan has two parts: a flat bottom, and a ring that closes with a buckle. All recipes that use springform pans in this book call for 9-inch or 10-inch pans.

Tart Pans: I use a removable-bottom tart pan with fluted sides, sometimes called a French tart pan. Recipes here call for 10-inch and 12-inch pans.

Muffin Pans and Mini Muffin Pans: I use the 12-cavity muffin pans; each cavity in the standard-size pans should hold about ½ cup; the capacity of the cavities in a mini muffin pan is variable. I always line full-size muffin pans with pleated paper liners.

Pizza Pan: The thin-crust pizzas in Chapter 8 are all about 10 inches in diameter. Therefore, you may use anything from a 10- to 15-inch-diameter round pan or even a rectangular cookie sheet or pan that's wider than 10 inches for baking them.

Sauté Pan: The Tarte Tatin on page 59 is made in a 10-inch nonstick sauté pan with sloping (not straight) sides.

HAND TOOLS

Knives: Three knives are essential in every kitchen: a good paring knife, a chopping (or chef's) knife, and a serrated knife for slicing bread and through cake layers. A thin-bladed slicing knife is also useful for slicing cakes and other desserts at serving time.

Spatulas: Small and large offset spatulas are essential for evenly spreading out batters before baking, spreading fillings onto dough, and finishing cakes. I also like to use a wide griddle spatula for moving around finished cakes and desserts.

Graters: A box grater with diagonally set holes, large and small, is better than one that has only holes that look like they were formed by a nail piercing the sheet metal. Microplane and Cuisipro are two brands of graters that come in all sizes and degrees of fineness for grating zests, nutmeg, or cheese or shaving chocolate.

Pizza Wheel: A plain sharp one and a serrated one (sometimes both come mounted on the same handle) are useful for cutting dough and, of course, pizza.

Thermometers: A small instant-read thermometer looks like a dial set at the top of a very long nail. It's useful for determining the internal temperature of dough, for testing doneness, as well as in heated mixtures such as meringue.

Rolling Pin: I prefer the wooden type without handles that is a straight cylinder, about 16 inches by 2 inches.

Pastry Brush: A natural bristle pastry brush works better than one with synthetic bristles. Silicone brushes with thin bristles work well for brushing egg wash or sprinkling syrup on cake layers.

Spray Bottle: A spray bottle is used to spritz the oven when baking certain types of bread. Be careful not to hit the pilot light and knock out your oven heat.

X-Acto Knife or Single-Edge Razor: Either of these blades make nice deep cuts when slashing the tops of breads.

Baking Stone: A baking stone gives your breads a crisp bottom crust, but you can also use an upside-down jelly-roll pan that doesn't warp under intense heat.

Pastry Bag and Tips: Nylon or cloth bags can be cleaned in the top rack of a dishwasher or in a washing machine. I use a ½-inch plain piping tube (Ateco #806) and a ½-inch open star tube (Ateco #824).

PAPERS AND FOIL

Parchment Paper: Try to find parchment paper that comes in large individual sheets, rather than on a roll.

Silicone Pan Liners: These reusable liners are great for anything that spreads. Don't use them as pan liners for general baking. That way they don't get worn out.

Cake Cardboards: These are available in a variety of sizes and shapes. Round ones the same diameter as your cake will make cake finishing a breeze. Rectangular ones make unmolding easy.

MEASURING TOOLS

Liquid Measures: These are usually made from glass or clear plastic and are graduated for fractions of cups. Newer measuring cups make it possible to read the quantity from the top, rather than the side of the cup—a definite improvement. I have several each in 1-, 2-, 4- and 8-cup sizes. Not having to rinse out the cup before measuring another ingredient makes things easier.

Dry-Measure Cups: For measuring dry ingredients such as flour, confectioners' sugar, or cornstarch. Spoon the ingredient into the cup and level it off for accurate measurement. Sugar is the only dry ingredient I scoop when measuring.

Measuring Spoons: Graduated metal measuring spoons are essential. I like to have several sets so that if one gets wet measuring liquid ingredients, there is another set of dry ones waiting.

Scales: There are any number of fairly inexpensive battery-operated scales available. These make quick work of weighing out chocolate or other ingredients measured by weight.

ELECTRICALS

Stand Mixer: A heavy-duty mixer such as a KitchenAid is an essential baker's tool. You could use a heavy-duty handheld mixer, but they are much less convenient. If you are investing in a stand mixer, buy an extra bowl and whisk. They will save you time when you need to whisk several mixtures for a single dessert.

Food Processor: A food processor (fitted with its metal blade) is useful for grinding nuts and mixing doughs.

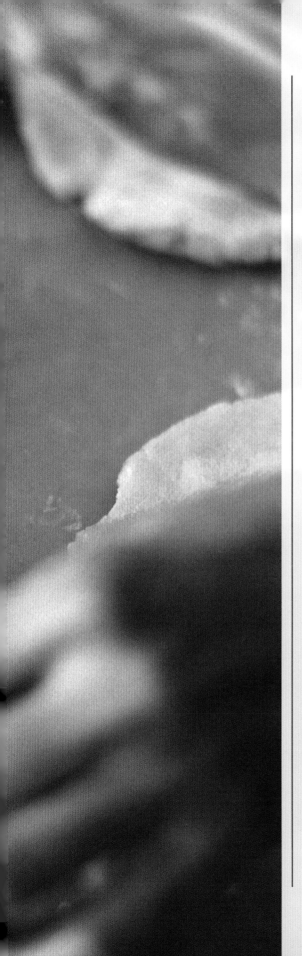

sweet pastry dough & tarts

Sweet-crusted tarts are a welcome dessert, teatime sweet, or snack any time of the year. All the tarts in this chapter are made with a sweet, crumbly crust that is as delicious as it is easy to prepare. And aside from being easy both to mix and to work with, the dough bakes to golden perfection every time. Fillings vary from the humble sweet potato to flavorful combinations of chocolate, nuts, citrus, and other fruit. Serve any of these and you'll quickly gain a reputation as an accomplished baker.

A

B

sweet pastry dough

If you've long shied away from preparing pastry, this is a perfect dough to begin with as you conquer your fear. It's easy both to make and to use, and it always bakes through dry and golden on the bottom, ensuring a successful tart with no filling leaks or inconsistent patches.

Makes about 18 ounces dough, enough for two 10-inch tarts, or the bottom and top crust for a 10-inch tart

2 cups all-purpose flour (spoon into a dry-measure cup and level off)

⅓ cup sugar

½ teaspoon baking powder

¼ teaspoon salt

8 tablespoons (1 stick) unsalted butter, cold, cut into 10 pieces

2 large eggs

1 To mix the dough by hand, combine the flour, sugar, baking powder, and salt in a medium bowl and stir well to combine.

2 Cut each piece of butter into 4 or 5 smaller pieces and add all of them to the bowl.

3 Use both hands, palms upward, to reach under the dry ingredients to the bottom of the bowl, and lift them up through the contents of the bowl several times to distribute the pieces of butter evenly among the dry ingredients (A).

4 Use your fingertips to pinch the pieces of butter into smaller pieces, alternating with rubbing the mixture between the palms of your hands and occasionally repeating step 3. Continue rubbing in the butter until no visible pieces remain and the whole mixture is cool and powdery.

5 Add the eggs and use a fork to break them up. Use one hand to move the bowl back and forth across the work surface in a straight line while you stir up from the bottom with the fork until the dough is almost completely mixed (B).

6 Invert the dough to a floured work surface (C) and gently knead it into a consistent mass (D and E). Continue with step 10.

7 To mix the dough in a food processor, combine the flour, sugar, baking powder, and salt in the work bowl fitted with the metal blade. Pulse several times to mix.

8 Add the butter and pulse repeatedly at 1-second intervals until the butter is finely mixed into the dry ingredients.

9 Add the eggs and pulse again until the dough forms a ball. Invert the dough to a floured work surface and carefully remove the blade.

10 Divide the dough in half, then flatten each half into a disk. Use immediately or wrap in plastic and refrigerate for up to 3 days.

variations

Nut dough: Add ½ cup ground nuts such as almonds or hazelnuts to the dough. No adjustments are necessary, since the ground nuts won't absorb the eggs.

Cocoa dough: Use 1⅔ cups all-purpose flour and 3 tablespoons alkalized (Dutch process) cocoa powder, sifted after measuring, in place of the 2 cups flour.

C

D

E

essential tips for sweet pastry dough

- Sweet dough is easy to work with because of its relatively low butter content. Most pastry doughs contain much more butter (both for tenderness and flavor), and therefore they may soften to an unmanageable consistency if your kitchen is warm or you take too long rolling out the dough. Usually less butter means less tenderness, but in this case, sugar provides the extra tenderness needed to achieve a baked crust that isn't tough or hard.

- Baking powder is another ingredient that contributes to this dough's ability to bake through dry and golden even under a liquid filling. Normally when we add baking powder to a dough it causes it to puff up. In this case, however, the filling exerts enough weight to prevent the dough from rising upward, causing it to press firmly against the bottom of the pan when it expands, so that it maintains constant contact with the hot pan bottom and bakes through efficiently. The most common cause of a tart's bottom crust not baking through is the dough shrinking slightly and losing contact with the hot pan bottom.

- Because of this dough's ability to bake through so efficiently, it never needs to be partially prebaked, saving time and fuss whenever you bake a tart.

forming a tart crust from sweet pastry dough

Makes one 10-inch tart crust

½ batch Sweet Pastry Dough (page 14)

Flour for the work surface and dough

One 10-inch tart pan with removable bottom

Because of its relatively high sugar content, Sweet Pastry Dough can become soft and sticky if excessively handled. Follow the instructions for using the chilled dough until you feel confident enough to try rolling freshly prepared dough. Whether working with chilled or fresh dough, try the alternative method for rolling the dough directly on the tart pan bottom (step 6) to simplify transferring the dough to the pan.

1   Remove one of the pieces of dough from the refrigerator, unwrap it, and place it on a floured work surface. Gently knead the dough until it is slightly softened and malleable. Shape it into a disk again and use the palm of your hand to press it about ¼ inch thick.

2   Flour the work surface and the dough and gently roll the dough to a 13-inch-diameter disk, adding pinches of flour under and on top of the dough as needed. Picture the dough as the face of a clock: Roll back and forth from 6 to 12 and back again, without rolling over the edges in either direction. Slide the dough around to make sure it doesn't stick to the work surface, then add a few more pinches of flour to both the work surface and the surface of the dough. Turn the dough a little so that the spot that was at 12 o'clock is now at 2 and repeat. After you have rolled over the dough 3 or 4 times, turning it a little in between, it should be large enough for the pan and still of even thickness.

3   Fold the dough in half and slide both hands under it, palms upward, and transfer it to the pan, lining up the fold with the diameter of the pan. Unfold the dough into the pan. Don't be concerned if the dough cracks or tears—you can always press it back together. Evenly fit the dough into the pan, making sure it's flat against both the bottom and sides of the pan.

4   Trim away any excess dough at the rim of the pan by rolling over the rim with the rolling pin or scraping away excess dough with the back of a paring knife.

5   Finish off the top edges of the crust by using your thumb to press the dough from inside the pan against the side of the pan and at the same time using your index finger to press down on the top of the crust.

6   Alternately, remove the bottom from the tart pan and place it on the work surface. Flour the metal disk, place the disk of dough in the center of it, and roll the dough as in step 2 (A). When the dough reaches the edge of the pan bottom, flour the work surface around the dough and roll it to 2 more inches in diameter or 1 inch beyond the edge of the metal disk. Run a thin metal spatula under the overhanging perimeter of dough to make sure it isn't stuck to the work surface (if it is, gently slide a long spatula or a thin tart pan bottom underneath). Fold the extra dough inward all around onto the rolled dough on the metal disk and gently transfer the pan bottom to the tart pan (B). Lift the folded-over dough and press it against the side of the pan, then perform steps 4 and 5 above (C).

7   Use the crust immediately or wrap it in plastic and chill for up to 24 hours.

A

B

C

essential tips for rolling tart crusts

- Always knead and gently soften the dough before attempting to roll it. A chilled, hard dough will break apart when rolled.

- Flouring the work surface and dough is essential to prevent sticking. Use small pinches of flour and repeat, adding them often, and you won't add more than a couple of teaspoons of extra flour to the dough.

- You can also roll the dough on a thin, flexible cutting board. After the dough is rolled, slide a long metal spatula or knife under it to make sure it isn't stuck, then slide the dough to the edge of the board. Line up the edge of the cutting board with the far end of the tart pan and gently slide the disk of dough off the cutting board and into the pan.

- Make sure you have pressed the dough against the side of the pan (step 3) before cutting off any excess or the pan sides might not be completely covered with dough.

- Practice finishing off the top edges of the crust by pressing inward on the side with your thumb and downward on the top with your forefinger at the same time (see photo C at left), making a straight, even, finished edge that won't crack when baking.

chocolate hazelnut tart

Makes one 10-inch tart, 8 to 10 servings

2 cups whole hazelnuts

1 cup dark corn syrup

½ cup sugar

4 ounces bittersweet chocolate,
cut into ¼-inch pieces

4 tablespoons unsalted butter,
cut into 8 pieces

3 large eggs

Pinch of salt

2 tablespoons dark rum or bourbon,
optional

One 10-inch tart crust made from
Sweet Pastry Dough (page 14)

The filling of this tart recalls *gianduja*, the delicious chocolate hazelnut confection of Italy's Piemonte region. I like to use a plain crust with this filling so that all the chocolate emphasis is within, plus the pale crust and dark filling provide fun color contrast. Purchasing hazelnuts with their skins already removed makes preparing the filling much easier.

1 Set an oven rack in the lowest level of the oven and preheat to 350°F.

2 If the hazelnuts are not already skinned, place them in a small roasting pan or jelly-roll pan and toast them in the oven until the skins darken and loosen, 10 to 15 minutes. Pour the hazelnuts onto a clean kitchen towel and rub them vigorously in the towel to loosen their skins, then go over them one by one and peel off any remaining skins (if you purchased skinned hazelnuts, toast them lightly). Place the skinned nuts on a jelly-roll pan and set a small saucepan on top of them. Rock the saucepan back and forth over the nuts, applying firm pressure, to crush them into halves and quarters.

3 Combine the corn syrup and sugar in a medium saucepan and stir well to mix. Place on medium heat and bring to a full boil, stirring occasionally. Off heat, add the chocolate and butter and gently shake the pan once or twice to submerge them. Wait 2 minutes, then whisk smooth.

4 Whisk the eggs into the chocolate mixture, one at a time, followed by the salt and rum, if using.

5 Pour the filling into the prepared crust and bake the tart until the dough is baked through and deep golden on the top edges and the filling is set, 35 to 40 minutes.

6 Cool the tart on a rack. Unmold the cooled tart and slide it from the pan bottom to a platter.

Serving: Serve the tart in wedges. A spoonful of whipped cream is a nice touch.

Storage: Keep the tart loosely covered at room temperature until serving. Wrap and store leftovers at room temperature.

variations

Walnuts, pecans, toasted almonds, and macadamias all make excellent substitutes for the hazelnuts. One of the best fillings for this tart I've ever made used an assortment of odds and ends of nutmeats I had in the freezer.

old-fashioned sweet potato tart

Makes one 10-inch tart, 8 to 10 servings

3 medium sweet potatoes,
1½ to 1¾ pounds

½ cup sugar

½ teaspoon ground cinnamon

Generous pinch freshly grated nutmeg

Pinch of salt

3 large eggs

1 cup light cream or half-and-half

1 teaspoon vanilla extract

One 10-inch tart crust made from Sweet Pastry Dough (page 14)

A flavorful change from the eternal pumpkin pie, sweet potato tart is as Southern as you can get. This version is loosely based on one by Leah Chase, proprietor of the Dooky Chase restaurant in New Orleans, Louisiana. There seems to be a lot of confusion about sweet potatoes versus yams, and some people even use the terms interchangeably. You can easily find a sweet potato in a supermarket or farmers' market in the United States, and the color of its flesh or skin varies. Yams are another species of tuber altogether, which have a completely different flavor. They grow mostly in South America, though I'm sure some Latino markets in other places carry them.

1 Set an oven rack in the lowest level of the oven and preheat to 375°F.

2 Bake the sweet potatoes in the oven until they feel soft when pressed with a fingertip at the thickest part, about 1 hour. Cool and peel them, trimming away any dry spots on the pointed ends after peeling.

3 Place the sweet potatoes in a shallow bowl and use a potato masher to reduce them to a heavy puree. Stir in the sugar, spices, and salt.

4 Whisk in the eggs, one at a time, followed by the cream and vanilla.

5 Pour the filling into the prepared crust. Place the tart on the lowest rack of the oven and immediately lower the temperature to 350°F. Bake until the edge of the crust is deep golden and the filling is set, about 40 to 45 minutes.

6 Cool the tart on a rack. Unmold and slide the tart from the pan bottom to a platter. Serve at room temperature.

Serving: In New Orleans they often decorate each portion of the tart with a pecan half, then serve it with whipped cream or vanilla ice cream.

Storage: Keep the tart at a cool room temperature until serving, or wrap and refrigerate. Bring to room temperature before serving.

variations

Add ¼ cup finely ground pecans to the dough when preparing it. Scatter ½ cup chopped pecans over the filling before baking.

pear & walnut tart

Makes one 10-inch tart, 8 servings

POACHED PEARS

Ice water

2 tablespoons lemon juice

5 ripe Bartlett pears, about 2 pounds

½ cup sugar

1 vanilla bean

1 2- to 3-inch cinnamon stick

1 tablespoon clear pear brandy, optional

WALNUT FILLING

1 cup walnut pieces

½ cup light brown sugar, firmly packed

¼ teaspoon ground cinnamon

Pinch of salt

6 tablespoons unsalted butter, softened

1 large egg

1 large egg yolk

¼ cup all-purpose flour (spoon into
a dry-measure cup and level off)

½ teaspoon baking powder

½ cup walnut pieces, finely chopped

APRICOT GLAZE

¾ cup apricot preserves

2 tablespoons water

Confectioners' sugar for finishing

One 10-inch tart crust made from
Sweet Pastry Dough (page 14)

variations

For the filling, use pecans or blanched almonds, granulated sugar for brown, and 1 teaspoon of vanilla for cinnamon.

Cover the crust with 1 pint blueberries, spreading the filling over them before sprinkling with the nuts. Omit the glaze.

Substitute peeled peach or nectarine quarters, or unpeeled apricot, plum, or prune halves, for the pears.

This was always one of the most popular items sold by my Total Heaven Baking Company in the early 1980s. Poaching the pears first is a little extra work, but you can do it for up to five days in advance of assembling the tart; just chill them in their poaching liquid. The variations with this tart are almost infinite—just change the fruit or the nuts in the filling.

1   To poach the pears, half-fill a 4-quart pan with ice water and add the lemon juice. Peel, halve, and use a melon-ball scoop to core and stem the pears, adding each half to the ice water. Skim out the ice and pour away all the water except what's needed to cover the pears by 1 inch. Add the sugar, vanilla bean, and cinnamon stick and stir gently. Cut a piece of parchment or wax paper the same diameter as the pan and cut six to eight 1-inch holes in it. Press the paper down on top of the pears so that it is fully submerged. (This will keep the pears from floating up while they are cooking.) Place the pan over medium heat and bring to a full boil. Cover, remove from the heat, and allow the pears to sit in the hot liquid until completely cooled. If the pears are perfectly ripe, they won't need any more cooking; if they are less ripe, boil them for another 2 minutes. Once the pears are cool, use a slotted spoon to lift them gently to a plastic container and pour the pear brandy, if using, on top. Pour in enough of the poaching syrup to cover the pears and transfer the vanilla bean to the container. Cover and refrigerate until needed.

2   Before assembling, set a rack in the lowest level of the oven and preheat to 350°F.

3   For the filling, combine the walnut pieces, sugar, cinnamon, and salt in the bowl of a food processor fitted with the metal blade. Pulse until finely ground. Use a thin metal spatula to scrape away any mixture stuck to the bottom and sides of the bowl. Add the butter, egg, and yolk and pulse until smooth. Mix the flour and baking powder together and then add to the bowl and pulse again until absorbed. Scrape the sides of the bowl again and pulse 2 or 3 more times. Remove the blade and scrape any filling stuck to it into the prepared tart crust. Scrape the remaining filling into the crust and smooth the top. Evenly scatter the chopped walnuts on top.

4   Drain the pear halves on paper towels and arrange them on the filling, wider sides close to the edge of the crust, ends pointing toward the center. (Do a dry run on a plate and trim the sides of the pear halves if necessary.) Bake until the edge of the crust is deep golden and the filling is set, about 30 minutes.

5   Cool on a rack. Meanwhile, prepare the glaze. Stir together the preserves and water in a small saucepan and bring to a boil, stirring occasionally, over low heat. Strain into a bowl, then rinse the pan and return the strained glaze to it.

6   Dust the tart well with confectioners' sugar and wait until it melts on the pears. Blot the pears with a paper towel. Reheat the glaze and reduce it slightly, then pour a small spoonful of glaze onto each pear. Unmold and slide the tart to a platter.

Serving: Cut the tart into wedges, centering one of the pear halves in each serving.

Storage: Keep the tart loosely covered with foil (plastic wrap will stick to the glaze) until serving. Wrap and store leftovers at room temperature.

citrus-scented chocolate tart

Makes one 10-inch tart, 8 to 10 servings

1¼ cups light cream or half-and-half

⅓ cup sugar

6 tablespoons unsalted butter,
cut into 10 pieces

8 ounces semisweet chocolate (55 to 65%
cocoa solids), cut into ¼-inch pieces

3 large eggs

Pinch of salt

1 teaspoon finely grated lemon zest

2 teaspoons finely grated orange zest

1 tablespoon lemon juice, strained
before measuring

2 tablespoons orange juice, strained
before measuring

1 tablespoon orange liqueur, such as
Cointreau or Triple Sec, optional

1 teaspoon vanilla extract

One 10-inch tart crust, made from Sweet
Pastry Dough, Cocoa Dough variation
(page 14)

The flavor of this creamy chocolate filling is beautifully enhanced by lemon and orange zests and a little of each fruit's juice, both of which tie into the chocolate's natural acidity. I like to bake it in a cocoa-flavored crust to emphasize the tart's chocolate richness, but you may also use a plain or nut-enriched sweet dough. This tart also makes a delicious base for berries or orange or tangerine segments, or try hiding a thin layer of sliced bananas under the chocolate filling.

1 Set an oven rack in the lowest level of the oven and preheat to 350°F.

2 Whisk the cream and sugar together in a small saucepan and place over medium heat and bring to a boil. Off heat, add the butter and chocolate to the saucepan and shake the pan to submerge them. Let stand 1 minute; whisk smooth.

3 Add the eggs and salt; whisk them in, followed by the citrus zests, juices, liqueur, and vanilla.

4 Pour the filling into the prepared crust and bake until the crust is baked through and the filling is set, about 25 minutes.

5 Cool the tart on a rack. Unmold it and slide it from the pan bottom to a platter.

Serving: Serve the tart at room temperature with some slices of peeled orange, or decorate the edge of the tart with halved orange slices.

Storage: Keep the tart at room temperature until serving. Wrap and store leftovers at a cool room temperature.

variations

For a pure chocolate flavor, omit the citrus zests and juices. Or scatter 1 cup fresh raspberries on the crust before pouring over the plain or citrus-scented filling; don't be tempted to add more berries, as they'll exude a lot of juice during baking. Or thinly slice a couple of poached pear halves (see Pear and Walnut Tart, page 20) and arrange them on the crust before adding the plain filling.

shredded apple custard tart

Makes one 10-inch tart, 8 to 10 servings

3 large tart apples such as Granny Smith, about 1½ pounds

⅓ cup sugar

3 tablespoons all-purpose flour

3 large eggs

1 teaspoon vanilla extract

⅔ cup light cream or half-and-half

Ground cinnamon for sprinkling on the filling

½ cup walnut pieces, coarsely chopped

One 10-inch tart crust made from Sweet Pastry Dough (page 14)

I remember the pastry chef at the hotel where I worked in Zurich in the early 1970s improvising a tart like this one afternoon when we didn't have a lot of work to do. It's also a model for tarts made with other fruits.

1 Set a rack in the lowest level of the oven and preheat to 350°F.

2 Peel, halve, and core the apples. Set a box grater in a shallow bowl and grate the apple halves over the grater's largest holes, or use the largest grating blade of your food processor. Scrape the grated apples into a large strainer and set it back over the bowl for the apples to drain while preparing the other ingredients. Don't be concerned if the apples darken slightly, but don't take too long with the rest of the filling either.

3 Evenly whisk the sugar and flour together in a mixing bowl. Add the eggs and vanilla and whisk smooth. Whisk in the cream.

4 Stir the drained apples into the custard mixture and scrape it into the prepared tart crust. If the apples mound in the center of the tart, use a fork to distribute them more evenly.

5 Sparingly sprinkle the top of the tart with cinnamon and evenly scatter on the chopped nuts. Bake the tart until the edge of the crust is deep golden and the filling is set, 40 to 45 minutes.

6 Cool the tart on a rack, then unmold and slide it from the pan bottom to a platter.

Serving: Cut the tart into wedges. It needs no accompaniment.

Storage: Keep the tart at a cool room temperature until serving. Wrap and refrigerate leftovers and bring them to room temperature before serving again.

variations

Scatter 3 cups rinsed, dried, and picked over blueberries onto the tart crust and pour the custard cream over them. Omit the cinnamon and walnuts. Substitute 3 cups blackberries or raspberries for the blueberries, but just pick through them for any stems or blemished berries—washing either will turn them to puree.

Substitute 4 or 5 ripe peaches (about 2 pounds), peeled, halved, and each half cut into 3 wedges. Arrange the peach wedges cut side up on the tart crust, making one row of wedges perpendicular to the edge of the tart and filling in the center with the remaining wedges. Pour the custard cream over the peaches, omitting the cinnamon and walnuts. The top may be glazed with the apricot glaze from the recipe for Pear and Walnut Tart, page 20. Substitute unpeeled quarters of apricots or prune plums for the peaches.

You may finish the top of the tart with an unbaked crumb topping for any of the variations above, including the apple tart. Use the crumb topping in the recipe for Strawberry Cream Cheese Crumble Tart, page 45, omitting the almonds.

bakewell tart

Makes one 10-inch tart, about 10 servings

One 10-inch unbaked tart crust made from Sweet Pastry Dough (see pages 14 and 16)

¼ cup strawberry or seedless raspberry jam

8 ounces almond paste, cut into ½-inch cubes (see Note)

¼ cup sugar

3 large eggs

8 tablespoons (1 stick) unsalted butter, softened

1 tablespoon lemon juice

⅓ cup all-purpose flour (spoon into a dry-measure cup and level off)

variation

Bordeaux Fruit Tart: This is my take on the old-fashioned French tart Infante de Bordeaux that calls for an icing to be spread over baked almond filling. I like to use it as a base for really juicy fruit, such as pineapple, oranges, or perfectly ripe strawberries, which would drain too much liquid into a typical tart crust spread with pastry cream.

Prepare the tart filling using the ground almonds and sugar (see Note) instead of the almond paste, and using melted butter in place of the softened butter. Omit the jam and spread the filling in the crust and bake. Cool the tart and arrange 3 cups of sliced fruit on the surface. Just before serving, blot excess moisture from the surface of the fruit and brush on apricot glaze (see page 20) for light-colored fruit, or raspberry glaze (see page 46) for red fruit. Use a very sharp knife to cut the tart since there is nothing to adhere the fruit to the surface beneath.

I love British recipes like this one for Bakewell Tart—the only definitive statement you can make about it is that absolutely no one can agree on what it is. According to some, it was originally a custard tart with some ground almonds added for flavor and a layer of jam spread on the crust. Some time late in the 19th century, the almonds became more prominent in the filling. Purists like to refer to it as Bakewell pudding, probably from the British tradition of referring to all sweets served at the table as "puddings." My thoroughly delicious, but non-authentic, version calls for a type of frangipane filling made with almond paste (or you can easily substitute ground almonds). By the way, Bakewell is a town in Derbyshire, not a reference to the quality of the outcome. Thanks to my dear friend Kyra Effren for guiding me through the intricacies of Bakewell.

1. Set a rack in the lowest level of the oven and preheat to 350°F.

2. Use the tines of a fork to pierce the bottom of the crust all over at 1-inch intervals. Evenly spread the jam on the tart crust and set aside.

3. Combine the almond paste and sugar in the bowl of an electric mixer fitted with the paddle attachment. Beat on medium speed until reduced to small crumbs. Add one of the eggs and continue beating until the mixture is smooth and free of lumps.

4. Use a rubber spatula to scrape the side of the bowl and the beater, beat again for a minute, then add the butter. Continue beating until the mixture lightens somewhat, 2 to 3 minutes.

5. Beat in the lemon juice, and the second egg, continuing to beat until smooth. Scrape the bowl and beater again and add the last egg. Beat smooth and decrease to the lowest speed. Add the flour and beat until it is just absorbed.

6. Use a large rubber spatula to give a final mixing to the batter and scrape it into the prepared crust. Use a small offset spatula to spread the filling evenly.

7. Bake the tart until the crust is deep golden and the filling is set and a light golden color, 30 to 40 minutes.

8. Cool on a rack; unmold and slide the tart from the pan base to a platter.

Serving: Serve wedges of the tart with spoonfuls of whipped cream.

Storage: Keep the tart at room temperature before and after serving. Cover leftovers with plastic wrap.

Note: If you don't have any almond paste, combine 1 cup blanched almonds, ½ cup sugar, and ½ teaspoon almond extract in the bowl of a food processor fitted with the metal blade. Pulse until finely ground, then let the machine run continuously for 1 minute at a time until the mixture begins to become pasty. Stop the machine and use the end of a narrow metal spatula to scrape the bottom and sides of the bowl, pulse again a few times for even consistency, and use instead of the almond paste.

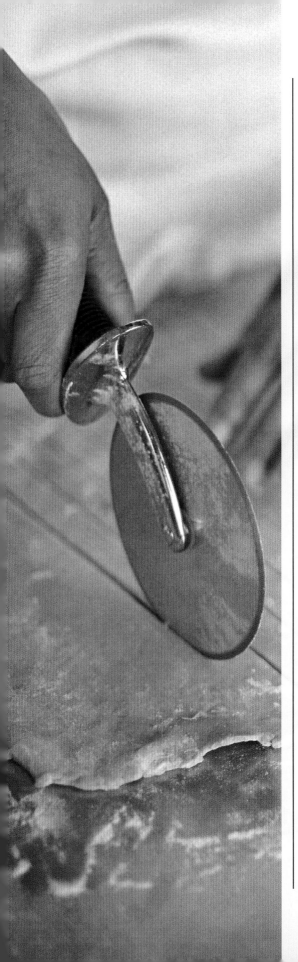

02

flaky pastry dough & tarts

When I first tried baking, back when I was a teenager, I hated making flaky pastry dough. All the caveats about keeping everything cool, over handling, and worst of all, the variable amount of water needed to pull the ingredients together to form a dough so filled me with dread that the dough and subsequent tart were ruined before I even got started. This dough takes all the fear out of preparing a rich, flaky crust. No variables, ease of mixing and handling, and best of all, a perfectly baked result every time will make you look forward to working with this type of dough. The tarts are both sweet and savory, including a tailored free-standing version of everyone's favorite, apple pie. Two types of tangy lemon tart, a chocolate cream tart, and my favorite savory combinations—spinach and bacon, cheese and onion, and smoked salmon and avocado—round out the assortment.

flaky pastry dough

Flaky dough makes a wonderful container for many sweet and savory fillings. Its fragile texture after baking is more than equaled by its subtle buttery flavor, which always enhances but never competes with delicate fillings.

Makes about 18 ounces dough, enough for two 10-inch tart crusts or one double-crust tart

2 cups all-purpose flour (spoon into a dry-measure cup and level off)

½ teaspoon salt

1 teaspoon baking powder

12 tablespoons (1½ sticks) unsalted butter, cold, cut into 12 pieces

2 large eggs (see Note)

Note: Even though a dozen large eggs equals 24 ounces, each individual egg isn't guaranteed to be 2 ounces. If you happen to use the two smallest eggs in the dozen, the dough might not start to form a ball after 4 or 5 pulses. If this happens, add ½ teaspoon water.

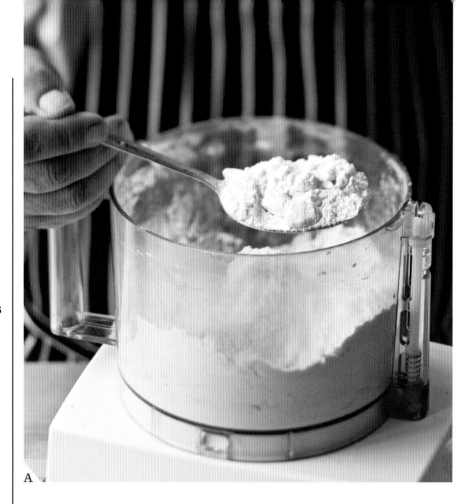

A

1 To mix the dough by hand, combine the flour, salt, and baking powder in a medium bowl and stir to combine.

2 Cut each piece of butter into 4 or 5 smaller pieces and add the pieces to the bowl. Using both hands, palms upward, reach under the dry ingredients to the bottom of the bowl and lift them up through the contents of the bowl several times to distribute the pieces of butter evenly.

3 Use your fingertips to pinch the pieces of butter into smaller pieces, alternating that with rubbing the mixture between the palms of your hands, as well as occasionally repeating step 2.

4 Continue rubbing in the butter until the largest pieces are no more than 1/4 inch across, but the whole mixture is still cool and powdery.

5 Add the eggs and use a fork to break them up. Move the bowl back and forth on the work surface while you stir from the bottom up with the fork until the dough is almost completely mixed.

6 Invert the dough to a floured work surface and gently press it into a consistent mass. Continue with step 11.

7 To mix the dough in a food processor, combine the flour, salt, and baking powder in the bowl fitted with the metal blade. Pulse several times to mix.

8 Add the butter and pulse repeatedly at 1-second intervals until the butter appears in small pieces as in step 4 (A).

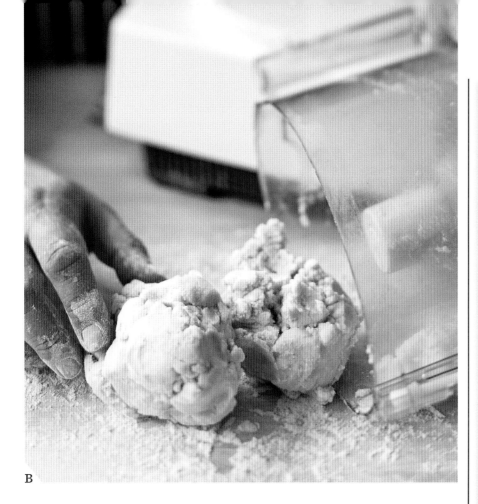

B

9   Add the eggs and pulse just until the dough almost forms a ball; pulsing too much at this point will incorporate the butter smoothly and cut down on flakiness.

10 Invert the dough to a floured work surface and carefully remove the blade. Gently press the dough into a cohesive mass (B).

11 Divide the dough in half, then flatten each half into a disk. Wrap in plastic and refrigerate until firm or as long as 3 days.

essential tips for flaky pastry dough

- The small pieces of butter turn into irregular layers when the dough is rolled out. When the dough begins baking, the butter melts and leaves tiny spaces throughout the dough. When the liquid in the dough evaporates, it forms steam, which slightly inflates all those little spaces. Once the starches in the dough coagulate, those spaces provide the open-textured flakiness characteristic of this dough.

- Starting with cold butter is important. If the butter melts during mixing, or later during rolling, it forms a paste with the flour rather than remaining in discernible pieces. No pieces of butter equals no flakiness.

- Unlike a dough that contains sugar, a flaky dough develops a slightly stronger elasticity during both mixing and rolling. Proteins in the flour change shape due to the addition of moisture and the presence of friction, and they form elastic strands of gluten. Overmixing can form too strong a gluten, causing a dough to shrink excessively (all pastry doughs shrink a little) during baking and become tough. Mix quickly and efficiently, allow the dough to chill and rest after mixing and again after rolling, and shrinkage will be minimized and tenderness maximized.

forming a tart crust from flaky pastry dough

Makes one 10-inch tart crust

½ batch Flaky Pastry Dough (page 26)

Flour for the work surface and dough

One 10-inch tart pan with removable bottom

essential tips for rolling tart crusts from flaky dough

- A thin cookie sheet with no sides or a thin flexible cutting board are helpful when rolling a flaky dough. If the kitchen is warm and the dough starts to soften, slide the cookie sheet or cutting board under the dough and refrigerate it until it is firm, about 10 to 15 minutes.

- Continue rolling directly on the cookie sheet or cutting board and transfer it to the pan as in step 3.

- A flaky dough tart crust needs to chill and rest after being rolled, too. Rolling activates the strands of gluten again and may cause excessive shrinkage if the crust is baked immediately. Give the crust at least a couple of hours of chilling before baking for best results.

Because of its relatively high butter content, Flaky Pastry Dough can become soft and sticky if excessively handled. Follow the instructions for using the chilled dough until you feel confident enough to try rolling the freshly prepared dough. In either case, you may also try the alternative method for rolling the dough directly on the tart pan bottom (step 6) to simplify transferring the dough to the pan.

1 Remove one of the pieces of dough from the refrigerator, unwrap it, and place it on a floured work surface. Use the rolling pin to press the dough, gently at first, in a series of strokes that are both parallel and close together. Turn the disk of dough about 30 degrees and repeat. While you're pressing the dough, be sure to add pinches of flour under and on the dough to prevent sticking. Moving the dough 30 degrees every time you press it will help to keep it round. Continue pressing the dough until it is malleable and about ¼ inch thick.

2 Flour the work surface and the dough and gently roll the dough to a 13-inch-diameter disk, adding pinches of flour under and on the dough as needed. If you picture the dough as the face of a clock, roll back and forth from 6 to 12 and back again, without rolling over the edges in either direction. Slide the dough around to make sure it isn't stuck to the work surface (if it is, gently slide a long spatula or a thin tart pan bottom underneath), then add a few more pinches of flour to both the work surface and the dough. Turn the dough so that the spot that was at 12 o'clock is now at 2 and repeat. After you have rolled over the dough 3 or 4 times, turning it a little in between, it should be large enough for the pan.

3 Fold the dough in half and slide both hands under it, palms upward, and transfer it to the pan, lining up the fold with the diameter of the pan. Unfold the dough into the pan. The dough will be slightly elastic after rolling, so it won't break apart unless it has softened excessively. Evenly fit the dough into the pan, making sure it's flat against both the bottom and sides of the pan.

4 Use the back of a knife or scissors to trim away all but ½ inch of excess dough at the rim of the pan. Fold the extra dough inward against the inside of the pan to reinforce the side of the crust. (This isn't necessary if the tart is going to have a top crust—in that case, just leave the extra dough in place until you add the top crust.)

5 Finish off the top edges of the crust by using your thumb to press the dough from inside the pan against the side of the pan and at the same time using your index finger to press down on the top of the crust.

6 Alternatively, remove the bottom from the tart pan and place it on the work surface. Flour the metal disk, place the disk of dough in the center of it, and roll the dough as in step 2. When the dough reaches the edge of the pan bottom, flour the work surface around the dough and roll it to 2 more inches in diameter or 1½ inches beyond the edge of the metal disk. Run a thin metal spatula under the overhanging perimeter of dough to make sure it isn't stuck to the work surface. Fold the extra dough inward all around onto the rolled dough on the metal disk and gently transfer the pan bottom to the tart pan. Lift the folded-over dough and press it

against the side of the pan (see photos on page 17), then perform steps 4 and 5 above. Wrap the tart pan in plastic and chill for at least 3 hours or up to 24 hours.

7 For a *full top crust*, roll the dough to an 11-inch disk, slide it to a cookie sheet or the back of a jelly-roll pan, cover with plastic wrap, and chill it until ready to fill and finish the tart. For a *lattice top crust*, roll the dough to an 11-inch square by starting with a square of dough and turning it 90 degrees every time you roll over it. Wrap and chill as in step 6.

baking an empty tart crust

Often a tart crust needs to be fully baked before adding a filling that doesn't require baking. This technique is known as baking it "blind." It's simple to do, but you'll need some dried beans to weigh down the crust during the initial baking time when it might puff up and distort.

One tart crust made from Flaky Pastry Dough, see opposite page, chilled

1 When you are ready to bake the tart crust, set a rack in the middle level of the oven and preheat to 350°F.

2 Pierce the chilled crust at 1-inch intervals with a fork. Line the bottom and sides of the crust with a 14-inch disk of parchment or wax paper (A) and fill with dried beans.

3 Bake the tart crust until it is dry looking and set, about 10 minutes. Remove the paper and beans and continue baking until the crust is evenly light golden, 15 to 20 additional minutes.

4 Cool the crust on a rack and use it the same day you bake it.

A

lattice-topped apple tart

Makes one 10-inch double-crusted tart, about 10 servings

APPLE FILLING

3 pounds tart apples, peeled, halved, cored, and cut into ½-inch dice (see Note)

½ cup granulated sugar

¼ cup light brown sugar

3 tablespoons all-purpose flour

1 teaspoon ground cinnamon

2 tablespoons cold unsalted butter

FINISHING

2 tablespoons granulated sugar

One 10-inch unbaked tart crust, edges untrimmed, and a square of dough for the top crust, both made from Flaky Pastry Dough (pages 26 and 28–29)

Note: The best apples for the filling are Northern Spies, available in the northeast and northern midwest US and in southern Canada. Failing those, a combination of equal parts Golden Delicious and Granny Smith works well, but cut the Granny Smith apples into smaller dice since they're so firm—otherwise they'll take too long to soften.

variations

Add the (unbaked) crumb topping on page 31 (omit the almonds or substitute walnut pieces) instead of the lattice.

Try adding ⅔ cup raisins or currants to the filling by reserving 2 cups of the seasoned filling and folding the raisins into the rest of the filling. Scrape the raisin-studded filling into the bottom crust, then top with the reserved filling to avoid burnt raisins at the top of the tart. Dried cranberries work well, too.

This is so much more practical to prepare and serve than a standard apple pie baked in a sloping pie pan. It's free-standing on a platter and only needs to be cut into wedges, with none of the sometimes destructive digging underneath the bottom crust to extract wedges from the other type of pan. It's also much more elegant looking than a plain apple pie. I like to use a little flour to thicken the juices of an apple filling such as this one—it's easy to do (just mix the flour with the sugar) and, unless you use too much, it provides just the slight thickening needed so the juices in the baked pie aren't watery. Dicing the apples makes them bake through more quickly than cutting them into wedges, plus it makes the filling less bulky when placed in the bottom crust, creating only a small gap between the filling and top crust after the tart is baked.

1 Set a rack in the lowest level of the oven and preheat to 375°F. Slide a sheet of aluminum foil onto the bottom of the oven to catch drips when the filling comes to a simmer close to the end of the baking time.

2 Put the apples in a large bowl and mix the sugars, flour, and cinnamon in a small bowl. Scatter 2 tablespoons of the sugar mixture onto the bottom of the tart crust. Scatter the rest over the apples and use a large rubber spatula, repeatedly digging upward from the bottom of the bowl, to mix.

3 Scrape the filling into the prepared crust and redistribute the apple pieces so that the top of the filling is level rather than domed. Dot the filling with shreds of the butter.

4 Use some water and a brush to moisten the extra dough at the edge of the pan. Use a pizza wheel or serrated pastry wheel to cut the square of dough into ten 1-inch-wide strips. Place 5 of the strips parallel and equidistant from each other on the filling, letting the ends of the strips touch the moistened area of the bottom crust. Place the next 5 strips at either a 45- or 90-degree angle to the first strips.

5 Use moistened fingers to press the ends of the strips gently against the overhanging edge of the bottom crust. Use the back of a knife to trim the overhanging dough even with the rim of the pan.

6 To finish, gently brush a little water on the strips of dough and scatter on the sugar. Bake the tart until the crust is well colored and baked through and the filling is gently bubbling, about 45 to 55 minutes.

7 Cool the tart on a rack. Slide it from the pan bottom to a platter to serve.

Serving: Cut wedges of the tart and serve with a scoop of vanilla ice cream if you wish.

Storage: Keep the tart at room temperature on the day it's baked. For longer storage, continue to keep it at room temperature, but cover loosely with plastic wrap.

shaker lemon tart

Makes one 10-inch double-crust tart, about 10 servings

1 pound lemons, about 3 medium or 4 small

2 cups sugar

5 large eggs

¼ teaspoon salt

Sugar, for finishing

One 10-inch unbaked tart crust, made from Flaky Pastry Dough (page 26)

This is my version of what's often known as Shaker lemon pie. The Shakers were a Christian religious sect that practiced communal living and have left behind a legacy of delicious plain cooking and beautifully designed hand-crafted furniture and household accessories. This four-ingredient lemon filling is a perfect example of Shaker cooking at its best. This is usually made with thin lemon slices. I find it easier to quarter the lemons and remove the seeds and then chop them in the food processor.

1 Place the lemons in a large saucepan or Dutch oven and cover them by 2 inches with cold water. Place on medium heat and bring to a full boil. Pour off the water and replace with fresh cold water, then bring to a boil and continue cooking at a steady boil for 10 minutes. Use a slotted spoon to remove the lemons to a bowl and cover them with cold water. Let the lemons stand until completely cooled, then drain them.

2 Set a rack in the lowest level of the oven and preheat to 375°F.

3 Quarter the lemons and catch any seeds in a strainer set over a bowl, so that any juice is collected in the bowl. Then as you seed the lemon quarters, simply drop them into the bowl with the juice.

4 Place the solid lemon pieces into a food processor and pulse them until they are chopped into pieces no larger than ¼ inch across. Pour the contents of the work bowl back into the bowl with the lemon juice and stir in the sugar, eggs, and salt. Pour into the tart crust.

5 Bake the tart until the crust is deep golden and the filling is set, about 30 to 35 minutes.

6 Cool the tart on a rack. Unmold it and slide the tart to a platter to serve.

Serving: Serve wedges of the tart with lightly sweetened whipped cream.

Storage: Keep the tart at room temperature if serving the same day. Wrap and refrigerate leftovers and bring them to room temperature again before serving.

chocolate meringue tart

Makes one 10-inch tart, 8 to 10 servings

CHOCOLATE CREAM FILLING

2 cups whole milk

½ cup sugar

1 3-inch cinnamon stick

3 3-inch-long strips orange zest, removed with a vegetable peeler

1 cup light cream or half-and-half

⅓ cup cornstarch

4 large eggs

8 ounces bittersweet chocolate (65 to 70% cocoa solids), cut into ¼-inch pieces

2 teaspoons vanilla extract

MERINGUE TOPPING

4 large egg whites

¾ cup sugar

Pinch of salt

One 10-inch tart crust made from Flaky Pastry Dough (pages 26 and 28–29), baked and cooled

variation

Lemon cream meringue tart: Decrease the milk to 1 cup; combine the milk and cream with the sugar in step 1. Omit the cinnamon stick, orange zest, and chocolate. Whisk the cornstarch and eggs into ½ cup lemon juice, strained before measuring, instead of the cream in step 2.

Though a chocolate cream tart is often covered with whipped cream, it's more traditional to use a light meringue. For best results, don't have the chocolate cream too cold or a layer of watery condensation will develop between the filling and the meringue.

1 For the chocolate cream, combine the milk and sugar in a medium saucepan and whisk to dissolve the sugar. Add the cinnamon stick and orange zest. Set the pan over low heat and bring to a full boil.

2 Meanwhile, pour the cream into a large heat-proof bowl and whisk in the cornstarch. Whisk the eggs into the cream mixture, one at a time.

3 When the milk mixture boils, remove the pan from the heat and use a slotted spoon to remove and discard the cinnamon stick and strips of zest. Whisk about ³/₄ cup of the hot milk into the cream and egg mixture.

4 Return the remaining milk to a boil and, beginning to whisk before pouring, whisk the cream and egg mixture into the boiling milk, continuing to whisk constantly until the cream comes to a boil. Cook, whisking, for 30 seconds.

5 Remove the pan from the heat and whisk in the chocolate until the chocolate is melted and the cream is smooth. Whisk in the vanilla.

6 Scrape the chocolate cream into the cooled tart shell and spread it evenly. Press plastic wrap against the surface of the cream and refrigerate the filled tart until the cream has cooled to about 70°F.

7 Once the filling has cooled, remove the tart from the refrigerator. Set a rack in the middle level of the oven and preheat to 400°F.

8 For the meringue, fill a saucepan halfway with water and bring it to a boil. Decrease the heat so that the water boils gently. Combine the egg whites, sugar, and salt in the bowl of an electric mixer and place the bowl over the pan of simmering water. Whisk gently until the egg whites are hot (about 140°F) and the sugar is dissolved, about 2 minutes.

9 Place the bowl on the mixer with the whisk attachment and whip the meringue on medium-high speed until it has risen in volume and is very fluffy, 2 to 3 minutes. Decrease the speed to medium and continue whipping until the meringue cools to room temperature. Press the palm of your hand against the outside of the bowl; if you can't feel any heat, the meringue is ready.

10 Use a rubber spatula to scrape the meringue onto the chocolate filling. Spread the meringue evenly over the filling, making sure that it touches the edge of the crust all around. Bake the tart until the meringue is golden, 3 to 4 minutes, watching it constantly.

11 Cool the tart on a rack, then chill until serving. Unmold the tart and slide it from the pan base to a platter.

Serving: Use a thin, sharp knife to cut the tart, wiping the knife after each cut.

Storage: Wrap leftovers and store in the refrigerator.

spinach & bacon tart

Makes one 10-inch tart, about 10 servings

1 pound baby spinach or 1 10-ounce
package frozen spinach, thawed

4 ounces thin-sliced bacon,
cut into ¼-inch dice

½ cup finely diced white or yellow onion

Salt

Freshly ground black pepper

Freshly grated nutmeg

1½ cups light cream or half-and-half

1 cup coarsely grated sharp cheddar,
Gouda, or Swiss Gruyère

3 large eggs

One 10-inch unbaked tart crust made
from Flaky Pastry Dough (page 26)

Tart fillings made from greens such as spinach are always difficult to salt properly: too much and the tart's inedible, too little and you risk expiring from boredom after a forkful or two. Adding bacon to this spinach filling helps, because the spinach itself then may be very lightly salted since you'll have little bursts of salty bacon flavor in every bite.

1   For the filling, rinse the spinach and place it in a colander to drain. Place the spinach in a large saucepan and place over high heat. Cover the pan and let the spinach steam, uncovering and stirring it occasionally, until it is completely wilted and cooked through, about 5 minutes. Drain in the same colander and allow to cool. Once cooled, squeeze the moisture from handfuls of the spinach, then coarsely chop by hand. If using frozen spinach, just wring out the excess moisture.

2   Cook the bacon over medium heat in a shallow sauté pan, stirring occasionally to keep the pieces separate. Once the bacon has colored nicely, take off the heat and use a slotted spoon to transfer the cooked bacon to a plate lined with a paper towel. Pour off all but 1 tablespoon of the bacon fat from the pan.

3   Set a rack in the lowest level of the oven and preheat to 375°F.

4   Place the pan on medium heat and add the onion. Once it starts to sizzle, decrease the heat to low and continue cooking, stirring occasionally, until the onion is wilted and just beginning to color, about 10 minutes. Add the spinach and bacon to the pan and season with a little salt, several grindings of pepper, and a tiny pinch of nutmeg. Stir everything together until evenly combined.

5   Scrape the mixture into a bowl and stir in the cream and grated cheese. Taste for seasoning. At this point, it should taste like well-seasoned creamed spinach. Add a little more salt and pepper if necessary. Beat in the eggs one at a time. Scrape the filling into the prepared crust and spread it evenly.

6   Bake the tart until the crust is well colored and baked through and the filling is set, about 35 to 40 minutes.

7   Cool the tart on a rack and unmold it. Slide it from the pan bottom to a platter to serve.

Storage: Keep the tart at room temperature on the day it's baked. Loosely cover with plastic wrap and continue storing leftovers at room temperature for up to one day.

smoked salmon & avocado tart

Makes one 10-inch tart, 8 to 10 servings

2 to 3 perfectly ripe Hass avocados, about 1 to 1¼ pounds

2 tablespoons lime juice

1 tablespoon finely minced seeded jalapeño or serrano chile, or a few drops hot sauce, optional

Salt

Freshly ground black pepper

¼ cup finely minced white onion

2 medium ripe plum tomatoes, about 8 ounces, stemmed, halved, seeded and cut into ¼-inch dice, about ½ cup

4 ounces best smoked salmon, thinly sliced and cut into ½-inch squares

3 to 4 large leaves of Boston, romaine, or iceburg lettuce, rinsed, thoroughly dried, any thick ribs removed, and shredded

1 bunch chives, finely sliced, about ½ cup, or chopped cilantro leaves

One 10-inch tart crust made from Flaky Pastry Dough (page 26), baked and cooled

No, I shouldn't admit it, but, yes, I could eat a whole one of these. Smoked salmon and avocados are two of my favorite foods, and I like them even better together. I first tasted the combination at Bouley restaurant in New York. It came in a tiny portion served as an "amuse" right after my friends and I had ordered our lunch. I resolved to try it as a tart, and this is the result. Make sure the lettuce in the bottom of the tart shell is completely dry or it will defeat its purpose of keeping the crust from softening from contact with the moist avocado and salmon. Normally I would prefer not to cut smoked salmon into small pieces, but it's essential here or it would be impossible to cut through the tart without having the soft avocado mixture squish out in all directions.

1 For the filling, halve one of the avocados and remove the pit. Scoop the flesh from the skin into a mixing bowl. Quickly repeat with the remaining avocado(s). Sprinkle on the lime juice, hot sauce, if using, a large pinch of salt, and a couple of grindings of pepper. Use a small rubber spatula to fold in the seasonings, being careful not to overmix and mash the avocado. Press plastic wrap against the surface and refrigerate until right before serving.

2 Half an hour before serving the tart, use a large fork to mash the avocados so that there are no pieces larger than about ¼ inch. Taste for seasoning and adjust, remembering that the salmon is salty. Add the minced chile (if using), onion, tomatoes, and salmon to the avocado; use a small rubber spatula to fold everything together.

3 Evenly scatter the lettuce in the bottom of the tart crust. Scrape the avocado mixture onto the lettuce in 6 or 8 places to make it easier to spread. Use a small offset spatula to spread the filling smoothly in the crust.

4 Sprinkle the chives on top of the filling. Unmold the tart and slide it from the pan bottom to a platter. Serve immediately or within 20 minutes at the latest.

Serving: Use a thin, sharp knife to cut the tart into wedges. Garnish with lime wedges if you wish.

Storage: Try to avoid having leftovers; this isn't a good keeper.

gomser cholera
(Swiss potato & cheese pie from Goms in the Valais)

Makes one 9-inch pie, about 10 servings

4 tablespoons unsalted butter

2 large white onions, about 1 pound, peeled and finely chopped

2 large tart apples (about 1 pound) such as Granny Smith, peeled, halved, cored, and thinly sliced

Salt

Freshly ground black pepper

Freshly grated nutmeg

1 batch Flaky Pastry Dough (page 26), divided into two pieces, one slightly larger than the other

1 pound Yukon Gold potatoes, boiled until tender, cooled, peeled, and sliced ¼ inch thick

1 pound Goms or other Swiss raclette cheese, rind removed and thinly sliced

Egg wash: 1 egg well beaten with a pinch of salt

One 9 x 2-inch round cake pan, buttered

No one seems to really know how this delicious pie came to be named for a disease. One flimsy explanation states that people stayed indoors and cooked what they had, rather than venturing out to do food shopping during the 1830 cholera epidemic. The village of Goms in the Upper Valais is also well known for the quality of the cheese produced there, but any real Swiss raclette cheese will do nicely. This makes an excellent brunch or lunch dish with a salad and then some sorbet and crisp cookies for dessert.

1   For the filling, melt the butter on medium heat in a sauté pan or Dutch oven with a cover. Add the chopped onion and cook until it starts to sizzle. Lower the heat, cover the pan, and let the onion sweat until very soft, about 20 minutes. Add the sliced apples and continue to cook uncovered until the apples are tender and the water they have exuded has evaporated. Cool slightly and season with salt, pepper, and nutmeg.

2   When you're ready to bake the pie, set a rack in the lowest level of the oven and preheat to 375°F.

3   Roll the larger piece of dough on a floured surface and fit it into the pan, letting any excess dough hang over the edge of the pan. Place a layer of half the sliced potatoes into the pan and season sparingly with salt and pepper. Spread half the onion and apple mixture over them, then top with half the cheese slices. Repeat with the remaining potatoes, onion and apple mixture, and cheese.

4   Trim the excess dough at the rim of the pan to ½ inch and fold it in over the filling.

5   Roll the remaining dough to a disk the size of the top of the pie and trim evenly. Arrange on the filling so that the top crust comes right to the edge of the pan and gently press it to the downturned edge of the bottom crust. Brush with the egg wash and trace a lattice pattern with the back of a fork.

6   Bake the pie until the crust is deep golden and the filling is well heated through, about 45 minutes. Cool briefly on a rack and serve warm or at room temperature.

Storage: Keep at room temperature on the day it is baked. Wrap leftovers tightly in plastic and store at room temperature for up to two days. Reheat at 350°F for 15 minutes and cool slightly before serving again.

cookie dough & tarts

The French name for cookie dough, *pâte sablée* (sandy dough), says it all: When baked, this dough has a crumbly, sandy texture that pairs well with rich, creamy fillings. Preparing the dough in the food processor is especially efficient when you use ground nuts as an ingredient, as the nuts are processed and then simply left in the work bowl. Fillings range from a rich and elegant layered combination of chocolate and chestnut creams, to the smooth and satisfying cream cheese and sour cream filling for a New York cheesecake— which actually isn't a tart at all, but does use a baked cookie dough crust as a base.

A

D

> ESSENTIAL TECHNIQUE

baked cookie dough tart crust

I like to include some ground almonds in this dough for extra flavor and texture, but you may omit them. Since the almonds don't absorb any liquid, the dough will work exactly the same way with or without them; no need to make adjustments. This recipe makes enough for two crusts as all the other pastry dough recipes do, but the instructions in steps 4 through 12 are for rolling and baking a single crust from half the dough.

Makes about 1½ pounds of dough, enough for two 10-inch tart crusts

¼ cup slivered or whole blanched almonds, optional

¾ cup confectioners' sugar, sifted after measuring

2½ cups all-purpose flour (spoon into a dry-measure cup and level off)

¼ teaspoon salt

8 ounces (2 sticks) unsalted butter, cold, cut into 16 pieces

2 large egg yolks

1 teaspoon vanilla extract

One 10-inch tart pan with removable bottom

1 Combine the almonds and confectioners' sugar in the bowl of a food processor and pulse repeatedly until finely ground, about 1 minute. No visible pieces of almond should remain. Use a thin metal spatula to scrape away any of the mixture caked up in the corner where the bottom meets the side of the bowl.

2 Add the flour and salt and pulse a couple of times to mix. (If not using the nuts, start here and add the sugar.) Add the butter and pulse repeatedly until no visible pieces remain. Add the yolks and vanilla and pulse until the dough forms a ball.

3 Invert the dough to a floured surface and carefully remove the blade. Divide the dough into 2 equal pieces. Shape each piece of dough into a thick disk and wrap individually in plastic wrap. Refrigerate until firm, at least 1 hour. You may prepare the dough several days in advance and keep it refrigerated, or double wrap and freeze the second piece, defrosting it in the refrigerator overnight before use.

4 To form a tart crust, remove one of the pieces of dough from the refrigerator, and allow it to soften at a cool room temperature for about 20 minutes, just until it is soft enough to roll without cracking, but still firm. Unwrap it, and place it on a floured surface. Use the palm of your hand to press it to a thickness of ¼ inch.

5 Flour the work surface and the dough and gently roll the dough into a 13-inch disk, adding pinches of flour under and on top of the dough as needed (A and B).

B

C

E

F

6 Fold the dough in half and slide both hands under it, palms upward, and transfer it to the pan, lining up the fold with the diameter of the pan. Unfold the dough into the pan. If the dough cracks or tears you can press it back together (C and D).

7 Evenly fit the dough into the pan, making sure it's flat against both the bottom and side of the pan (E). Trim away any excess dough at the rim of the pan by rolling over it with a rolling pin (F) or scraping it away with the back of a paring knife.

8 Finish off the top edges by pressing outward against the side of the pan with your thumb and down at the same time at the top of the crust with your index finger.

9 Slide the tart pan onto a cookie sheet, cover it with plastic wrap, and refrigerate it for several hours or overnight before baking.

10 Set a rack in the middle level of the oven and preheat to 350°F. Pierce the chilled tart crust all over at 1-inch intervals with a fork. Line the crust, bottom and sides, with a 14-inch disk of parchment or wax paper and fill with dried beans or other small weights (G).

11 Bake the tart crust until it is dry looking and set, about 10 minutes. Remove the paper and beans, and bake until the crust is evenly light golden, 15 to 20 minutes.

12 Cool the crust on a rack and use it the same day you bake it.

G

new york cheesecake

This isn't a tart, but it does utilize a cookie dough base—my favorite way of preparing a cheesecake. A baked pastry base makes the cheesecake so easy to unmold, even if you use a springform pan, and it tastes much better than those cookie crumb crusts that are so loaded with butter that they never really become firm.

Makes one 9-inch cheesecake, about 12 servings

½ batch Cookie Dough Tart Crust (page 40), made with or without ground almonds

CHEESECAKE BATTER

1 pound cream cheese, softened at room temperature for at least 3 hours

1 cup sugar

4 large eggs

1½ cups sour cream

2 teaspoons vanilla extract

1 tablespoon lemon juice, strained before measuring

One 9 x 3-inch round cake pan or a 9-inch springform pan, the bottom buttered and lined with a disk of parchment; one small roasting pan to hold the cake in water

Serving: A rich cheesecake needs no accompaniment, but some crushed, sugared strawberries wouldn't hurt either. Bring the cake to room temperature at least 2 hours before serving.

Storage: Store the cake wrapped in plastic in the refrigerator for up to several days before serving.

1   Roll the cookie dough to a 9½-inch disk according to the directions on page 40. Slide the piece of rolled dough onto a flexible cookie sheet or cutting board. Place the pan on the dough and cut around the base of the pan using a paring knife or small pizza wheel. Remove the scraps and slide the disk of dough into the prepared pan. Press it into place and about ⅛ inch up the side of the pan to allow for shrinkage during baking. Chill the dough-lined pan for up to 1 day or at least 1 hour before proceeding.

2   When you are ready to bake the cheesecake, set a rack in the lower third of the oven and preheat to 325°F.

3   Combine the cream cheese and sugar in the bowl of an electric mixer fitted with the paddle attachment and beat on low speed until smooth, about 30 seconds. Use a rubber spatula to scrape down the bowl and beater.

4   Add 1 egg, beat just until smooth, still on low speed, and scrape. Repeat for each of the 3 remaining eggs.

5   In a bowl, whisk the sour cream with the vanilla and lemon juice and add to the mixer bowl. Mix on low speed until just combined. Set the filling aside. If you notice any lumps, use a small rubber spatula to pass the batter through a fine-mesh strainer into a clean bowl.

6   If using a springform pan, wrap the bottom and sides of the pan in a double layer of aluminum foil. Pierce the chilled dough at 1-inch intervals with the tines of a fork and bake it until it is dry and golden, about 15 minutes.

7   While the crust is baking, set the roasting pan on the stove. Have ready a 4-cup measure filled with hot water.

8   As soon as the crust is baked, place it in the roasting pan and butter the side of the pan. Pour the cheesecake batter over the baked crust. Quickly add ½ inch of hot water to the roasting pan and place it in the oven. This quick succession of steps is necessary to ensure that the crust doesn't cool after baking and possibly shrink.

9   Bake the cheesecake until the top is lightly colored and it is set in all but the very center, 45 to 55 minutes. Remove the pan from the water bath and place the cheesecake on a rack. Immediately run the point of a small paring knife around the inside of the pan at the top to loosen the top ½ inch of the cake from the side of the pan. This will prevent cracking.

10 Cool completely, wrap loosely in plastic, and chill for several hours or overnight before serving.

11 To unmold the chilled cheesecake, have a couple of cardboard rounds, plastic wrap, and a platter ready. Use a small paring knife to loosen the cake from the side of the pan. Place the pan over high heat for a couple of seconds to melt the butter under the paper and loosen the cake from the pan. If you used a springform, remove the side of the pan.

12 Cover the top of the cake with plastic wrap and a cardboard and invert. Lift off the pan and paper. Replace with another cardboard and invert again. Remove the top cardboard and plastic wrap. Slide the cheesecake from the cardboard onto the platter or wrap the cake, still on the cardboard, and refrigerate until needed.

chocolate chestnut tart

Makes one 10-inch tart, about 10 servings

CHESTNUT FILLING

1½ pounds fresh chestnuts, or one
14- to 16-ounce jar peeled chestnuts

1 teaspoon salt

2 cups milk

⅓ cup sugar

1 vanilla bean, split lengthwise

1 tablespoon dark rum

4 tablespoons unsalted butter, softened

CHOCOLATE FILLING

⅔ cup heavy whipping cream

2 tablespoons sugar

7 ounces bittersweet chocolate (65 to 70% cocoa solids), melted and cooled

2 tablespoons unsalted butter, very soft

10 crystallized violets or large chocolate shavings for finishing

One 10-inch Cookie Dough Tart Crust (page 40), with or without ground almonds, baked and cooled

This is a showstopper dessert for a fall or winter party. The crumbly cookie dough crust contrasts perfectly with the rich chestnut and chocolate fillings, which form elegant layers when the tart is cut. Fresh chestnuts are easily available from October through January, the best time to enjoy this type of dessert. You may substitute peeled chestnuts that come in a jar, but they tend to be really expensive.

1 For the chestnut filling, pierce the rounded end of each chestnut with the point of a small knife and place the nuts in a large saucepan. Cover with water and bring to a boil. Add the salt and continue cooking at a low boil until the chestnuts are tender and one peels easily, 30 to 45 minutes. If using chestnuts from a jar, rinse, drain, and taste a small piece of one for tenderness. If they seem hard, boil them as above for 30 minutes.

2 Drain the chestnuts in a colander and cover with a kitchen towel to keep them warm so that they peel easily. Peel the chestnuts, removing the outer shell and as much of the interior brown skin as possible.

3 Rinse the pan and return the peeled chestnuts to it along with the milk, sugar, and vanilla bean. Use a potato masher to crush the chestnuts into small pieces, but not a puree. Bring to a boil over medium heat and decrease the heat so that the milk just simmers. Cook, stirring often, until the chestnuts are very soft, about 20 minutes. If the liquid become too thick before the chestnuts are tender, add water a couple of tablespoons at a time to prevent scorching. Remove the vanilla bean.

4 Cool the cooked chestnuts to room temperature and then puree them in a food processor for 30 seconds, scrape down the sides, and continue to alternate pureeing and scraping until when you taste a small spoonful of the cream there is no graininess at all in it. Once they are reduced to a perfectly smooth cream, add the rum and the butter and pulse to mix in.

5 Scrape the filling into the crust and use a small offset spatula to spread it evenly.

6 For the chocolate filling, combine the cream and sugar in a small saucepan and whisk to dissolve the sugar. Place over medium heat and cook until the sugar is dissolved and the mixture is hot, about 175°F. Pour the cream into a bowl to cool to room temperature.

7 Pour the cooled cream into the cooled chocolate and whisk smooth. Whisk in the butter (if it's not very soft, the butter will form lumps).

8 Scrape the chocolate filling over the chestnut filling and use a small offset spatula to spread it evenly. Arrange 10 crystallized violets equidistant from each other on the chocolate filling next to the crust, or sprinkle with chocolate shavings. Unmold the tart and slide it from the pan base to a platter.

Serving: Use a thin, sharp knife wiped with a damp cloth after each cut to divide the tart into wedges.

Storage: Cover leftovers with plastic wrap and keep at a cool room temperature or in the refrigerator. Bring to room temperature again before serving if refrigerated.

strawberry cream cheese crumble tart

Makes one 10-inch tart, about 8 servings

ALMOND CRUMB TOPPING

1¼ cups all-purpose flour (spoon into a dry-measure cup and level off)

⅓ cup sugar

¼ teaspoon baking powder

¼ teaspoon ground cinnamon

⅛ teaspoon salt

¼ cup slivered or whole blanched almonds, coarsely chopped into ¼-inch pieces

8 tablespoons (1 stick) unsalted butter, melted

STRAWBERRY CREAM CHEESE FILLING

1 pound cream cheese, softened

1 cup confectioners' sugar, sifted after measuring

1 teaspoon finely grated lemon zest

1½ teaspoons vanilla extract

1 pound strawberries, rinsed, hulled, and halved or quartered if large, or left whole if very small (reserve 1 perfect whole berry)

Confectioners' sugar in a shaker, for finishing

1 unbaked Cookie Dough Tart Crust (page 40), prepared up to the end of step 9

Jelly-roll pan lined with parchment or foil for baking the crumb topping

I've often confessed in the past to being addicted to crumb topping. Recently I even found a new way to enjoy it—atop a tart that has a prebaked crust and a creamy filling. This does necessitate the extra step of baking the crumb topping separately, but you can do that while baking the tart crust. The crisp crumb topping with a hint of chopped almonds is a perfect contrast to this tart's light cream cheese filling and juicy strawberries.

1   Set racks in the upper and lower thirds of the oven and preheat to 350°F.

2   For the topping, in a medium bowl, stir together the flour, sugar, baking powder, cinnamon, and salt. Stir in the almonds. Use a rubber spatula to stir in the butter. Let the mixture stand for a few minutes, then use your fingertips to break the mixture into ¼- to ½-inch crumbs. Scatter the crumbs on the prepared pan.

3   Bake the tart crust in the lower third of the oven and the crumb topping in the upper third. After 10 minutes, remove the paper and beans from the tart shell and place it on the upper rack and the crumbs on the lower one.

4   Continue baking the tart shell until it is dry and light golden, another 15 to 20 minutes. Bake the crumb topping until it is deep golden and firm, another 10 to 15 minutes.

5   Cool the crust and the topping on racks. If the crumbs have clumped together during baking, let them cool completely and then use a bench scraper or table knife to chop them coarsely.

6   For the cream cheese filling, place the cream cheese in the bowl of an electric mixer fitted with the paddle attachment and beat on medium speed just until it is smooth. Beat in the confectioners' sugar, lemon zest, and vanilla and continue beating until lightened, about 1 minute.

7   To assemble the tart, spread half the cream cheese filling on the bottom of the tart crust and arrange the berries on it, cut side down. Spread the remaining filling over the berries. Evenly scatter the crumb topping over the filling. Right before serving, lightly dust the topping with confectioners' sugar and place the reserved berry in the center of the tart.

Serving: Unmold the tart and slide it off the pan base to a platter. Serve wedges of the tart; it needs no accompaniment.

Storage: You may have all the components ready, but don't assemble the tart until a few hours before you intend to serve it. Keep it at a cool room temperature until you do. Wrap and refrigerate leftovers and bring to room temperature before serving again. The crust will soften after it has been refrigerated.

variations

Substitute raspberries or blueberries, or use a combination of all three berries. Peeled and diced perfectly ripe peaches or mangoes are also good choices.

french raspberry tart

Makes one 10-inch tart, 8 to 10 servings

PASTRY CREAM

¾ cup whole milk

¼ cup heavy whipping cream

¼ cup sugar

3 large egg yolks

2 tablespoons all-purpose flour

1 teaspoon vanilla extract

RASPBERRIES AND GLAZE

¾ cup seedless raspberry jam

2 tablespoons water

3 half-pint baskets fresh raspberries, about 1 pound, picked over but not washed

10-inch Cookie Dough Tart Crust (page 40), with or without ground almonds, baked and cooled

This is a classic: a cookie dough crust topped with a thin layer of pastry cream, lots of flavorful fresh raspberries, and a bit of raspberry glaze to bind them together. Strawberries are an obvious substitute, but I only like to make this with small, perfectly sweet, height-of-season strawberries. Larger, out-of-season berries have less flavor and produce a lot of water when they are cut. Mulberries, blackberries, and blueberries in season sidestep the water issue. See the variation for making an accompanying glaze for these berries.

1 For the pastry cream, whisk the milk, cream, and half the sugar in a small saucepan. Place over low heat and bring to a full boil.

2 Meanwhile, in a bowl, whisk the yolks and then whisk in the remaining sugar. Sift over and whisk in the flour.

3 When the milk mixture boils, whisk it into the yolk mixture. Strain the mixture back into the pan and place over medium heat. Use a small, pointed-end whisk to whisk constantly, being sure to reach into the corners of the pan, until the cream comes to a full boil and thickens. Continue to cook, whisking constantly, for 30 seconds. Off heat, whisk in the vanilla.

4 Scrape the cream into a glass or stainless-steel bowl and press plastic wrap against the surface. Chill until cold.

5 A few hours before you intend to serve the tart, make the glaze. Combine the jam and water in a small saucepan. Bring to a boil over medium heat, stirring often. Strain the glaze into a bowl, rinse the saucepan, return the glaze to the saucepan, and cook over low heat until reduced to about 1/2 cup, about 10 minutes.

6 Use a small offset spatula to spread the cooled pastry cream in the tart crust.

7 Put the berries in a bowl and drizzle on the slightly cooled glaze. Use a small rubber spatula to fold the berries and glaze together gently. Scrape the berries into the tart crust on the pastry cream and arrange them in an even mound.

8 Unmold the tart and slide it from the pan base to a platter.

Serving: Use a sharp, thin knife to cut the tart into wedges.

Storage: Keep at a cool room temperature until serving. Wrap and chill leftovers.

variations

Omit the glaze, arrange the berries in the crust, and dust with confectioners' sugar immediately before serving.

Substitute strawberry jam for the glaze. Arrange strawberries on the pastry cream and use a brush to apply a thin coat of the jam.

To substitute any of the other berries mentioned above, use a neutral-flavored jelly such as currant or apple instead of the jam. Omit the water. Crush 1/2 cup of the berries, add them to the jelly, and bring to a boil over medium heat, stirring occasionally. Strain and reduce the glaze as above. Continue with the recipe at step 6, above.

04

quick puff pastry

Some purists may still make the laborious type of puff pastry that involves preparing a dough and wrapping it around a square of softened butter before beginning the rolling and folding process. I abandoned it a long time ago, especially since I know that no one, including me, has the time for long versions of recipes when equally good and faster versions exist. Making quick puff pastry, sometimes also referred to as rough puff pastry, is a one-step mixing process immediately followed by rolling and folding that's completed without chilling the dough either after mixing or after any of the folds. It does take a bit of time to prepare, but still only about a third of the time (or less) that the traditional version takes. If you're really pressed for time, there is an even faster version made in the food processor that will take about twenty minutes.

quick puff pastry

There is only one inviolable rule for preparing quick or any other kind of puff pastry: Make sure it's cool in your kitchen or the dough will turn into a gooey mess. That said, mixing the dough is no more complicated than making any other pastry dough—in fact, you can do part or all of the mixing in the food processor. Keep a ruler handy as you roll or you might wind up with an odd-shaped piece of dough that's difficult to maneuver.

Makes about 1½ pounds dough

10 ounces (2½ sticks) unsalted butter, cold

2 cups all-purpose flour (spoon into a dry-measure cup and level off)

¾ teaspoon salt

⅔ cup cold water

Storage: The dough keeps well in the refrigerator for up to 5 days. Some people like to add a couple of teaspoons of distilled white vinegar to that first amount of water added to the dough in step 4, as a preservative. Double wrap and freeze for up to 1 month. Defrost the dough in the refrigerator overnight before using.

A

1 Cut 2 sticks of the butter into ¼-inch cubes. Scrape them onto a plate in one layer and refrigerate them.

2 Put the flour and salt in a bowl and stir a couple of times to combine. Cut the remaining 4 tablespoons of butter into thin slivers and add to the bowl. Rub in the butter, squeezing it with your fingertips, rubbing the butter and flour mixture between the palms of your hands and reaching down to the bottom of the bowl. Repeat until the flour and butter are evenly mixed. This only takes a couple of minutes; the mixture should remain cool and powdery. Alternatively, pulse the flour, salt, and butter slivers in a food processor fitted with the metal blade until no visible pieces of butter remain, then pour the mixture into a bowl.

3 Add the chilled butter cubes (A) and use a rubber spatula to fold them in.

4 Set aside 2 tablespoons of the measured water and pour the remaining water on the flour and butter mixture (B). Use the rubber spatula to fold everything together, scraping from the bottom of the bowl upward (C). If there are a lot of dry bits of unmoistened flour, sprinkle on the remaining water, 1 tablespoon at a time, folding it in as before.

5 Scrape the dough from the bowl to a floured work surface and lightly flour the dough. Use your hands to squeeze and shape the dough into a cylinder, and then press down to flatten it into a rectangle (D).

6 Flour the surface and the dough, and starting at the narrow end of the rectangle farthest from you, use a rolling pin to press the dough firmly in parallel strokes close to each other (E). If there are sticky pieces of butter on the surface of the dough, seal them with a large pinch of flour, making sure to clean off anything stuck to the rolling pin before continuing. Repeat the pressing motion again from the close to farther narrow end of the dough.

7 Press the dough once along the width; it should now be a rectangle about ½ inch thick. Once again, flour under and on top of the dough and roll the dough away and back toward you in the length and once in the width, without rolling over the ends in the same direction, to make a rectangle about 18 inches long and 8 inches wide.

B

C

D

E

F

G

H

8 Fold the two 8-inch ends of the dough in toward the middle of the rectangle, leaving a 1-inch space in the middle. Fold the bottom up to the top to form 4 layers of dough (F, G, and H). Reposition the dough do that the folded edge that resembles the spine of a book is on your left. Rolling and folding the dough is known as "giving the dough a turn."

9 Repeat steps 6, 7, and 8.

10 Repeat steps 6, 7, and 8 again.

11 Wrap the dough and refrigerate it for at least 3 hours to firm up and rest its elasticity before attempting to use it. **>**

variation

Food Processor Mixing Prepare the first part of the dough in the food processor as described in step 2, but leave it in the work bowl. Add the chilled butter cubes and give three 1-second pulses. Add half the water and pulse once; add the remaining water and pulse twice. The dough will not form a ball. Remove the blade by its handle and do step 5, page 50. Press the dough in both directions as in step 6, then roll it to a rectangle that's about 10 x 20 inches. Fold the 10-inch side farthest from you down over the middle and the 10-inch side closest to you over that to make a 3-layered rectangle that's about 6 x 10 inches. Position one of the 6-inch sides closest to you and roll upward, jelly-roll-style, to make a fat cylinder. Flour the work surface, position the cylinder of dough with the seam on the bottom, flour the top of the dough, and press with the palm of your hand to make the dough into a rectangle. Resume at step 11.

> ESSENTIAL TECHNIQUE

rolling puff pastry

Follow these simple instructions for all the recipes in this chapter. Some recipes might call for the dough to be rolled in sugar instead of flour, but the technique remains the same.

1 Flour the work surface and place the chilled puff pastry on it. Flour the dough. Press the dough in parallel and successive firm strokes with a rolling pin in both directions, until it is somewhat more malleable. Repeat dusting the surface and the dough with pinches of flour.

2 Roll back and forth away and back toward you without rolling over the ends (which would make them thinner and possibly make them stick to the surface).

3 To roll in the other direction, move the piece of dough 90 degrees and repeat step 2.

4 Keep a ruler nearby and measure the dough to see whether it is the size specified in the recipe. Repeat rolling in both directions until the dough is about 1/2 inch larger all around than the size you need.

5 Slide the dough to a cookie sheet (if it's a large piece, you might have to fold it and then unfold it on the sheet) and cover loosely with plastic wrap.

6 Chill the dough until firm for easier cutting and shaping.

essential tips for quick puff pastry

- Quick puff pastry works like the flaky pastry dough on page 26, except here the butter is in larger pieces, consequently making larger layers throughout the dough. There is even more butter than flour by weight, so the dough not only bakes up flaky, but the many spaces that fill with steam actually rise up (puff) away from each other.

- When mixing the liquid into the dough, be careful not to overmix, which might render the dough elastic and consequently difficult to roll and form the layers.

- Cold, cold, cold: Make sure everything is cold before you start mixing the dough. If you're the least bit apprehensive, or if the butter seems to be softening before you start rolling the dough, refrigerate the dough, wrapped in plastic, for 1 hour after step 5.

- Pay attention to the corners of the dough every time you roll over it. You want real 90-degree corners, so that the dough folds up into a symmetrically layered package that's easy to roll out again. A bench scraper is a handy tool for straightening the corners: Hold it perpendicular to the work surface and push in on the dough with the flat side of the blade to straighten it.

- As with all pastry doughs, resting is as important as careful mixing and rolling. Let the dough rest after turning it, then again once you've formed a pastry from the dough.

- Save any scraps generated by cutting out rounds of dough. Wrap and chill them and when they are firm, press them together, then roll them into a rectangle twice as long as it is wide. Fold the dough over to make a square, wrap, and refrigerate. This dough is best used for the base of the thin apple tart, the cheese straws, or the sugared puff pastries that follow.

- If you intend to keep the puff pastry in the refrigerator and use it over the course of several days, when preparing the dough, stir a tablespoon of strained lemon juice or distilled white vinegar into the water. The acidity will help prevent the dough from becoming gray as it sits.

"thin" apple tart
tarte fine aux pommes

This name refers to what I call a bistro apple tart—a dinner-plate-size or two-portion puff pastry tart topped with thin apple slices and a bit of glaze. It's a lovely tart, but it's pretty impractical if you are serving more than a couple of guests. The recipe below incorporates all the same elements, but with a slightly more generous yield. It's more practical, too, since it can be baked in advance and reheated if you want to serve it warm.

Makes one large 10 x 15-inch tart, about 12 servings

½ batch (12 ounces) Quick Puff Pastry (page 50)

APPLE TOPPING

4 large Golden Delicious apples, about 2¼ pounds

4 tablespoons unsalted butter, melted

⅓ cup turbinado sugar or granulated light brown sugar

APRICOT GLAZE

¾ cup best-quality apricot preserves

2 tablespoons water

Crème fraîche or sweetened whipped cream for serving

One 10 x 15-inch jelly-roll pan lined, bottom and sides, with buttered foil

1 Roll the dough to a 12 x 16-inch rectangle, according to the instructions on page 50.

2 Fold the dough in quarters and arrange it in the pan, unfolding it to fit the pan. Press the dough into the bottom and sides of the pan and leave the excess dough at the rim of the pan untrimmed for the moment. Cover loosely with plastic wrap and chill until a few hours before you intend to serve the tart.

3 When you are ready to serve the tart, set a rack in the lowest level of the oven and preheat to 400°F.

4 Peel, halve, and core the apples. Use a small sharp paring knife to slice through each apple half across the core, to make ⅛-inch slices. Keep the apple halves together as you slice through them to make arranging the apples easier.

5 Remove the tart crust from the refrigerator and pierce it all over with a fork at 1-inch intervals.

6 Eliminate the first couple of smaller slices from the ends of each apple half and press on it gently with the palm of your hand to fan it out away from you so that it's about 6 inches long. Slide a spatula under the apple slices and arrange them in the top left corner of the pan in the length of the pan. Repeat with another apple half, then use an apple quarter to fill in the first row. Make 2 more rows right next to each other in the same way.

7 Paint the apple slices with the butter and evenly sprinkle with the sugar. Bake the tart until the pastry is baked through and the apples have taken on some color, about 30 minutes.

8 Place the tart on a rack and use a sharp paring knife to trim away the overhanging dough. Cool the tart completely and keep it at room temperature until you intend to serve it.

9 For the glaze, stir the preserves and water together in a small saucepan and bring to a boil over low heat, stirring occasionally. Strain into a bowl, rinse the pan, return the glaze to the pan, and bring the glaze to a boil again. Let it reduce until slightly thickened, about 5 minutes.

10 If you wish to serve the tart warm, reheat for 10 minutes at 350°F and cool slightly first. Pull on the foil lining to slide the tart to a cutting board. Flatten the foil that was on the side of the tart and slide a long spatula between the tart and the foil. Pull away the foil, holding the tart in place with your other hand. Paint the apples with the glaze.

Serving: Use a sharp knife to slice the tart into three 15-inch strips. Cut across the strips every 3¾ inches to make 12 servings. Arrange each serving on a dessert plate and spoon some crème fraîche or whipped cream beside it.

Storage: Wrap leftovers and keep at room temperature for up to a day or two. Leftover apple tart benefits from reheating.

A   B   C

ground beef empanadas
empanadas de picadillo

Makes eight 6-inch empanadas

⅔ batch (1 pound) Quick Puff Pastry (page 50)

PICADILLO

2 small (about 8 ounces total) Yukon Gold or boiling potatoes

½ large white or yellow onion (about 4 to 5 ounces), peeled and coarsely chopped

1 small red or green bell pepper (about 4 to 5 ounces), coarsely chopped

3 large cloves garlic, crushed, peeled, and coarsely chopped

3 tablespoons olive or mild vegetable oil

1 teaspoon ground cumin

1 pound lean ground beef

¾ cup tomato puree

¾ cup water

½ teaspoon salt

1 teaspoon distilled white vinegar

2 tablespoons capers in brine, rinsed and drained

3 tablespoons sliced pimiento-stuffed green olives

¼ teaspoon hot chili powder, or to taste (optional)

One cookie sheet or jelly-roll pan lined with parchment paper or foil

Typical empanadas are made from complicated, ancient forms of puff pastry and are usually fried. I recently had leftover puff pastry and leftover picadillo and decided to try some baked empanadas; these are the result. Picadillo (*picado* means "chopped" in Spanish) is a fairly dry ragout made from ground beef and seasonings. This quantity is about twice as much as you need for eight empanadas. Serve the rest with rice.

1 Roll the dough according to the instructions on page 52 to a 12-inch square. Slide the dough to a cookie sheet and refrigerate until firm, about 15 minutes. Cut the square of dough into two 6 x 12-inch rectangles and roll each to a 12-inch square. Stack them on a cookie sheet with plastic wrap between and on top and refrigerate until you are ready to form the empanadas.

2 For the picadillo, put the potatoes in a small saucepan and cover them with water. Bring to a boil over medium heat and boil for a minute. Slide the pan off the heat and leave the potatoes in the water until you need to add them to the picadillo; they'll be about three-quarters cooked when you do.

3 Put the onion, bell pepper, and garlic in a food processor fitted with the metal blade and pulse to chop fine, but do not puree.

4 Put the oil in a wide saucepan or Dutch oven with a cover and add the vegetables. Cook over medium heat until they start to sizzle, then decrease to medium-low and cook, stirring occasionally, until they are soft and beginning to turn golden, about 20 minutes. Stir in the cumin and cook, stirring, for 30 seconds.

5 Add the ground beef and use a wooden spoon to mash it into the vegetables, continuously jabbing the spoon downward into the meat so that it cooks in separate grains and not clumps. Continue jabbing and stirring until the meat is reduced to fine granules and is starting to sizzle in the pan, about 5 minutes.

6 Add the tomato puree, water, salt, and vinegar and stir them in. Bring to a boil, then regulate the heat so that the mixture simmers actively for about 10 minutes. If the liquid seems to be evaporating too quickly, decrease the heat.

D   E   F

7 Peel and cut the potatoes into 1/2-inch dice. Add the
   potatoes, capers, olives, and chili powder, if using, to the
   pan and stir. Simmer until the potatoes are tender and most
   of the liquid has boiled off, 15 to 20 additional minutes.

8 Cool the picadillo completely before filling the empanadas.
   When you are ready to bake, set a rack in the middle level
   of the oven and preheat to 400°F.

9 Cut each piece of chilled dough into four 6-inch disks
   (A and B), refrigerating them again as you cut them. Wrap
   and refrigerate the scraps for another use.

10 Place one of the disks on a floured surface and sprinkle
   lightly with flour. Roll over once away and back toward you
   to make a 7 1/2- to 8-inch oval (C). Brush some water on the
   edge of the oval closest to you and place 3 tablespoons of the
   filling on it (D). Fold the bottom half of the oval over to join
   the top edge (E) and transfer to the pan. Use your finger to
   press the two layers of dough firmly together, about 1/8 inch
   in (F). Repeat with the rest of the dough and filling.

11 Use the point of a paring knife to cut a 1-inch vent hole in
   each empanada over the thickest part of the filling. Bake
   until the emapnadas are deep golden and the filling is
   bubbling slightly, about 20 minutes.

12 Slide to a rack and cool the empanadas for 5 minutes before
   serving on a platter.

Serving: Empanadas make a great lunch with a salad. They're
also good at room temperature or for a picnic. Cool them on a
rack to keep them crisp if you want to serve them that way.

Storage: You can assemble the empanadas and bake them
later the same day, but they have to be eaten on the day they're
baked. Wrap and refrigerate leftovers, reheat them at 350°F
for 10 minutes, and cool them slightly before serving.

variation

Chicken Empanadas Substitute 1 pound skinless boneless
chicken thighs cut into 1-inch dice for the ground beef. Cook the
same way, stirring occasionally (no need to jab) after adding the
meat to the vegetables. Before adding the potatoes, use 2 forks
to shred the meat.

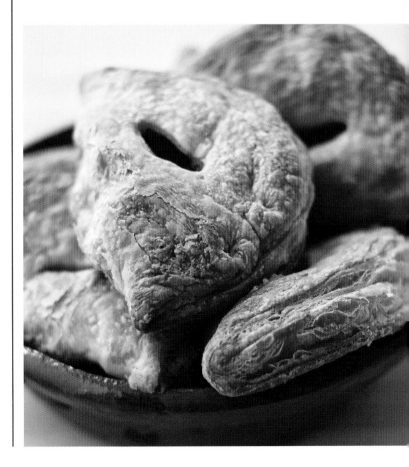

just add sugar

There are any number of wonderful puff pastries that only require rolling the dough in sugar before shaping it. Though these are simple, absolutely nothing can equal the flavor of fresh-from-the-oven all-butter puff pastry that has had sugar caramelized on it. When you begin rolling the dough, the amount of sugar it has to absorb might seem excessive. Every time you roll over the dough, redistribute half the sugar underneath it and half on top of it and roll with a firm but gentle pressure to avoid making the dough too thin too quickly. Remember that any leftover sugar can either be sprinkled on the pastries before they're baked or, as in the case of the Butterfly Wings, the pastries can be dipped into the sugar after they are cut and before they are placed on the pan.

½ batch (12 ounces) Quick Puff Pastry (page 50)

1 cup sugar

2 cookie sheets or jelly-roll pans, lined with parchment paper.

ox tongues

This is the easiest and most simple variation.

Makes 24 individual pastries

1 Roll the dough according to the instructions on page 52 to an 8 x 12-inch rectangle. If the dough gets soft, slide it onto a cookie sheet and refrigerate it for 15 minutes.

2 Use a 2-inch plain round cutter to cut the dough into 24 disks. Wrap and refrigerate the scraps and use them for another pastry.

3 One at a time, place the disks on a heavily sugared work surface and sprinkle with additional sugar. Roll over the disk to make it into a 3- to 3^1/$_2$-inch oval.

4 Arrange the ovals on the prepared pans and refrigerate them for 30 minutes.

5 When you are ready to bake them, set a rack in the middle level of the oven and preheat to 375°F.

6 Pierce the chilled ox tongues all over with a fork and sprinkle more sugar on them. Bake one pan at a time until the sugar is caramelized to a deep golden color, 10 to 15 minutes.

7 Watch the ox tongues carefully after half the baking time has elapsed. Hotter areas in the oven and other variables such as the thickness of the dough will cause them to be done at different times. If necessary, use a wide spatula to remove individual pastries from the pan to a cooling rack as they are done.

8 Cool on a rack and serve them on the day they are baked for best flavor.

Storage: Keep leftovers between wax paper in a container with a tight-fitting lid.

banderillas

Named for the darts that are used during a bullfight, these are a popular Mexican puff pastry.

Makes 16 individual pastries

1 Cover the work surface with half the sugar and the top of the dough with the other half of the sugar, then roll the dough, according to the instructions on page 52, to an 8 x 12-inch rectangle. If the dough gets soft, slide it onto a cookie sheet and chill for 15 minutes.

2 Use a sharp pizza wheel to trim the edges of the dough and then to cut it into two 8 x 6-inch rectangles. Pierce the dough all over with the tines of a fork.

3 Cut one of the pieces of dough into eight 1 x 6-inch strips. Place the strips on one of the prepared pans as they are cut. Repeat with the second piece of dough.

4 Arrange the pastries on the prepared pans and refrigerate them for 30 minutes.

5 Bake and cool as for ox tongues, above.

butterfly wings

A variation of the ever-popular palmier, or elephant ear, these are more tailored and elegant in appearance.

Makes about 24 individual pastries

1 Cover the work surface with half the sugar, then top the dough with the rest, and, according to the instructions on page 52, roll to an 8 x 12-inch rectangle. If the dough gets soft, slide it onto a cookie sheet and chill for 15 minutes.

2 Use a sharp pizza wheel to trim the edges of the dough. Fold each of the 12-inch sides of the dough almost in toward the middle, leaving a 3/4-inch gap where they meet. Fold the left (4-inch) side of the dough over to meet the right side. Finally, fold the top (now 6-inch) side down to meet the bottom edge. Give the layered strip of dough a good press with the palm of your hand and wrap and refrigerate for 1 hour. Reserve the extra sugar on the work surface.

3 Cut the chilled package of dough into 1/4-inch slices. Working with one at a time, dip the bottom cut side into the reserved sugar and place the pastry on one of the pans, leaving 2 inches all around to allow for expansion.

4 Bake and cool as for ox tongues, opposite.

sacristains

The name of these pastries means sacristan or church/sacristy caretaker in French. All my efforts to find out why they have this name have been unsuccessful, but I can attest to the fact that they're delicious.

Makes about 48 small individual pastries

½ batch (12 ounces) Quick Puff Pastry (page 52)

Egg wash: 1 egg well beaten with a pinch of salt

⅔ cup ground almonds

⅔ cup sugar

½ teaspoon ground cinnamon

2 jelly-roll pans lined with parchment

1 Roll the dough according to the instructions on page 52 to a 12-inch square. Paint with the egg wash. Mix the almonds, sugar, and cinnamon together and evenly sprinkle on a 6 x 12-inch rectangle of the dough. Fold the other half of the dough over the sugar and almonds and press to adhere. Chill until firm, about 15 minutes.

2 Set racks in the upper and lower thirds of the oven and preheat to 375°F.

3 Roll the dough back to a 12-inch square and use a pastry wheel to cut into 24 1/2-inch-wide strips. Twist one of the strips into a corkscrew shape by pressing in opposite directions at the same time with the palms of each hand.

4 Arrange 12 sacristains on each of the prepared pans, pressing the ends against the side of the pan to prevent them from unraveling while baking.

5 Bake until deep golden, about 15 minutes, switching the pans from top to bottom and vice versa and rotating them from front to back at the same time halfway through the baking time.

6 Immediately remove the sacristains to a cutting board, trim off the ends, and cut them in half lengthwise. Work quickly because the pastry is still flexible when it's hot, but it becomes crisp as it cools and would shatter when cut.

variation

Cheese Straws Substitute 3/4 cup finely grated Parmigiano-Reggiano cheese for the almonds and sugar. Spread the cheese on the egg-washed dough and sprinkle with 1/2 teaspoon salt (it brings out the flavor in the cheese) and 2 teaspoons sweet Hungarian paprika. Proceed as for Sacristains, above.

NOTE: To substitute the grated cheese and paprika in the recipes for the Ox Tongues, Banderillas, or Butterfly Wings, roll the dough to the size and shape specified in the recipe. For the Ox Tongues, cut the dough, brush the tops with egg wash, and sprinkle with half of the cheese and paprika. Turn them over, repeat the egg wash, cheese, and paprika, then roll them into ovals. For the Banderillas, paint the two rectangles of dough with egg wash and sprinkle with half the cheese and paprika. Invert, paint, and sprinkle and then cut and place on pans. For the Butterfly Wings, paint the surface of the dough with the egg wash and sprinkle with the cheese and paprika before folding.

caramelized apple tart
tarte tartin

Makes one 9- to 10-inch tart,
about 8 to 10 servings

½ batch (12 ounces) Quick Puff Pastry,
page 50, or ½ batch (about 9 ounces)
Flaky Pastry Dough, page 26

2½ pounds Golden Delicious apples

¾ cup sugar

1 tablespoon lemon juice, measured
after straining

1 tablespoon water

3 tablespoons unsalted butter,
cut into 8 pieces

One 9- or 10-inch nonstick slope-sided
sauté pan

Serving: Serve the tart at room
temperature with some whipped cream.

Storage: Keep the tart loosely covered
at room temperature before and after
serving. Reheat leftovers for best flavor.

I first encountered Tarte Tatin in early 1974, when I lived briefly with the Pinelli family at their small hotel in Monte Carlo. Raymonde Pinelli loved apples in all forms and had beautiful 19th-century earthenware Calvados jugs in the shape of apples, which I have to confess I coveted. Raymonde's method of preparing Tarte Tatin involved repeatedly turning wedges of her favorite apples, *les Golden*, in a buttery caramel in a flimsy aluminum tart pan set atop a flame tamer on her big commercial range. She used a tender sweet dough to cover the apples before baking, which is pleasant enough, but buttery puff pastry, especially in combination with caramel, is much better. I retained one thing from her recipe, though: The apples need plenty of caramel and butter to achieve the best flavor.

1   Roll the dough according to the directions on page 52 to an 11-inch disk. Slide onto a cookie sheet, loosely cover with plastic wrap, and chill while making the filling.

2   Peel, halve, and core the apples. Cut each half into 3 wedges. Cover and set aside while preparing the caramel.

3   Set a rack in the middle level of the oven and preheat to 350°F.

4   Combine the sugar, lemon juice, water, and butter in the sauté pan and use a wooden spoon to mix. Place over medium heat and bring to a boil, stirring often so that the butter is absorbed by the syrup and does not separate from it.

5   At the boil, decrease the heat to medium low and continue cooking until the syrup begins to color. Check the color of the syrup by picking up a spoonful and letting it drip back into the pan; the caramel always looks darker when concentrated in the pan. Pull the pan from the heat as the caramel continues to darken but is not quite finished; it will continue to cook and color more deeply from the heat retained by the pan. If it stays too light, return the pan to the heat and cook until only slightly darker, removing the pan again and checking the color after a minute. At this point the caramel is safe from over-darkening.

6   Arrange the apple wedges in the caramel rounded side down, crowding them close together in a row perpendicular to the side of the pan. Fill in the center with more wedges, then scatter any remaining apple pieces over the others.

7   Place the pan over low heat to melt the caramel again. Remove from the heat and slide the disk of chilled dough onto the apples. Push the dough inward toward the center of the pan so that it fits inside the pan even though it's larger. This will compensate for any shrinkage while the dough is baking.

8   Bake the tart until the dough is baked through and the apples have absorbed the caramel and are no longer watery, about 50 to 60 minutes.

9   Cool the tart in the pan on a rack until it is lukewarm. To unmold the tart, invert a platter onto the pan and invert again, firmly grasping the platter with one hand and the handle of the pan with the other. Protect both hands with oven mitts in case some hot syrup drips out of the pan. Lift off the pan.

fig & raspberry croustades

Makes nine 5-inch croustades

CROUSTADES

½ batch (12 ounces) Quick Puff Pastry (page 50)

Egg wash: 1 egg well beaten with a pinch of salt

CRÈME ANGLAISE

1 cup whole milk

1 cup heavy whipping cream

⅓ cup sugar

½ vanilla bean, split lengthwise

3 3-inch strips lemon zest removed with a vegetable peeler

1 2-inch cinnamon stick

6 large egg yolks

FIG AND RASPBERRY FILLING

1 pint (about 12 ounces) fresh black or green figs

2 ½-pint baskets (about 8 ounces) fresh raspberries

¾ cup seedless raspberry jam

Cookie sheet or jelly-roll pan lined with parchment or foil

Serving: Place each croustade on a dessert plate and pass the crème anglaise at the table in a bowl or sauceboat.

Storage: Keep the croustades at room temperature and use them on the day they are baked.

A

D

Although I love this fig and raspberry combination, these tailored croustades can be filled with any sweet or savory mixture you like. Here fresh figs are mixed with whole raspberries, bound with some raspberry glaze, and finished with an unglazed fig half and berries and crème anglaise. Another presentation might use the pastry cream on page 46 on the bottom, topped with any single fruit or assortment of fruit you have on hand. Or try savory mixtures like creamed mushrooms, cultivated or wild; shredded roast duck (I buy a half roast duck in Chinatown), quickly stir-fried with scallions and a dash of hoisin sauce; or diced Japanese eggplant sautéed in olive oil and garlic with seeded, diced fresh tomatoes and a handful of shredded basil. The recipe calls for a half batch of puff pastry, which makes 9 croustades. Place any extra unbaked ones on a cookie sheet in the freezer until they're frozen solid, wrap them individually in plastic, and store in a sealed plastic bag in the freezer; they'll defrost in a few minutes.

B

C

E

F

1 Roll the dough according to the directions on page 52 to a 15-inch square. Slide onto a cookie sheet or flexible cutting board and chill until firm, about 15 minutes.

2 Use a sharp pizza wheel to trim the edges and cut the dough into 9 5-inch squares. Fold over each square of dough to form a triangle. Make a cut over the fold on either side, 1/2 inch from the cut edge to within 1/2 inch of the point of the triangle (A). Unfold the triangles back into squares.

3 Pierce the inner squares at 1/2-inch intervals with a fork (B) and paint them lightly with the egg wash. Fold the outer corners of each square over to the opposite inside corners, one at a time (C and D). With a floured fingertip press the borders down and indent the sides of each croustade at 1/4-inch intervals with the dull side of a paring knife (E and F). Arrange on the prepared pan and chill until firm or cover and chill overnight.

4 When you are ready to bake the croustades, set a rack in the middle level of the oven and preheat to 375°F. Arrange the chilled croustades on the prepared pan. Bake the croustades until they are well risen and deep golden, 25 to 30 minutes. Remove the pan from the oven and empty the squares by loosening the sides of the inner squares with a fork and lifting them out. Remove any unbaked dough from the centers of the croustades and return them to the oven for another 5 minutes. If you want to use the squares of dough removed from the croustades as covers for the filling, return them to the oven with the croustades. Cool the croustades on a rack and use them the day they are baked.

5 For the crème anglaise, whisk together the milk, cream, sugar, vanilla bean, lemon zest, and cinnamon stick in a saucepan. Bring to a boil over low heat. Meanwhile, set a fine strainer over a bowl and set the bowl in a larger bowl of ice water. Whisk the yolks in a third bowl. When the milk mixture boils, use a slotted spoon to remove and discard the vanilla bean, lemon zest, and cinnamon stick. Whisk about a third of the hot milk mixture into the yolks. Return the remaining milk mixture to a boil and, beginning to whisk >

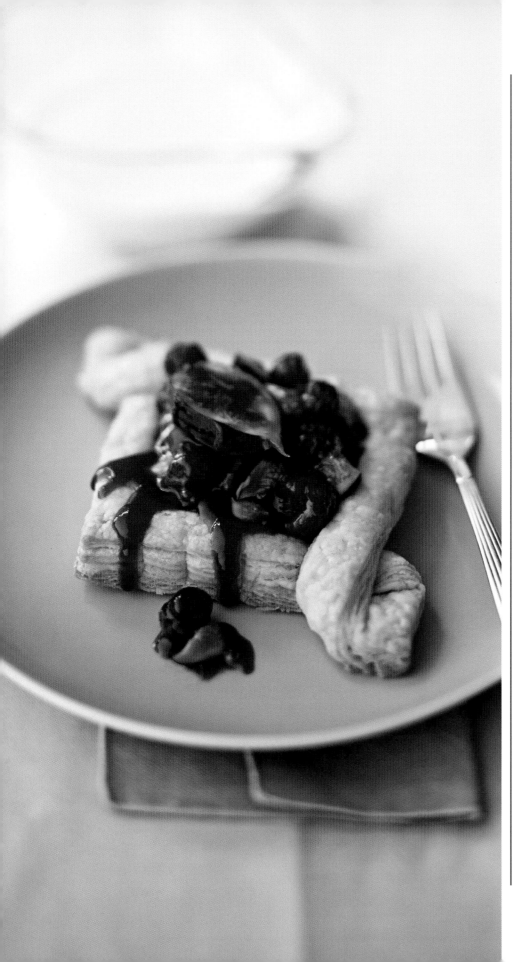

before you pour, whisk in the yolk mixture. Continue whisking until the cream thickens slightly, about 15 seconds (the cream thickens only a little now, but thickens further as it cools). Immediately strain the cream into the prepared bowl and remove the strainer. Whisk the hot cream until it cools slightly, about 30 seconds. Let it continute to cool in the ice-water bath. Once the cream is cold, pour it into a plastic container, cover, and chill until needed.

6   For the filling, reserve 5 whole figs and 18 whole raspberries to finish the croustades. Stem, peel, and dice the remaining figs and place them in a mixing bowl with the remaining raspberries. Cover and reserve at room temperature.

7   All the previous steps may be done up to one day in advance. Only proceed to the steps below when you are ready to serve the croustades; if the fruit sits after it's combined with the jam, before or after filling the croustades, it will turn watery.

8   Cook the jam in a small saucepan over low heat until it comes to a boil, stirring occasionally. Let the jam reduce slightly, about 5 minutes, then pour it into a bowl to cool for at least 15 minutes.

9   To assemble the croustades, fold the cooled raspberry jam into the fruit mixture, then spoon some of the mixture into the center of each croustade. Finish the top with a stemmed fig half, cut side up, and a couple of raspberries. Spoon some of the crème anglaise next to it on the plate.

one-step breads & rolls

These are one-step breads in the sense that to make the dough, you will simply combine all the ingredients at once rather than creating a sponge separately that's mixed into the rest of the dough ingredients after it has fermented. I would like to correct a misconception about bread baking right up front: You do not need to beat up your dough. Rather, the gentle mixing method used here assures maximum flavor, because flavor-bearing pigments in the flour don't dissipate as they do with prolonged mixing. Another misconception about bread baking is that it requires a big time commitment. This is only half right: You do need to be around in order to take care of the various steps, but none of the individual steps is actually time-consuming. Because I've designed these recipes using the one-step process, these are breads to bake and eat in one day, unlike their artisan cousins, which can take four or five days to create.

A
B

one-step bread dough

Using this new mixing technique means this bread is ready in hardly any time at all. I like to add a little olive oil to this dough for flavor as well as tenderness—a little secret touch that many bread bakers use.

Makes 1¾ pounds dough, enough for any of the loaves or rolls in this chapter

3⅔ cups bread flour or unbleached all-purpose flour (spoon flour into a dry-measure cup and level off)

1½ teaspoons non-iodized salt or fine sea salt

2½ teaspoons (1¼-ounce envelope) active dry yeast, not rapid-rise or instant

1⅓ cups warm tap water, about 100°F

1 tablespoon olive oil, plus ½ teaspoon for oiling the bowl

1 Mix the flour and salt together in a small bowl and set aside.

2 In a large bowl, whisk the yeast into the water. Wait 30 seconds, then whisk again to make sure all the yeast is dissolved. Whisk in the oil.

3 Use a large rubber spatula to mix in half the flour to make a paste. Add about half the remaining flour, mixing it in by repeatedly digging down to the bottom of the bowl with the spatula until the spatula is parallel to the bottom of the bowl and folding upward (A). Add the last of the flour and repeat the folding motion until all the flour is absorbed and there are no dry bits stuck to the side of the bowl (B).

4 Cover the bowl with a clean kitchen towel or plastic wrap and let the dough rest for 10 to 15 minutes (C).

5 Repeat the digging and folding motion in the dough using a clean rubber spatula (D). Cover and let the dough rest for 10 to 15 minutes again.

6 Lightly oil a bowl large enough to hold twice the quantity of dough you now have. Scrape the dough onto a lightly floured work surface. Flour your hands, not the top of the dough, and pat the dough into a rough rectangle. Fold one of the narrow ends of the dough over the middle, then fold the other end over to make 3 layers. Turn the dough 90 degrees so that the folded side is facing you and repeat the folding. Invert the dough into the oiled bowl and cover it with a kitchen towel or plastic wrap. Let the dough rest for 15 minutes, then repeat the folding.

7 Lightly oil the bowl again if necessary and put the dough back in the bowl. Turn the dough over so that the top is oiled. Cover with plastic wrap and let the dough rise until it has doubled in bulk, 45 minutes to 1 hour.

8 Use the dough immediately to shape any of the loaves or rolls in this chapter.

C

D

variations

Part Whole-Wheat Dough: Substitute
1 cup whole-wheat flour for an equal
amount of the white flour in the recipe.

Mixed-Grain Dough: Substitute 1/2 cup
whole-wheat flour and 1/2 cup whole-
grain rye flour for 1 cup of the white flour
in the recipe.

essential tips for one-step bread dough

- Using bread flour makes this dough and the resulting bread even easier to
  prepare. Once difficult to obtain, bread flour (look for the "better for bread"
  statement on the sack) has become a common supermarket item.

- Make sure the water is no hotter than 110°F or the yeast might die as soon as it
  hits the water. This is the single greatest cause of failure in home bread baking.

- Mixing, resting, mixing, and turning the dough makes it smooth and elastic
  without any of the effort of kneading. There really isn't any need to use a mixer,
  as none of the mixing is strenuous.

- Controlled mixing helps preserve the natural sweet wheat flavor in flour.
  That flavor dissipates when dough is mixed too long or too fast.

- The short rests followed by the rising contribute to developing flavor in the
  dough. Never try to rush the dough by putting it in an excessively warm place.

- The initial mixing and turning will take about 1 hour at a 70°F room temperature. The rising until doubled in the bowl should take another 45 minutes to
  1 hour—longer if it's cooler in the room and less long if it's a little warmer.

- Time preparing the dough so that you can proceed immediately to the shaping,
  rising, and baking of your dough.

- If you know you'll have, or need, 3 or 4 hours between mixing and baking the
  bread, cover and refrigerate the dough at the beginning of step 1. Deflate the
  dough and bring it back to room temperature before forming.

crusty ring bread

Makes one 10-inch ring-shaped loaf

1 batch One-Step Bread Dough (page 64)

Flour for shaping

Cornmeal or parchment for the pan

Cookie sheet, jelly-roll pan, or round pizza pan (only for the ring loaf) at least 12 inches across

Spray bottle filled with warm water

Serving: Use a sharp serrated knife to cut the loaf into thick slices.

Storage: Keep the loaf uncovered on the day it is baked. If it's humid and the crust softens, crisp it in a 350°F oven for a few minutes and cool it again before serving.

This loaf, like a giant bagel, increases the surface area for crust and makes for a chewy, crusty loaf that's great for serving with a meal, especially if a hearty soup or tasty sauce is on the menu. See the end of the recipe for other easy shapes. This and any of the variations that follow may be made with any of the dough variations on page 65.

1 Invert the risen dough to a floured surface, scraping it from the bowl without folding it over on itself. Turn the dough over so that what was the smooth top surface when it was rising is now uppermost.

2 Gently round the piece of dough without deflating it too much by pushing inward at the bottom with your flat upturned palms all around the piece of dough; you'll see the outside skin of the dough tighten and it will become more spherical. Cover the dough with a clean flat-weave kitchen towel and let it rest for 10 minutes.

3 Gently press the ball of dough to flatten it. Lightly flour the top of the dough and the fingertips of one hand. Point these fingertips and use them to make an opening in the center of the flattened dough. Once your fingertips are touching the work surface, rotate your hand to widen the opening (A and B).

4 Dust the pan with cornmeal and transfer the loaf to it (C and D). Widen the opening in the center of the loaf by pushing outward with one hand from the inside, until it is about 5 inches in diameter. Cover with the kitchen towel and let rise until almost doubled, about 1 hour at a 70°F to 75°F room temperature.

5 About 20 minutes before the loaf is risen, set a rack in the lower third of the oven and preheat to 400°F.

6 Remove the towel and use a single-edge razor or X-Acto knife to make 4 diagonal slashes through just the outside skin at the very top of the loaf. Place the pan in the oven and spray water all over the sides of the oven to create steam; quickly close the oven door.

7 Five minutes later, repeat the spraying. Continue baking until the loaf is deep golden and has an internal temperature of over 200°F to 210°F, a total of 30 to 40 minutes.

8 Slide the loaf to a rack to cool.

variations

Boule Loaves: A boule (ball) is a French name for a spherical loaf. After step 2 above, use a bench scraper or knife to divide the dough into 2 equal pieces (they'll bake better and more quickly than a large loaf). Round both loaves as in step 2 and place them on the cornmeal-dusted pan and resume at covering in step 4. At step 6, slash the top of the loaf in a diagonal lattice pattern—4 or 5 cuts parallel and equidistant from each other in one direction, then another 4 or 5 at a 45-degree angle to the first ones. Bake as above, but they should be done in a little less than 30 minutes.

Bâtard Loaves: No, I'm not going to provide a translation . . . A bâtard is a fatter form of a baguette and is easy to shape. Divide the risen dough in half and round each piece

A

B

C

D

separately. Cover and let rest 10 minutes. Working with one ball of dough at a time, invert it and pull it into a rough rectangle with the long ends facing you. Roll the far end of the dough over about 1 inch and gently press it into place. Continue rolling and sealing until you get to the end. Pinch the last edge into place. Invert and cover. Repeat with the second piece of dough and let rest 5 to 10 minutes. Keeping the seam on the bottom, roll the dough back and forth under your palms into a fat sausage shape that is a little shorter than the length of your pan. Roll over and taper the ends. Place the loaves on the cornmeal-dusted pan. Cover and let rise until almost doubled. Before baking, slash each loaf in 3-inch cuts in the center of the loaf that are almost parallel to the sides. Bake as for the boules, above.

Seeded Twist:

1 cup white sesame seeds, or equal parts black and white seeds

Form the dough as for bâtards, but roll each piece to about 20 inches. You may need to stop and cover the dough and let it rest for 10 minutes to avoid tearing when making it so long. Don't point the ends. Position one of the lengths of dough parallel to the edge of the work surface and bring one end to meet the other in a hairpin shape. Twist the opposite ends 2 or 3 times in opposite directions at the same time. Repeat with the other piece of dough. Paint one loaf with water and slide it to a piece of parchment or wax paper. Generously sprinkle the entire outside of the loaf with half the seeds, letting the excess fall onto the paper. Use the palm of one hand to press the seeds gently to make them adhere. Transfer the loaf to the pan and repeat with the other loaf. Bake as for bâtards, above.

tiger rolls

Also called Dutch crunch rolls, these have a crisp topping made from rice flour, and are popular in both the Netherlands and the UK. In the US, they're found largely in San Francisco. The tasty topping derives a lot of its flavor from the yeast in it and its crunch from the rice flour, which, being mostly starch, contributes no elasticity and therefore bakes to a hard, crunchy texture. Rice flour is available in most Asian markets. Dutch crunch topping is equally appropriate on a larger loaf, such as a bâtard, page 66, or twist, page 67. However, in the case of the bâtard, no slashing is necessary before baking the loaf.

Makes 12 rolls

1 batch One-Step Bread Dough (page 64) or the part whole-wheat variation (page 65)

2½ teaspoons (1¼-ounce envelope) active dry yeast

⅓ cup warm water, about 100°F

2½ teaspoons sugar

¼ teaspoon salt

2 teaspoons olive or vegetable oil

½ cup rice flour

Cookie sheet or jelly-roll pan lined with parchment paper or foil

1   Invert the risen dough to a floured work surface without folding it over on itself. Turn the dough over and, without deflating it too much, pull it into a rough rectangle. Cut the dough into 12 equal pieces.

2   Round each piece of dough under the cupped palm of your hand on a clean, flour-free work surface. Arrange the rolls on the prepared pan, cover with a clean kitchen towel, and set aside.

3   For the topping, whisk the yeast into the warm water, then whisk in the remaining ingredients, one at a time. Cover the bowl and set aside for 15 minutes.

4   Once the topping has rested for about 15 minutes, stir it down and evenly spread it on the rolls with the back of a spoon or a small offset spatula. Don't overload the rolls with topping or it will puddle underneath.

5   Let the rolls continue to rise, uncovered, until they have doubled in bulk, about 45 minutes to an hour. About 20 minutes before the loaf is risen, set a rack in the middle level of the oven and preheat to 375°F.

6   Bake the rolls until the topping is set, crackled, and lightly colored, 25 to 30 minutes. Cool the rolls on a rack and serve them on the day they are baked.

Serving: These rolls make good little sandwiches, or even dinner rolls.

Storage: Keep the rolls uncovered at room temperature the day they are baked. Wrap and freeze for longer storage. Defrost; reheat at 350°F for about 5 minutes, then cool before serving.

variations

Round or Long Sandwich Rolls: Use any of the variations of One-Step Bread Dough on pages 64–65 for these. After rounding off the rolls in step 2 above, cover and let them rest again. For round rolls, leave them as they are. For long rolls, one at a time, roll over them with the palm of one hand to elongate and make them about ¾ inch in diameter and about 4½ inches long. Arrange the rolls on the prepared pan as they're formed. For the round rolls, use the palm of your hand to flatten them once they are on the pan to retain a round shape. Omit the crunch topping and dust the rolls with flour before covering. Bake as above.

Poppy Seed Knots: You can use sesame seeds, white or black or a combination; nigella seeds; or even caraway seeds if using any rye flour (see Variations on page 65). Apply just a pinch of caraway seeds, though—don't encrust the entire roll with them.

1 cup poppy seeds in a small bowl

Form the rolls as above. One at a time, pick up a cylinder of dough and stretch it to about 6 inches in length. Tie it into a loose single knot so that one of the ends is on the bottom of the roll and the other protrudes slightly at the top. Arrange the rolls on the work surface. Brush a roll with water and invert it into the poppy seeds, pressing gently to make the seeds adhere. Arrange on the prepared pan. Allow to rise and bake as for Tiger Rolls.

salt sticks

These, like good bagels and bialys, used to be a New York standby but seem to have all but disappeared from the typical bagel store assortment. These are more tender than the classics, but not a bad substitute, all things considered. If you can get some chunky opaque pretzel salt, by all means use it; the rolls will taste pretty much the same, but they'll look terrific.

Makes 16 6-inch rolls

1 batch One-Step Bread Dough (page 64)

Egg wash: 1 large egg white, well beaten in a small bowl

¼ teaspoon kosher or other coarse salt or pretzel salt

2 cookie sheets or jelly-roll pans lined with parchment paper or foil

1. Invert the risen dough to a floured work surface without folding it over on itself. Turn the dough over and, without deflating it too much, pull it into a rough rectangle. Cut the dough into 16 equal pieces, each about 4½ ounces.

2. Round each piece of dough under the cupped palm of your hand on a clean flour-free work surface. Cover with a clean kitchen towel and let them rest for 5 minutes.

3. One by one, roll over the pieces of dough with the palm of one hand to elongate to about 6 inches, without pointing the ends.

4. Arrange the rolls on the prepared pans 2 inches apart all around to allow for expansion. Cover the rolls with a kitchen towel and let them rise until they just start to puff, about 20 minutes.

5. Set racks in the upper and lower thirds of the oven and preheat to 375°F.

6. Once the rolls have begun to rise, brush them with the egg white and sprinkle with the salt. Let the rolls continue to rise, uncovered, until they have doubled in bulk.

7. Bake the rolls until they're deep golden and firm, 20 to 25 minutes, switching the bottom pan to the top rack and vice versa and also turning the pans from back to front halfway through the baking time.

8. Cool the rolls on a rack and serve them on the day they are baked.

Serving: These rolls are great with butter for breakfast, warmed or not, or even split and toasted.

Storage: Keep the rolls uncovered at room temperature the day they are baked. Wrap and freeze for longer storage. Defrost; reheat at 350°F for about 5 minutes, then cool before serving.

variation

Soft Sesame Breadsticks: These are a slightly longer and thinner version of the salt sticks above.

1 cup white sesame seeds

2 cookie sheets or jelly-roll pans lined with parchment or foil

1. Prepare salt sticks up to the end of step 2. Elongate them as in step 3, but make them about 8 inches long.

2. Have ready a bowl of water and the sesame seeds arranged in a wide 8-inch area on a piece of parchment or wax paper.

3. One by one, use one hand to dip a formed breadstick into the water, then lift it out, letting it drain, and arrange it on the sesame seeds. Use the dry hand to coat it all over with the seeds and transfer it to the work surface afterward. Repeat with the remaining sticks.

4. Dry the water dipping hand and use both hands to transfer the breadsticks to the prepared pans, allowing 2 inches all around for expansion.

5. Resume with step 4, above.

Serving: These are more a snack, or a good accompaniment to hors d'oeuvre or first courses, but not really a roll.

06
pan breads

Pan breads are versatile and easy to shape. As their name indicates, they're risen and baked in a pan—usually a loaf pan—which makes them perfect for slicing. They're great for sandwiches, toast, croutons, and all manner of bread-based dishes, both sweet and savory. Because the dough for pan breads is quickly made by machine, this type of loaf can become a flavorful solution to industrially made white bread. The same dough also makes excellent dinner rolls and perfect hamburger and hot dog buns. The flavoring variations in the recipes that follow the chapter's master recipe all expand upon the almost endless possibilities of this simple bread. Use them as guidelines for developing your own combinations; just remember not to overdo the quantity of anything you decide to add to the dough to flavor it.

A

B

perfect white pan bread

Makes two 9 x 5 x 5-inch loaves

6½ cups bread flour (spoon into
a dry-measure cup and level off)

1 tablespoon sugar

1 tablespoon salt

4 tablespoons unsalted butter,
cut into 8 pieces

1½ cups milk, scalded

1 cup warm tap water, about 110°F

2½ teaspoons (1¼-ounce envelope)
active dry yeast

Two 9 x 5 x 3-inch loaf pans, buttered
or oiled

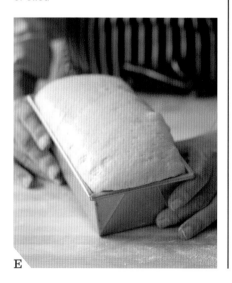

E

Despite its wonderful texture and flavor, a loaf such as this is more than easy to prepare. In addition, it's the basis for all the recipe variations in this chapter; some use a full recipe, some use half. After you try this once, you'll never settle for supermarket sandwich bread again. Many thanks to my friend Kyra Effren for sharing all her wisdom about this bread, which she has been making two to seven times a week for 50 years.

1 Stir the flour, sugar, and salt together and set aside.

2 Stir the butter into the hot milk, pour it into a shallow bowl, and let it cool to room temperature.

3 Once the milk has cooled, pour the water into the bowl of an electric mixer and whisk in the yeast. Wait 1 minute, then whisk again to make sure the yeast is completely dissolved. Whisk in the cooled milk and butter mixture.

4 Use a large rubber spatula to stir in about half of the flour mixture. Stir in the rest in 3 or 4 additions to form a rough dough in which there is no longer any unmoistened flour.

5 Place the bowl on the mixer fitted with the dough hook and beat on medium speed until the dough is somewhat smoother but not perfectly smooth, about 2 minutes. Stop the mixer and allow the dough to rest for 10 minutes.

6 Beat the rested dough on medium speed until it is smoother and more elastic, about 2 additional minutes.

7 Scrape the dough into a lightly oiled bowl large enough to hold twice the amount of dough and turn the dough over so that the top is now oiled. Gently press oiled plastic wrap against the surface of the dough. Let the dough rise until it has doubled in bulk. At a room temperature of 75°F, it should take about 1 hour.

8 Invert the dough to a lightly floured work surface and turn it over. Press to deflate the dough (A) and repeat step 7.

9 After the dough has risen for the second time, use a small flexible scraper to invert the dough to a lightly floured work surface. Divide the dough in half. Without deflating the dough too much, pull and stretch each piece into a rough 8- to 9-inch

C

D

square. Starting at the far end of the dough, tightly roll it toward you jelly-roll style, pinching the edge in place when you get to the end (B and C).

10 Place the formed loaves in the pans, seam side down, evenly pressing into place so that the top of each loaf is level (D). Cover with oiled plastic wrap and let rise until doubled, about 1 hour. When risen, the dough should be at least 1 inch above the rims of the pans (E).

11 When the loaves are almost completely risen, set a rack in the middle level of the oven and preheat to 400°F.

12 Once the loaves are completely risen, uncover and place them on the rack in the oven, short side inward and equidistant from each other and the sides of the oven. Bake until the bread is well risen, deep golden, and firm, with an internal temperature of over 200°F, about 45 minutes.

13 Unmold each loaf to a rack and cool on its side to prevent falling. If you want the crust to be very soft, have a tablespoon of melted butter ready when you unmold the breads and use a brush to paint all surfaces of each loaf with the butter.

Serving: Wait until the bread cools before attempting to slice it with a sharp serrated knife. Slice the bread about 1/2 inch thick and use for sandwiches or toast.

Storage: Keep the loaves at room temperature on the day they are baked. Slide leftovers into a plastic bag and keep at room temperature. Freeze for longer storage.

variations

To mix the dough by hand, use the method described on page 64 for One-Step Bread Dough. Resume the recipe above with step 7.

Hamburger or Sandwich Rolls: You can make 6 large rolls or 8 smaller ones from a half batch of the dough. After dividing the dough in half and forming a loaf, divide the remaining dough into 6 or 8 equal pieces. Round each and place on a parchment paper-lined cookie sheet or jelly-roll pan. Cover and let rest for 15 minutes. Press each with the palm of your hand to flatten it. Cover again and let rise until doubled in size, 20 to 30 minutes. Bake until firm and golden, about 20 minutes. For hot dog or sausage rolls, round the dough, then cover and let rest 10 minutes. Roll each round by hand to form an even 6-inch-long cylinder. Place on the pan and continue as for hamburger rolls.

essential tips for pan breads

- Review Essentials for One-Step Bread Doughs, page 65.

- As in all other yeast-risen baked goods, the most important part of this recipe is having the water between 100°F and 110°F when you add the yeast. If the water is too hot, the yeast will die immediately and you'll wait in vain for the dough to rise.

- Avoid deflating the dough too much by pressing on it while forming the loaf. The shaping process will deflate the dough enough.

- Don't skimp on the rising time either in the bowl or before baking or the loaf will be tough and dry after baking.

- Refrigerating baked bread will hasten staling. If you want to bake a few loaves in advance for a special occasion, double-wrap completely cooled loaves in plastic and freeze them. Defrost at room temperature and warm slightly at 350°F for 5 minutes, then cool before serving.

gruyère & walnut bread

Makes one 9 x 5 x 5-inch loaf

1 batch dough for Perfect White Pan Bread (page 72), completed up to the end of step 5

2 cups coarsely grated Swiss Gruyère, loosely packed, chopped into ¼-inch pieces

2 cups chopped walnuts, lightly toasted

2 teaspoons coarsely ground black pepper or crushed red pepper, optional

Two 9 x 5 x 3-inch loaf pans, buttered or oiled

Serving and Storage: As in the master recipe.

Gruyère and other aged cheeses are a perfect pairing with the slight bitterness of walnuts in this easy and delicious bread.

1   Add the cheese and nuts to the mixer bowl before beginning with step 6, and then continue with the master recipe. In a mixer fitted with the dough hook, beat the rested dough on medium speed until it is smoother and more elastic, about 2 additional minutes. Remove the dough to a lightly oiled bowl and turn it over so that the top is oiled. Press plastic wrap against the surface and let the dough rise until it has doubled in size.

2   Continue with the rising, shaping, proofing, and baking in the master recipe.

variations

Substitute any aged cheese such as sharp cheddar, Cantal, or Parmigiano-Reggiano for the Gruyère. Grate the Parmigiano fine as you would for serving with pasta. You can also substitute chopped toasted pecans for the walnuts.

oatmeal & honey bread

Makes two 9 x 5 x 5-inch loaves

COOKED OATS

1½ cups rolled oats

¼ cup dark flavorful honey

2 tablespoons unsalted butter, cut into 5 or 6 pieces

1½ cups boiling water

DOUGH

4 cups bread flour (spoon into a dry-measure cup and level off)

2 cups whole-wheat flour

1 tablespoon salt

1½ cups warm tap water, about 110°F

3½ teaspoons (1½ envelopes) active dry yeast

1½ cups uncooked rolled oats for finishing

Two 9 x 5 x 3-inch loaf pans, buttered or oiled

This makes an excellent breakfast or brunch bread when toasted, the best way to enjoy this moist-textured bread. The addition of whole-wheat flour to the dough emphasizes the nutty flavor of oatmeal.

1   For the oatmeal, place the oats in a stainless-steel bowl and drizzle the honey over them. Scatter the pieces of butter over all. Pour over the boiling water and stir once to mix. Let the mixture cool to room temperature.

2   Follow the instructions on page 72 for Perfect White Pan Bread; substitute the combination of bread and whole-wheat flour for the bread flour. At the middle of step 4, add the cooked oats along with the second half of the flour.

3   Continue with the master recipe to the end of step 9.

4   Place the uncooked rolled oats on a piece of parchment or wax paper and form them into a rectangle roughly equal to the top of one loaf.

5   Paint the top of one of the loaves with water and invert it onto the oats. Let the dough remain there for 1 minute, then lift and invert it into one of the prepared pans so that the oat-encrusted part is uppermost. Repeat with the other loaf.

6   Let rise, bake, and cool as in the master recipe.

Serving: Wait until completely cool before attempting to slice with a sharp serrated knife. Slice the bread a little under 1/2 inch thick and use it for sandwiches or toast.

Storage: Keep the loaves at room temperature on the day they are baked. Slide leftovers into a plastic bag and keep at room temperature. Freeze for longer storage.

chocolate spiral bread

Makes two 9 x 5 x 5-inch loaves

1 batch dough for Perfect White Pan
Bread (page 72), up to the end of step 5

¼ cup milk

¼ teaspoon ground cinnamon

3 ounces semisweet chocolate (55 to 65%
cocoa solids), melted and slightly cooled

¼ cup bread flour

1 tablespoon melted butter, for finishing

Two 9 x 5 x 3-inch loaf pans, buttered
or oiled

Once you've mixed the Perfect White Pan Bread up to the end of step 5, you can use it to make a couple of striking loaves that have a spiral of chocolate dough running through them. In this recipe, the chocolate colors the dough really well and imparts a faint chocolate flavor, but don't think that biting into a slice of this is going to be anything like chewing on a brownie.

1 Divide the dough into two pieces, one of which is twice as large as the other. Put the larger piece of dough into an oiled bowl and turn it so that the top is oiled; cover with plastic wrap and allow to rise until doubled. Return the smaller piece of dough to the mixer, still fitted with the dough hook

2 Whisk the milk and cinnamon into the chocolate and scrape the mixture into the mixer bowl. Mix on lowest speed until the dough evenly absorbs the chocolate liquid. Let the dough rest 10 minutes, then mix again on low for 2 more minutes. Put the chocolate dough into an oiled bowl and turn it so that the top is oiled; cover with plastic wrap and allow to rise until doubled.

3 Deflate the white and chocolate doughs and return them to the bowls to rise again until doubled.

4 Scrape the white dough from the bowl to a floured work surface and roll or press the dough into a 16-inch square (the square of dough is not as wide as the two pans, but will stretch an extra inch or two when it's being rolled). Press or roll the chocolate dough into an 8 x 16-inch rectangle. Brush the surface of the white dough with water. Position the rectangle of chocolate dough on it, leaving a 1-inch margin of white dough on the edge closest to you.

5 Fold over the inch of white dough onto the chocolate dough and then roll up the whole package jelly-roll-style to make one long cylinder of dough. (The extra white dough at the end attractively frames the chocolate spiral within.)

6 Cut the roll in half in the length and press each roll into one of the prepared pans, seam side down. Cover the pans with oiled plastic wrap and set aside to rise until doubled, about 1 hour. When risen, the dough should be at least 1 inch above the rim of the pan.

7 When the loaves are almost completely risen, set a rack in the middle level of the oven and preheat to 400°F.

8 Once the loaves are completely risen, uncover them and place them on the rack in the oven, short side inward. Bake until the bread is well risen, deep golden, and firm, with an internal temperature of 200°F to 210°F, about 45 minutes.

9 Unmold to a rack and cool the loaves on their sides. If you want the crust to be very soft, have a tablespoon of melted butter ready when you unmold the bread and use a brush to paint all surfaces of the loaves with the butter.

dark caraway rye bread

Makes one 9 x 5 x 5-inch loaf

4 cups bread flour (spoon into
a dry-measure cup and level off)

1½ cups whole-grain or medium rye flour

2 teaspoons salt

2 teaspoons ground caraway seeds

2 teaspoons whole caraway seeds,
optional

2 cups warm tap water, about 110°F

2½ teaspoons (1¼-ounce envelope)
active dry yeast

2 tablespoons molasses

One 9 x 5 x 3-inch loaf pan, buttered
or oiled

Many rye breads are made using a sourdough starter since rye flour can only develop gluten in the presence of acidity. Without using a sourdough, the best solution is to use a combination of rye flour and strong bread flour to impart the necessary elasticity to the dough, but even then part-rye doughs like this one tend to remain quite sticky. Try not to use too much flour in shaping the dough or it might not grow together well while it's rising and baking. I was amazed when I learned years ago that the flavor I had always associated with rye bread didn't come from rye flour, but from the addition of ground caraway seeds to the dough. If you can't find already-ground caraway, just grind up some seeds in a spice grinder. Molasses adds a note of dark richness to this bread and it ties in perfectly with the earthy rye flavor. Please note that the dough only rises once before being formed unlike the other doughs in this chapter.

1 In a bowl, mix the flours, salt, ground caraway seeds, and whole caraway seeds, if using. Set aside.

2 Pour the water into the bowl of an electric mixer and whisk in the yeast. Let stand 2 minutes, then whisk again. Add the flour mixture, then the molasses.

3 Use a large rubber spatula to mix the ingredients to a rough dough.

4 Place on the mixer fitted with the dough hook and continue with the master recipe from steps 5 through 7, on page 72.

5 Continue with the master recipe at step 9 (pages 72–73), but remember to form only a single loaf from the dough.

6 Let the loaf rise and bake it as in the master recipe, page 73.

Serving: Though delicious as toast, I love this untoasted as sandwich bread. Thinly sliced baked ham and Gruyère with dark mustard and a garlicky kosher pickle elevate this bread to the realm of haute cuisine.

Storage: Keep the loaves at room temperature on the day they are baked. Slide leftovers into a plastic bag and keep at room temperature. Freeze for longer storage.

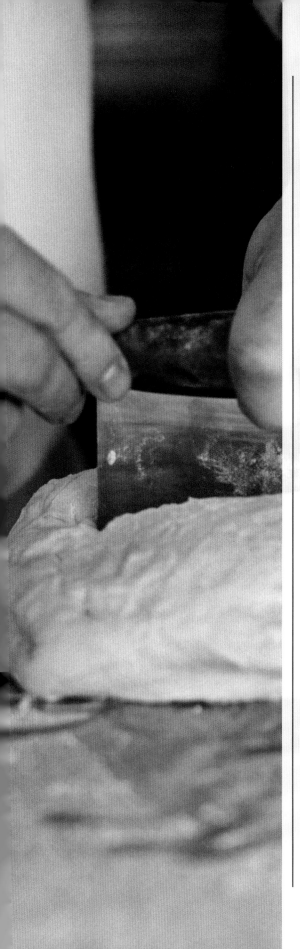

two-step & whole-grain breads

Using a sponge to make bread is nothing more than preparing a small amount of dough in advance and allowing it to rise in the refrigerator, usually overnight or over the course of the day. Sponges are easy to prepare, and the yeast multiplies in the sponge, so that when you add the sponge to the final dough it has much more impact than the same amount of yeast would have in a one-step dough. Consequently, since you are using less yeast in the final dough, the wheat flavor of the flour you are using stands out more. A bread made with a sponge has excellent flavor, a crisp crust, and an open crumb dotted with holes (though I would argue that it's not necessarily superior to a one-step bread—just different).

yeast-based sponge

Makes about 1 cup (about 9 ounces by weight)

½ teaspoon active dry yeast

¾ cup room temperature tap water, about 75–80°F

1 cup bread flour (spoon into a dry-measure cup and level off)

Though this sponge (also known as a starter or pre-ferment) needs more than 8 hours to rise completely before it can be used, it takes about 5 minutes to prepare, so it really doesn't add extra work to baking a loaf of bread. Using a sponge as part of a baked dough naturally increases the amount of yeast cells in the dough without using a large amount of yeast at the outset. This imparts a better flavor to the baked bread.

1 In a 1- to 2-quart bowl, whisk the yeast into the water. Wait a minute, then whisk again to make sure the yeast is completely dissolved.

2 Stir in the flour smoothly; the sponge will be like a thin batter. Cover the bowl with plastic wrap and let it rise for at least 1 hour at room temperature. The sponge will rise slowly.

3 Stir down the sponge and refrigerate it for 8 to 12 hours before using it in a recipe.

Storage: You may keep the sponge refrigerated for up to 16 hours, but after that the sponge will start to acquire an overly sour flavor.

essential tips for sponges & sponge-based bread dough

- Make sure the water is just room temperature when you add the yeast, or the sponge will rise too quickly.

- Never try to rush the sponge, or the resulting dough, or you'll defeat the entire purpose of using it. Each needs to rise slowly to develop the best possible flavor and texture.

- Note: This is emphatically not a sourdough sponge; that's made from flour and water only and ferments due to the natural yeasts in the wheat, not in the air as some erroneously believe. Sometimes a yeast-rich ingredient such as the water used to rinse raisins is added to boost the sourdough fermentation along.

- Although this sponge-based dough is mixed by machine, you still need to let it rest between gentle mixings. Mixing too fast or for too long overheats the dough and also destroys the natural flavor components in the flour.

- You can make this sponge and bread dough work around your schedule; it can be left alone for a few hours after mixing, but only if the room is cool. Letting either the sponge or dough ferment too much, however, will give an excessively yeasty taste to the dough and make the dough overly sticky and difficult to shape.

sponge-based bread dough

Use this recipe as a model for the variations in this chapter. Once the sponge is made, the dough comes together relatively quickly. This dough may also be formed and baked in the same way as any of the one-step breads in Chapter 5. Here, I'm giving you a machine mixing method, but you can also mix this by hand as for the One-Step Bread Dough, page 64.

Makes about 2½ pounds dough

3 cups bread flour (spoon into a dry-measure cup and level off)

2 teaspoons salt

½ teaspoon active dry yeast

1 cup warm tap water, about 100° to 110°F

1 batch Yeast-Based Sponge, opposite

1   Mix the flour and salt together and set aside.

2   In the bowl of an electric mixer fitted with the dough hook, whisk the yeast into the water. Wait 2 minutes, then whisk again to make sure all the yeast is dissolved. Use a large rubber spatula to stir in the sponge.

3   Use the same rubber spatula to stir the flour and salt into the liquid all at once.

4   Mix on medium speed for 2 minutes. Stop the mixer and let the dough rest for 10 minutes.

5   Mix again on medium speed for 2 minutes.

6   Lightly oil a bowl large enough to hold twice the quantity of dough you now have. Cover the bowl with plastic wrap and let the dough rest until it starts to puff visibly, about 30 minutes.

7   Scrape the dough from the bowl to a lightly floured work surface. Flour your hands, not the top of the dough, and pat it into a rough rectangle. Fold one of the narrow ends of the dough over the middle, then fold the other end over that to make 3 layers. Turn the dough 90 degrees so that the folded side is facing you and repeat the folding. Lightly oil the bowl again if necessary and invert the dough into the oiled bowl and cover it.

8   Let the dough rest for 15 minutes, then repeat step 7.

9   Lightly oil the bowl again if necessary and put in the dough. Turn the dough over so that the top is oiled. Cover with plastic wrap and let the dough rise until it has doubled in bulk.

variation

Part Whole-Wheat Dough: Substitute 1 cup whole-wheat flour for a cup of the bread flour.

The nutty flavor of whole-wheat flour pairs naturally with any nutmeats, but I like the flavor of hazelnuts with it best. Purchase the hazelnuts already skinned if you can; sometimes the skins are difficult to remove. Adding a handful of dark raisins or currants to this dough further complements the whole-wheat flavor.

Use this part whole-wheat variation of the dough; add 2 cups toasted, skinned, and coarsely crushed hazelnuts (or lightly toasted and coarsely chopped walnut or pecan pieces) about halfway through step 5 in the master dough recipe above. Follow the Apulian Olive Bread recipe on page 84, starting at step 2.

ciabatta
"slipper" bread

Makes two 10-inch-long loaves

2 cups bread flour (spoon into a
dry-measure cup and level off)

1½ teaspoons salt

½ teaspoon active dry yeast

¾ cup cool tap water, about 75°F

1 batch Yeast-Based Sponge
page 80 (see Note)

Olive oil for the rising bowl

Baking stone or inverted nonwarping
jelly-roll pan

Cornmeal for the peel

Spray bottle filled with hot water for
baking

Peel or rectangle of stiff cardboard

variation

Ciabatta Rolls: Unless you are a master at handling a peel, bake these on a pan dusted with cornmeal or lined with parchment paper. In step 10, at right, gently pull the dough into a 10-inch square. Use the bench scraper to cut it into 9 equal squares. Gently round each one by inverting and pulling the corners together. Invert again onto the prepared pan. Cover the rolls with a towel or oiled plastic wrap and let them rise until well puffed, but not completely double, about 30 minutes. Place the pan in the preheated oven (the stone isn't necessary) and mist with water. Repeat the misting again after 5 minutes. Bake the rolls as above until they are deep golden and light for their size, about 15 minutes. Cool on a rack and use or freeze.

A

Ciabatta's justly deserved popularity is due to its crusty exterior and airy interior, making it the ultimate crust-lovers' bread. Small versions make excellent sandwich rolls. Here we're using the sponge on page 80, and making a very soft dough. Don't be afraid to handle such a soft dough; just use plenty of flour on your hands and under the dough. You can brush away excess flour from the tops of the loaves before placing them in the oven, but many bakers leave a floury coating on the bread. It's best to use a baking stone for ciabatta, but if you don't have one and don't want to buy one, an overturned jelly-roll pan that won't warp when heated will do the trick. Use a wooden peel for sliding the loaves into the oven or improvise one with a piece of stiff cardboard. If you don't want to fuss with the peel or cardboard, just place the two loaves on a cornmeal-dusted or parchment-lined jelly-roll pan. After placing it in the oven, spray, and continue with the recipe at step 12.

1 Mix the flour and salt together and set aside.

2 In the bowl of an electric mixer fitted with the paddle attachment, whisk the yeast into the water. Use a large rubber spatula to scrape in and stir the sponge into the yeast and water.

3 Stir in the flour and salt; the dough will be very soft.

4 Beat on medium-low for 3 minutes. Stop and let the dough rest for 10 minutes.

B

5 Repeat step 4.

6 Continue with steps 6, 7, and 8 on page 81.

7 Turn the dough over so that the fold is underneath and form it into an 8-inch square. Cover with plastic wrap and a clean kitchen towel and let rise until puffed, about 30 minutes.

8 About 20 minutes before the dough is fully risen, set a rack in the middle level of the oven and place your baking stone or inverted jelly-roll pan on it (long side parallel to the oven door); preheat to 500°F.

9 Once the dough has risen, generously flour the work surface. Have the peel nearby and generously dust it with cornmeal. Place the spray bottle close to the oven.

10 Use an oiled bench scraper to cut the dough (cut straight down repeatedly, don't drag the blade through the dough) into two 4 x 8-inch rectangles (A).

11 Slide your flat upturned palms under one of the pieces of dough from the short ends until your fingertips meet in the middle. Lift the dough to the outermost edge of the peel, pulling it slightly until it is about 10 inches long (B). Open the oven and quickly slide the loaf from the peel to the far side of the baking stone or pan. Quickly close the oven and scatter more cornmeal on the peel and repeat with the second loaf, positioning it on the half of the stone closer to the oven door. Generously spray the inside of the oven with water to create steam.

12 Wait 5 minutes, then spray again.

13 Bake the ciabatte (the plural) until they are deep golden and their internal temperature is over 200°F, about 20–25 minutes. Transfer to a rack to cool.

Serving: Ciabatta is good with everything. For some no-nonsense hors d'oeuvre to serve with drinks before dinner, split a ciabatta or two horizontally and fill with thinly sliced prosciutto and mozzarella, a drizzle of olive oil, and some torn fresh basil. Replace the top of the loaf and cut lengthwise and then crosswise into 1½-inch pieces. Ciabatta is equally good with smoked salmon, a thin smear of cream cheese, plenty of ground pepper, and some finely cut chives or scallions.

Storage: Keep the ciabatta at room temperature on the day it is baked. This type of bread grows stale quickly, so wrap and freeze the second loaf if you don't need it immediately. Defrost and reheat at 350°F for 10 minutes, then cool and serve.

Note: Many bakers use a firmer Italian-style sponge called *biga* for making ciabatta, but this one works well, too. Make sure the sponge is well risen for best flavor and texture.

apulian olive bread

Real Cerignola green olives from Puglia make the best version of this bread. They're flavorful and somewhat firm and don't turn to puree when you're beating them into the dough. I often bake this as two smaller loaves—just divide the dough in half and round both pieces. For ease, you can also bake the loaf or loaves on a cornmeal-dusted or parchment-lined jelly-roll pan.

Makes one round 9- or 10-inch loaf

1 batch Sponge-Based Bread Dough (page 81)

6 ounces Cerignola or other large green olives, pitted and coarsely chopped, or ¾ cup green olives, coarsely chopped

Cornmeal for the peel

One baking stone or inverted nonwarping jelly-roll pan

Spray bottle filled with hot water for baking

Peel

1 Add the chopped olives about halfway through step 5 in the master dough recipe on page 81. Follow the master recipe to the end of step 9.

2 Invert the dough to a floured work surface without folding it over on itself. Turn the dough over so that what was the smooth top surface when it was rising is now uppermost. Gently round the piece of dough without deflating it too much by pushing inward at the bottom with your flat upturned palms all around the piece of dough; the outside skin of the dough will tighten and become more spherical.

3 Slide the dough to a cornmeal-dusted peel or cookie sheet and cover it with a kitchen towel or plastic wrap. Let the dough rise until it has almost doubled in size, about 1 hour.

4 About 20 minutes before the dough is fully risen, set a rack in the middle level of the oven and place the baking stone or inverted jelly-roll pan on it (long side parallel to the oven door); preheat to 500°F. Place a spray bottle filled with water within reach.

5 Use a single-edge razor blade or X-Acto knife to slash the top of the loaf 4 times, overlapping the ends of the slashes to form a crosshatch pattern.

6 Open the oven and quickly slide the loaf from the peel to the baking stone or pan. Grab the bottle, generously spray inside the oven, and close the door.

7 Wait 5 minutes, then spray again. Decrease the oven temperature to 400°F.

8 Bake the loaf until it is well risen and deep golden, and has an internal temperature of 200°F to 210°F, 50 minutes to 1 hour. Transfer to a wire rack to cool.

Serving: Use a sharp serrated knife to cut the cooled loaf into thick slices. This is a perfect bread to serve with cheeses.

Storage: Keep the loaf uncovered on the day it is baked. If it's humid and the crust softens, crisp it in a 350°F oven for a few minutes and cool again before serving.

variation

Garlic Lovers' Bread: This is a fun bread to serve with casual food such as fried chicken, anything barbecued, or even a big substantial salad, but it doesn't belong anywhere near delicately seasoned dishes. Many garlic breads use roasted garlic, but I'm borrowing a technique from Thai cooking and seasoning the bread with fried thin slices of garlic and some of the oil used to fry them.

6 to 8 large cloves garlic, peeled and thinly sliced lengthwise

½ cup olive oil

Combine the garlic and oil in a medium saucepan and place on low heat. Have a plate covered with a double thickness of paper towels ready near the stove. Once the garlic starts to sizzle and take on a little color, use a slotted spoon to stir it constantly or the sugars in the garlic will caramelize, causing all the slices to stick together. Once all the slices are an even light golden color, pull the pan off the burner and continue stirring for 1 minute, then use the slotted spoon to remove the garlic to the plate. Pour a couple of tablespoons of the oil into a small cup and let the garlic and oil cool to room temperature. Refrigerate the leftover garlic oil in a small covered jar and use it in cooking or salad dressings. Substitute the garlic and the reserved oil for the olives.

08
flatbreads

These are some of my favorite breads to make, because they combine easy preparation with delicious results. They span the globe from the Middle East to Italy, moving right across the Atlantic to some contemporary versions I've tasted in New York City. After visiting Istanbul several years ago and enjoying the incredibly fine baked goods available even in the street, I resolved to make versions of what I had tasted after I returned home—and these are the results. To duplicate all of them would require an entire book . . . so I have included a few of my favorites. I use a similar dough for a thin-crusted pizza (real Neapolitan pizza dough doesn't contain oil). My pizza crust is easy to press out thin and always bakes to a delicate texture no matter what the toppings.

middle eastern flatbread dough

Makes 1½ pounds dough, enough for several flatbreads

3 cups bread flour or unbleached all-purpose flour (spoon into a dry-measure cup and level off)

2 teaspoons salt

2½ teaspoons (1¼-ounce envelope) active dry yeast

1⅓ cups warm tap water, about 110°F

2 tablespoons olive oil

essential tips for middle eastern flatbread dough

- This very soft dough needs to develop quite a lot of elasticity and smoothness or it won't rise well in the oven. Use bread flour for best results.

- Don't let the dough rise more than indicated in the recipe at any point or it might over-ferment slightly and not rise well in the oven.

- Make sure to have any ingredients necessary for topping or finishing the dough ready when you start to prepare it or the dough might over-ferment while waiting.

It would be entirely possible to write a very thick book only on the subject of Middle Eastern flatbreads, so this recipe just skims the surface. I'm happy with the results of using the same dough for both thick and thin flatbreads used respectively as table breads or as wraps for a variety of accompaniments.

1 Mix the flour and salt together and set aside.

2 Whisk the yeast into the water in the bowl of an electric mixer fitted with the dough hook. Wait 2 minutes, then whisk again to make sure it's completely dissolved. Whisk in the oil.

3 Stir in about half the flour mixture until smooth, then stir in the rest. Beat on medium speed until fairly smooth, about 3 minutes. Stop the mixer and let the dough rest for 10 minutes.

4 Beat on low speed again until the dough is smoother and somewhat elastic, about 3 additional minutes.

5 Scrape the dough into an oiled bowl and turn it over (it's very soft, so it's best to use a flexible scraper) so that the top is oiled. Cover the bowl with plastic wrap. Let the dough rest until it starts to puff, 15 to 20 minutes.

6 Scrape the dough to a lightly floured work surface. Pat and stretch the dough into a rectangle 3 times longer than it is wide. Fold one third of the dough over the middle section, then fold the other side over that.

7 Turn the dough 90 degrees and repeat stretching and folding.

8 Return the dough to the bowl (it may be necessary to oil the bowl again) and turn it over so that the top is oiled. Cover with plastic wrap and let the dough rise until it has doubled in size, about 30 minutes. Use the risen dough in any of the recipes on page 90 to 91.

These recipes are but a few of the hundreds of slight variations possible in size, shape, dough and topping ingredients, and density of the finished bread. The soft dough might be difficult to shape, so flour the work surface well to prevent sticking. Form the larger variations on a rimless cookie sheet, flexible cutting board, or piece of stiff cardboard to facilitate transfer to the pan.

ekmek
basic turkish flatbread

The Turkish name for this merely means "bread," owing to the fact that this is so widely made. There are many variations of it, too, some made with a sourdough starter instead of yeast.

Makes 1 loaf

1 batch Middle Eastern Flatbread Dough (page 88), fully risen

Cornmeal for the pan

Cookie sheet or jelly-roll pan sprinkled with a light dusting of cornmeal or lined with parchment paper

Spray bottle filled with hot water

Serving: This is an excellent bread to serve with a meal. Cut into thick slices.

Storage: This bread is best on the day it's made. Wrap any leftovers and reheat them at 350°F for 10 minutes before serving again; it's delicious warm.

A

D

1 Without folding over the dough, scrape it to a floured work surface. Turn the dough over so that the smooth top surface is uppermost. Round the dough by repeatedly pulling upward all around the perimeter and pushing and pinching those flaps of dough into the center (A). Turn the dough over, cover it with a towel and let it rest for 5 to 10 minutes.

2 Without deflating the dough too much, stretch and pull it into an oval shape the length of your baking pan and half its width, about 5 by 15 inches (B). Slide both hands, palms upright, under the dough and transfer it to the prepared pan (C and D). Cover the dough with oiled plastic wrap.

3 Set a rack in the middle level of the oven and preheat to 500°F. Have a spray bottle filled with hot water nearby.

4 Let the loaf rise until it just starts to puff, about 20 minutes (E).

5 Use a fingertip to dimple the top of the loaf gently at 1-inch intervals without deflating it.

6 Place the pan in the oven, spray the inside of the oven all over with the water, and quickly close the oven door.

B

C

E

F

7 Wait 5 minutes and spray again. Decrease the heat to 400°F and continue to bake the bread until it is well risen, is deep golden, and has an internal temperature of 200°F to 210°F, about 20 minutes. Slide the bread to a rack to cool.

variations

Seeded Flatbreads:

2 tablespoons white or black sesame seeds, or a combination

Divide the dough into 2 equal pieces. Round a piece by repeatedly pulling upward around the perimeter and pushing those flaps of dough into the center. Repeat with the second piece. Invert both pieces of dough, cover with a towel, and let rest for 10 minutes. Preheat the oven and form the breads: Gently press each piece of dough into a disk 8 inches in diameter. Arrange on the prepared pan and cover. Let the dough rest until it starts to puff. Gently dimple the dough (F) and spray with a little water. Scatter seeds on each bread. Bake, cool, serve, and store.

Zatar Flatbreads: Zatar is a blend of herbs, white sesame seeds, and salt popular in Middle Eastern cooking. Many regional variations exist, and packaged blends are easy to find. Just be sure not to buy the finely ground variety, which, when combined with the oil, will form a paste unsuitable for topping.

Makes 4 medium flatbreads

⅓ cup zatar

4 tablespoons olive oil

One batch Middle Eastern Flatbread Dough (page 88), fully risen

1 Stir the zatar and oil together and set aside.

2 Divide the dough into four pieces, round, and let rest as in Seeded Flatbreads, above.

3 After preheating the oven, shape into four 6-inch disks, place on the prepared pan, cover, and allow to puff.

4 Dimple the formed loaves and spread each with a quarter of the topping. Bake, cool, serve, and store as above.

focaccia dough

Makes about 2¼ pounds dough, enough for 1 large thick-crusted focaccia or 2 smaller ones

4½ cups unbleached all-purpose flour or bread flour (spoon into a dry-measure cup and level off)

2 teaspoons salt

2½ teaspoons (one ¼-ounce envelope) active dry yeast

1¾ cups warm tap water, about 110°F

¼ cup olive oil

Focaccia, like pizza, means different things to different people. In a Roman pizzeria that makes typically Italian thin-crust pizza, it can be a similarly thin disk of the same dough brushed with olive oil and sprinkled with salt before it's baked for just a few minutes in a ferociously hot wood-burning oven. Thicker types of focacce (the plural) derive from the Italian region of Liguria, of which Genoa is the capital, and typically have some fat added to the dough. The fat, usually olive oil or freshly rendered pork lard, adds flavor, tenderness, and richness to the resulting focaccia. I like to use this version of the dough, which is more than easy to prepare, as a base for savory toppings beyond the traditionally Italian.

1   Stir the flour and salt together and set aside.

2   In a large mixing bowl, whisk the yeast into the water. Wait 2 minutes and whisk again to make sure the yeast is completely dissolved. Whisk in the oil.

3   Use a large rubber spatula to smoothly stir half the flour mixture into the liquid. Stir in the remaining flour mixture, using the spatula to dig up any unmoistened flour from the bottom of the bowl.

4   After all the flour is moistened, scrape any dry bits from the side of the bowl and incorporate them into the dough. Use the spatula to beat the dough vigorously for about 15 seconds. Cover the bowl with plastic wrap and let the dough rise until it has doubled in size, about 1 hour.

5   Use the dough with any of the seasoning and/or topping variations that follow.

essential tips for focaccia dough

• This dough is quickly made. For advance preparation, have all the ingredients ready, but make sure you'll be ready to follow through to the baking once you mix the dough. You may deflate and refrigerate the dough if you can't complete the process. Press it into the pan straight from the refrigerator. When cold it will take much longer to rise in the pan before baking, though.

• This soft dough is easy to mix, but not particularly easy to handle. If you have any difficulty turning the dough over once it's on the pan, just oil your hands to press the dough into the pan.

• Be creative about toppings and additions to the dough—just don't use too many different things at the same time or overload the top of the focaccia or it will not bake as well.

potato & gruyère focaccia

I first tasted a version of this made by my friend Amy Scherber, owner of Amy's Bread in New York. I liked it so much I developed a version of my own a few days later without ever finding out how she makes hers. Just recently Amy told me that for the topping she roasts the potatoes whole and unpeeled and then slices them once they're cold, another option you might want to try.

Makes one 12 x 18-inch focaccia,
12 approximately 4-inch squares

1 batch Focaccia Dough, left,
completely risen

2 medium Yukon Gold or other waxy
potatoes, about 12 ounces

Salt and freshly ground black pepper

½ cup coarsely grated Swiss Gruyère

2 tablespoons olive oil

One 11 x 17-inch or 12 x 18-inch jelly-roll
pan, greased with ¼ cup olive oil

Serving: Slide the still-warm focaccia to a cutting board and use a sharp serrated knife to cut it into 4 strips in the width and 3 in the length to make 4-inch squares. To serve the focaccia as an hors d'oeuvre, cut it into 2-inch squares.

Storage: Keep the focaccia on the rack until serving. Wrap leftovers in plastic and warm them in the oven before serving again.

1 Scrape the dough into the pan, being careful not to fold the dough over on itself. Reach under it and flip it over—now the top is coated with oil. Use the palms of your hands to press the dough into the pan. If it resists, cover, and let rest for 10 minutes, then press again to cover the entire bottom of the pan. Cover with plastic wrap and let rise until puffy, about 30 minutes.

2 Set a rack in the lowest level of the oven and preheat to 450°F.

3 Peel the potatoes and cut them as thin as you can; I use the little slicing blade on the side of a box grater. Slide into a saucepan, cover with water, and bring to a single full boil over medium heat. Drain, rinse, and set aside in a colander.

4 Once the focaccia is risen, use your index finger to dimple the top all over at 1-inch intervals. Cover with the potato slices, slightly overlapping them. Season with a little salt and pepper and evenly scatter on the cheese. Drizzle with the olive oil.

5 Place the focaccia on the oven rack and decrease the temperature to 425°F. Bake until the dough is firm and the topping is golden, about 30 minutes. About halfway through the baking time, use a wide spatula to lift the corner of the focaccia to check that the bottom is starting to color. If it is coloring too quickly, slide another pan under the pan the focaccia is in to insulate the bottom.

6 Slide the baked focaccia to a rack to cool so that the bottom doesn't become damp.

variation

Onion Focaccia: I know it doesn't sound very glamorous, but slowly cooked sliced onions are one of my favorite toppings for a focaccia. For a delicious variation, halve, seed, and thinly slice 1 pound red bell peppers and cook them along with the onions.

Makes one 12 x 18-inch focaccia,
12 approximately 4-inch squares

¼ cup olive oil

3 large white or yellow onions, peeled, halved,
and thinly sliced from stem to root end

1 batch Focaccia Dough, completely risen

Salt and freshly ground black pepper

1 Start cooking the onions before step 1 of the master recipe at left. Combine the oil and onions in a wide sauté pan that has a cover. Place on medium heat and when the oil starts to sizzle, decrease to low, cover the pan, and cook, stirring occasionally, until the onions are soft and translucent, about 30 minutes. Uncover the pan, season with a little salt, and increase the heat slightly. Cook until the liquid evaporates, 10 to 15 minutes. Scrape the onions into a thin layer on a cookie sheet lined with plastic wrap and cool quickly in the refrigerator or freezer.

2 Continue with the recipe above at step 4, substituting the cooled onions for the potatoes and cheese. Season with salt and pepper but do not drizzle with oil as there is plenty in the onions.

3 Bake, cool, serve, and store as above.

sage & dried tomato focaccia

Makes one 12 x 18-inch focaccia,
12 approximately 4-inch squares

Ingredients for Focaccia Dough (page 92)

1 small bunch fresh sage, stemmed, leaves stacked and cut into ¼-inch ribbons

⅓ cup sun-dried tomatoes, cut into ½-inch dice

2 tablespoons olive oil

1 teaspoon kosher or other coarse salt

One 11 x 17-inch or 12 x 18-inch jelly-roll pan, greased with ¼ cup olive oil

Sage and dried tomatoes make a flavorful focaccia topping but if you like, add them directly to the dough as in the variation below. See the end of the recipe for suggestions on other additions to the dough. Don't be afraid to be creative. Other dry cheeses, cured meats, and fresh or dried herbs beyond the ones suggested are fine too, as long as you don't overdo it.

1   Mix and let the dough rise as on page 92.

2   Scrape the dough into the prepared pan, being careful not to fold the dough over on itself. After the dough is on the pan, reach under it and flip it over—now the top is coated with oil. Use the flat palms of your hands to press the dough into the pan. If it resists, cover and let rest for 10 minutes, then press again to cover the entire bottom of the pan. Cover with plastic wrap and allow to rise until puffy, about 30 minutes.

3   Set a rack in the lowest level of the oven and preheat to 450°F.

4   Once the focaccia is fully risen, use your index finer to dimple the top all over at 1-inch intervals. Press pieces of the sage and tomato into the dough at about 1-inch intervals all over the top. Drizzle with the oil and sprinkle with the salt.

5   Place the focaccia on the oven rack and decrease the temperature to 425°F. Bake until the dough is firm and the topping is golden, about 30 minutes. About halfway through the baking time, use a wide spatula to lift a corner of the focaccia to check that the bottom is starting to color. If it is coloring too quickly, slide another pan under the pan the focaccia is in to insulate the bottom.

6   Slide the baked focaccia to a rack to cool slightly so that the bottom doesn't become damp. Serve and store as for the Potato and Gruyère Focaccia, page 93.

variations

Instead of topping the focaccia with the sage and tomatoes, add them to the flour and salt when mixing the master recipe, then continue with step 1 above. Or use any of the following as additions to the dough instead of the sage and dried tomatoes: 1/4 cup stripped and coarsely chopped fresh rosemary leaves, 2 tablespoons dried herbes de Provence or zatar, 1/2 cup dry grating cheese such as Parmigiano-Reggiano (reserve a tablespoon to sprinkle on top with the salt before baking), 1/2 cup pitted and coarsely chopped oil-cured olives, or 1/3 cup each diced thinly sliced mozzarella and prosciutto.

thin-crusted pizza

Makes 2½ pounds of dough,
enough for four 12-inch round pizzas
(see Note 1)

5 cups bread flour (spoon into
a dry-measure cup and level off)

2 teaspoons salt

2 teaspoons active dry yeast (see Note 2)

2 cups warm water, about 110°F

5 tablespoons olive oil, divided use

Note 1: You can divide the dough in thirds
or just in half to make three 10 x 15-inch or
two 12 x 18-inch rectangular pizzas.

Note 2: If you're preparing the dough early
in the day for the evening or even the day
before baking the pizzas, use only
1 teaspoon yeast.

essential tips for pizza

- Use a heavy-gauge pan with sides
for baking the pizza. Thin pans
don't hold enough heat to
sufficiently color and crisp the
bottom of the pizza before the
toppings dry out. And the pan
has to have sides or oil might drip
onto the bottom of the oven and
create smoke or even flames.

- Don't overdo the pizza toppings;
limit them to three to four.
Otherwise they will begin
cancelling each other out and
you won't taste the crust at all.

- Serve the pizza immediately
after baking for best results.

My quest for a thin-crusted pizza that's easy to prepare at home led me right to my friend Michael Ayoub, chef-owner of Fornino in Brooklyn, New York. Michael uses a long-rising dough made from a blend of different flours for his thin, delicate pizzas, but I wanted something that would work well if you decide you want to serve some pizza in a couple of hours. After a few false starts, including one that produced a perfect replica of a frozen pizza, I decided upon this dough, which is similar to a dough for a focaccia and is easy to press out thin into a pan. I decided on using an oiled pan for the pizza rather than a baking stone, another point that makes the process simpler to tackle. I like to proceed right from pressing the dough into the pan to adding the toppings and baking. Most domestic ovens won't hold two 10-inch pans side by side but you can bake the pizzas in succession, which isn't that much of a problem since they bake quickly.

1 Stir the flour and salt together in a large mixing bowl.

2 Whisk the yeast into the water and whisk in 2 tablespoons of the oil.

3 Use a large rubber spatula to stir the liquid into the flour, continuously scraping the side of the bowl and folding up any unmixed flour from the bottom of the bowl.

4 Once most of the flour is moistened, repeatedly slide the spatula between the side of the bowl and the dough and fold the dough over on itself to make it smoother. Cover the bowl with plastic wrap and set aside until doubled in bulk, about 1 hour.

5 Scrape the risen dough to a floured work surface and fold it over on itself several times to make it smoother. Use a bench scraper to divide the dough into equal pieces, depending on the size of the pans you're using (see Note 1, at left).

6 Fold the sides of each piece of dough into the top center to round it. Flip the pieces over so that the smooth sides are facing up. Generously flour each piece and loosely wrap them individually in plastic. They can be refrigerated for up to 24 hours.

7 About 20 minutes before forming and baking the pizzas, set a rack in the lowest level of the oven and preheat to your oven's highest setting, at least 550°F.

8 Use 2 more tablespoons of the oil to grease the bottom and sides of the pan and unwrap a piece of dough onto it (A). Turn the dough over so that the top is oiled too and press with the fingers of both hands to stretch the dough to fill the pan (B). If you're baking more than one pizza, repeat with the remaining pieces of dough. Only form as many crusts as you can bake pizzas immediately or the crusts that have to wait will rise on the pan and become thicker.

9 Spread and scatter the toppings on the crust to within 1/4 inch of the edge and drizzle with the remaining tablespoon of olive oil (C through F). Bake the pizza until the topping is bubbling and lightly browned and the bottom is well baked through, about 10 minutes. After about 5 minutes, use a metal spatula or pancake turner to lift the crust and check to see if the bottom is coloring.

A

B

C

D

E

F

10 Slide the pizza onto a cutting board and use a pizza wheel to cut into wedges. Serve immediately. Repeat for any remaining pizzas.

topping combinations for thin-crusted pizzas

The best advice I can give you is: Don't overdo it! The first pizza I ever had in an actual pizzeria was in New Jersey where I grew up (my grandmother made thick-crusted pizza at home on special occasions). We ordered it with "extra cheese." What arrived at the table was a disk of dough that seemed to be topped with about a gallon of lava-like melted cheese, still seething from the oven—there was easily enough mozzarella on that pizza to top a dozen or more traditional Italian pizzas.

Please note that for the sake of clarity all the topping quantities are given for a single 12-inch round pizza. A 10 x 15-inch pizza needs $1\frac{1}{2}$ times the topping quantities to cover it and a 12 x 18-inch pizza needs 2 times the quantities. The topping recipes and instructions following the combinations make more than you need for a single batch of pizza dough; pack, cover, and freeze extras for future pizzas. Finally, avoid adding cheese to any pizza that has anchovies.

Don't be afraid to be creative with your own ideas for pizza toppings, just remember a few simple rules: Limit your choices to 3 or 4 toppings per pizza. Use the quantities in the pizzas below as a guideline; toppings are meant to enhance, not overwhelm, the crust. Blanch or cook vegetables before using. And use freshly prepared ingredients; a pizza isn't a vehicle for disposing of leftovers. **>**

Pizza Margherita: The queen of all pizzas and the most popular one at Michael's Fornino pizzeria, it's actually named in honor of Italy's Queen Margherita di Savoia. Devised by Neapolitan pizzaiolo Raffaele Esposito in 1889, the pizza's red (tomato), white (mozzarella), and green (basil) toppings mimic the colors of the newly united Kingdom of Italy's flag and the Margherita was so named after the queen chose it as her favorite among the ones Esposito prepared.

Thinly spread the crust with 1/3 cup Tomato Topping (right). Scatter on 8 large leaves of basil that have been stacked and cut into 1/4-inch shreds, followed by 1/2 cup grated low-moisture mozzarella or finely diced fresh mozzarella. Drizzle with olive oil (see the photos on page 97).

Variation: Don't tell the Neapolitan pizza mafia, but I like to scatter a large clove of garlic, cut into paper-thin slivers, on the tomato topping. The garlic melts to a mild and creamy flavor and texture while the pizza is baking.

Pizza di Patate: This potato pizza is different from the potato focaccia on page 93. Cover the pizza crust with thin slices of blanched potato (page 93) and light salt and pepper. Scatter on 2 teaspoons finely chopped fresh rosemary (or 1 teaspoon dried oregano) and 1/2 cup finely grated Parmigiano-Reggiano or Pecorino Romano. If using Romano, which is quite salty, omit the salt from the toppings. Drizzle with olive oil.

Pizza Salsiccia e Peperoni (sausage and pepper pizza): First mix together 1/4 cup Tomato Topping with 1/2 cup each Onion and Pepper toppings (right). Spread on the pizza. Scatter on thin slices of a cooked link of Italian sausage, sweet or hot as you wish, and 1/2 cup grated ricotta salata, mozzarella, Parmigiano, or Pecorino. Drizzle with olive oil.

Variations: Substitute a couple of ounces of soppressata, other dried sausage, or even prosciutto, thinly sliced, stacked, and cut into 1/2-inch shreds, for the freshly cooked sausage. Scatter the dried sausage on the pizza after removing it from the oven.

Pizza con le Alici (anchovy pizza): Drain and chop 1 ounce (half a 2-ounce can) anchovies packed in oil and stir them into 1/2 cup Tomato Topping (right). Evenly spread on the pizza crust and top with a large clove of garlic cut into paper-thin slivers, 1 teaspoon dried oregano, and 2 tablespoons olive oil.

Pizza con le Cipolle: (onion pizza): Spread the crust with 2/3 cup Onion Topping (mix anchovies into it as above if you like). Top with 1/3 cup pitted and quartered Gaeta or Kalamata olives, 1 teaspoon dried oregano, and 1 tablespoon olive oil. Scatter with 1/2 cup grated cheese of your choice if you haven't added anchovies.

Variation: Use 1/2 cup each of Onion Topping and Pepper Topping (below); omit the olives. Sprinkle with 1/2 cup grated cheese and 1/2 teaspoon dried oregano.

recipes & instructions for preparing pizza toppings

Each of the following makes enough for several pizzas. You needn't prepare all of them—look through the pizzas at left, select the ones you want to bake, and prepare the necessary toppings accordingly.

Tomato Topping: In Italy or any pizzeria elsewhere that has a wood-burning oven, it's common to use fresh or canned chopped tomatoes as a pizza topping. In an oven that heats to close to 1,000 degrees, the excess water from the tomatoes easily evaporates. In a home oven, chopped tomatoes can produce a watery topping for a thin-crusted pizza, so I took Michael Ayoub's advice for a cooked pureed tomato topping.

Run a 28-ounce can of imported Italian San Marzano plum tomatoes through a food mill into a large saucepan. Add 4 large sprigs basil tied together with kitchen twine and 3 cloves of garlic, peeled and halved. Bring to a boil, decrease heat to a very gentle simmer, place a cover ajar on the pan, and cook for 30 minutes. Cool, remove the garlic and basil, and refrigerate covered if not using immediately. Makes about 3 cups.

Onion Topping: Peel, halve, and thinly slice a large white onion (about 8 to 10 ounces) from stem to root end. Pour 2 tablespoons olive oil into a wide sauté pan, add the onions, salt lightly, and set over high heat. When the onions begin to sizzle, reduce the heat to low and cook them slowly, stirring occasionally, until they are soft and light golden, about 20 to 30 minutes. Let cool.

Pepper Topping: Cut 2 red, green, or yellow bell peppers, or a combination, by standing them up, stem upward, and cutting away the four walls of the pepper. Slice away the bottom. Cut the pepper pieces in 3/8-inch strips. Oil a jelly-roll pan and add the pepper strips. Salt lightly. Bake in a preheated 375°F oven on the middle rack, stirring occasionally, until soft but not charred, about 20 minutes. If the pepper strips char at all while baking, they'll turn to cinders on the pizza.

Potato Topping: Peel, slice, and blanch 1 1/2 pounds Yukon Gold potatoes according to the instructions on page 93. Only make as much as you need; this topping doesn't freeze well.

Cheeses: Grate mozzarella or ricotta salata on the largest holes of a box grater. For harder cheese such as Parmigiano or Pecorino, use the smaller holes to make thin shreds.

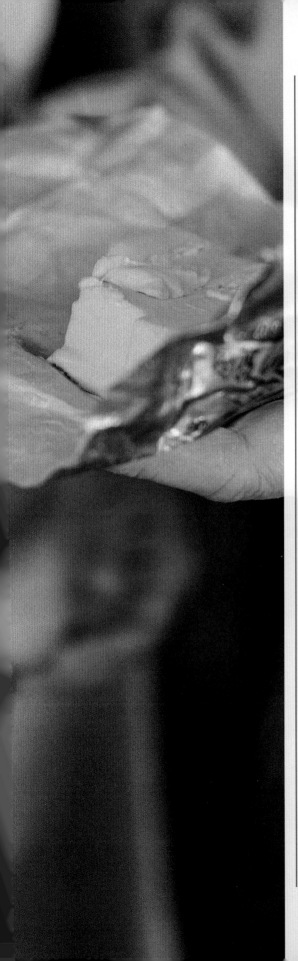

09

brioche

Tender, buttery, and just slightly sweet, brioches are among the world's finest breakfast pastries. And yes, brioche is considered a pastry, not a bread. I have a special affection for brioche because the first class I ever taught, in February 1979, was on preparing brioche dough and making various buns and loaves from it. This chapter begins with some simply formed or adorned breakfast loaves and buns, then takes off to cover some fruited and other more elaborate ones, before finishing up with the world's most elegant pizza—a double-crusted affair created by a French chef for a Sicilian prince.

brioche dough

Makes about 1¾ pounds dough

SPONGE

⅓ cup milk

2½ teaspoons (1 envelope) active dry yeast

¼ cup warm tap water, about 110°F

¾ cup bread flour (spoon into a dry-measure cup and level off)

DOUGH

2 large eggs, at room temperature

2 large egg yolks, at room temperature

3 tablespoons sugar

All the sponge, above

2 cups bread flour

1 teaspoon salt

8 tablespoons (1 stick) unsalted butter, softened

If you have an electric mixer to do all the work, brioche dough is as easy to prepare as the batter for a pound cake. This is a variation on the brioche dough I learned from my teacher Albert Kumin. His recipe called for starting with the butter and beating the other ingredients into it. I've revised the method to incorporate the butter at the end, the more traditional manner of preparing the dough.

1 For the sponge, warm the milk in a small pan over low heat; pour it into a small bowl and allow it to cool to 100°F.

2 Whisk the yeast into the warm water in a medium bowl. Wait 2 minutes, then whisk again to make sure all the yeast has dissolved. Whisk in the cooled milk. Use a rubber spatula to stir the flour into the liquid. Cover the bowl with plastic wrap and let the sponge ferment until more than doubled, about 30 minutes.

3 Once the sponge has risen, use a rubber spatula to break up the eggs and yolks in the bowl of an electric mixer fitted with the dough hook. Stir in the sugar. Scrape the risen sponge into the bowl and mix it into the eggs. Add the flour and salt to the bowl and stir in. Mix on medium speed until the dough comes away from the sides of the bowl, 3 to 4 minutes.

4 Add a third of the butter and continue mixing until the butter is completely absorbed. Repeat with the remaining two thirds of the butter, mixing to incorporate after each addition.

5 Continue to mix until the dough is very smooth, elastic, and shiny, 4 to 5 additional minutes (A and B).

6 Scrape the dough into a buttered bowl and turn it over so that the top is buttered. Cover with plastic wrap and let rise until doubled in size, about 30 minutes.

7 Scrape the dough to a lightly floured surface and press it into a square about ½ inch thick. Use the dough immediately in any of the recipes that follow, except the pizza; wrap and chill it for easier handling if you wish, but it's not strictly necessary except for the pizza.

A

B

- Be sure that both the milk and the water are just lukewarm (110°F maximum) or the yeast will not survive and the dough won't rise. Don't be afraid to use an instant-read thermometer to verify the temperature of the liquid.

- Don't let the sponge rise beyond a little more than doubled or it will lose some of its leavening power and also contribute a sour flavor to the dough.

- Make sure the butter is sufficiently soft or it will form lumps when added to the dough.

- Be careful that the dough doesn't get over-risen after mixing or after shaping or it might not retain an even shape during baking.

- After rising, brioche dough is pretty sticky, but it's still possible to form it into the shapes you need to make. For best results, flour your hands, rather than the work surface or the dough, for ease and accuracy in rounding and shaping the dough.

- If you're making any variation in which the dough needs to be rolled out, chill the dough thoroughly for several hours or it will be impossible to roll.

- For advance preparation, bake, cool, wrap, and freeze brioches. Reheat them at 350°F for 10 minutes and cool before serving.

brioche breakfast loaf

Delicately sweet and buttery as is, slices of this loaf acquire an ethereal flavor when lightly toasted. It's a perfect backdrop for any jam or preserves. A day old or lightly toasted, it's an excellent sandwich bread for such delicate fillings as a tarragon-flavored chicken salad or smoked salmon with chive-flavored cream cheese. With cocktails or dinner it also makes a nice raft for a thick slice of a terrine of foie gras. The great American gastronome James Beard used to make exquisite onion sandwiches for tea or cocktails using buttered brioche and paper-thin slices of sweet onion, such as Vidalia.

Makes one 9 x 5 x 5-inch loaf

1 batch Brioche Dough (page 100) prepared up to the end of step 7

Egg wash: 1 large egg well beaten with a pinch of salt

One 9 x 5 x 3-inch loaf pan, buttered

1 Scrape the risen dough from the bowl to a floured work surface. (If you're using chilled dough, let it soften at room temperature until it is no longer ice cold.) Flour your hands and gently round the dough without deflating it too much by pushing inward at the bottom with your flat upturned palms all around the piece of dough; the outside skin of the dough will tighten and become more spherical.

2 Stretch the rounded piece of dough into a rough rectangle and slide both hands under it, palms upward, and transfer it to the prepared pan.

3 Cover the pan with a piece of buttered plastic wrap and let the dough rise until it comes about $1\frac{1}{2}$ inches above the rim of the pan. Freshly made dough should rise within about 30 minutes, and chilled dough will require 1 hour or more.

4 About 20 minutes before the loaf is completely risen, set a rack in the lower third of the oven and preheat to 375°F.

5 Immediately before placing the risen loaf in the oven, brush the top with the egg wash, being careful not to drip any egg wash down the side of the pan. Use a single-edged razor or X-Acto knife to slash the top skin of the dough lengthwise, down the middle of the loaf. Bake the loaf until it is well risen, is deep golden, and has an internal temperature of 200°F to 210°F.

6 Unmold the loaf to a rack and cool it on its side to prevent deflating.

Serving: Cool completely before slicing. Serve plain or toasted with any of your favorite spreads except butter, which it doesn't need.

Storage: Keep lightly covered at room temperature on the day it's baked. Wrap and chill or freeze leftovers.

variations

Raisin Brioche Loaf: Add 1 cup dark or golden raisins or currants to the dough about 1 minute before the end of the mixing process when preparing Brioche Dough (step 5, page 100). After forming the loaf and transferring it to the pan (step 2 of Breakfast Brioche), pick off any raisins on the top that would burn during baking. If you can get some really delicious candied orange peel (avoid the supermarket variety), cut it into $3/8$-inch dice and use it to replace a third to all of the raisins.

Poppy or Almond Brioche Loaf: Before slashing the top of the loaf, sprinkle it generously with poppy seeds or crushed sliced almonds.

Chocolate Brioche Loaf: Whisk together 4 ounces bittersweet (not unsweetened) chocolate, melted and cooled, 3 tablespoons water, $1/2$ teaspoon baking soda, and $1/8$ teaspoon ground cinnamon. Add the mixture to the Brioche Dough after it is completely mixed (step 5, page 100) and continue to mix until the chocolate mixture is fully incorporated, sprinkling in $1/2$ cup flour as you do.

A

B

sugared brioche rolls

This is a popular use for brioche dough as a breakfast roll in France. The rolls are sprinkled with pearl sugar, large opaque sugar granules, right before baking. If you live near an IKEA store (and who doesn't?) they carry the Swedish version at a reasonable price. This is the master recipe for the variations that follow, including my take on currant-studded Bath Buns, the Mexican Buns called *conchas* (shells), and Jam-Filled Crumb Buns.

Makes 12

1 batch Brioche Dough (page 100)

Egg wash: 1 egg well beaten with a pinch of salt

½ cup pearl sugar or other coarse clear or opaque (not colored) sugar granules

Cookie sheet or jelly-roll pan lined with parchment paper or foil

1 Divide the dough into 12 equal pieces. Round the pieces under the cupped palm of one hand, moving your hand in a small circle (A and B). If the dough is sticky, flour your hand, not the dough or the work surface or the dough will just slide around instead of rounding.

2 Place the rolls on the pan with 2 inches between each roll and the sides of the pan.

3 Cover the rolls with buttered plastic wrap and let rise until doubled in size, about 1 hour or longer depending on how cold the dough is.

4 About 20 minutes before the rolls are fully risen, set a rack in the middle level of the oven and preheat to 375°F.

5 Once the rolls have risen, neatly paint them with the egg wash, making sure to clean each side of the brush against the side of the egg wash container after each dip so that the brush is not too sodden. You don't want to leave puddles of egg wash under the rolls. Immediately sprinkle with the pearl sugar.

6 Bake the rolls until they are well risen and deep golden, about 20 minutes.

7 Cool the rolls on a rack and serve them soon after they are baked.

Serving: These really don't need an accompaniment, but you might like jam or marmalade.

Storage: Keep the rolls loosely covered at room temperature until serving. Bag and freeze for longer storage. Defrost and bring to room temperature before serving.

variations

Bath Buns Many different version of these exist, some of which are almost indistinguishable from the sugared brioche rolls above. My favorite version incorporates some currants in the dough and on the outside of each bun.

When preparing the master recipe for Brioche Dough, add 1 cup currants right before completing the mixing process (step 5, page 100). Prepare exactly as for sugared brioche rolls, above, adding a pinch of currants on top of each bun in the center before sprinkling on the pearl sugar. Let rise, bake, cool, serve, and store as above. **>**

A

Mexican Buns Called *conchas,* or shells, because of the traditional pattern pressed into the topping with a round tool like a cookie cutter, these are not only delicious but also quite slick looking. The topping recipe is meant to be divided in half so that you can make half vanilla- and half chocolate-topped buns. For all vanilla, omit the cocoa; for all chocolate double it.

CONCHA TOPPING

6 tablespoons unsalted butter, softened

3/4 cup confectioners' sugar

2/3 cup unbleached all-purpose flour (spoon into a dry-measure cup and level off)

1 teaspoon vanilla extract

2 teaspoons alkalized (Dutch process) cocoa powder, sifted after measuring

1   Before beginning with step 1 on page 103, make the topping. Beat the butter in an electric mixer fitted with the paddle attachment on medium speed. Decrease the speed to low and beat in the confectioners' sugar and flour. Mix until smooth, then scrape the bowl and beater. Increase the speed to medium and beat in the vanilla extract. Beat for a few seconds longer, then scrape the topping, which should have

the consistency of a soft dough, to a lightly floured work surface. Roll the topping into a fat cylinder and divide it in half. Knead the cocoa powder into one half to color it (it's light colored, but will darken as it bakes).

2   Roll each batch of topping into a cylinder again and cut each cylinder into 6 equal pieces. Cover with plastic wrap and set aside at room temperature until needed.

3   Form the dough into 12 buns as step 1 of the Sugared Brioche Rolls recipe (page 103). Arrange the buns on the prepared pan and cover them with a kitchen towel; let rest until they start to puff slightly, 10 to 30 minutes, depending on the starting temperature of the dough. While the buns are resting, form each piece of the topping into a flat 2$^{1}/_{2}$-inch disk, pressing it with the palm of one hand to shape.

4   Once the buns have risen a little, flatten each one and press a disk of the topping against it. Use a paring knife with the blade perpendicular to the topping to press 5 equidistant lines through only the topping (A). Press in 5 more lines at a 45- or 90-degree angle to the first set of lines. Cover the buns with a kitchen towel or plastic wrap and let rise until doubled in size. Bake, cool, serve, and store as for the Sugared Brioche Rolls. In Mexico these are always eaten with hot chocolate.

Jam-Filled Crumb Buns Vary these by using any type of jam or preserves you like. They're also great with the prune or apricot filling in Chapter 10, Danish Pastry.

1/2 cup strawberry or seedless raspberry jam, or any other jam of your choice

Egg wash: 1 egg well beaten with a pinch of salt

Crumb Topping (page 103), unbaked

Form the dough into 12 buns as in the Sugared Brioche Rolls (page 105). Arrange the buns on the work surface and cover them with a clean kitchen towel; let them rest until they start to puff slightly, 10 to 30 minutes, depending on the starting temperature of the dough. Pick up and invert one of the buns; supporting the rounded (top) side with your fingers, use your thumbs to make a 1/2-inch cavity. Drop in about 1 1/2 teaspoons of jam, then pinch the dough to enclose the jam and seal the bottom of the bun. Arrange the buns on the pan, rounded side up, as they are formed. Cover the buns with a kitchen towel and let rest again until they begin to puff slightly, 10 to 30 minutes. Flatten each bun, paint with egg wash, and cover with the crumb topping, pressing it on. Cover the pan and let the buns rise until they are doubled in size. Bake, cool, serve, and store as above.

pizza alla campofranco

Makes one 12-inch pizza, about
8 generous servings

2 tablespoons olive oil

2 pounds plum tomatoes, peeled,
quartered, and seeded (see Note)

One batch Brioche Dough (page 100),
pressed flat on a floured cookie sheet,
covered with plastic wrap, and chilled
in the refrigerator until firm, at least
2 hours or up to 18 hours

Freshly ground black pepper

½ cup grated Parmigiano-Reggiano

½ cup torn basil leaves

12 ounces fresh mozzarella, thinly sliced

4 ounces prosciutto, thinly sliced and
shredded

One 12-inch tart pan with a removable
bottom

The town for which this unusual pizza is named is in Sicily. Pizza alla Campofranco was probably invented by a *monzù* (the *monzù* were French-trained chefs who worked for the nobility in Sicily and Naples) in the home of Don Antonio Lucchesi Palli, Prince of Campofranco. During the prince's life he was a right-hand man to King Ferdinand of the Kingdom of the Two Sicilies. Naples was also a part of the kingdom, which explains why they were making pizza—a Neapolitan specialty—in Campofranco. The Kingdom of the Two Sicilies ceased to exist when Garibaldi conquered both Sicily and Naples in 1860, and the Kingdom of Italy was established in early 1861, but this unusual pizza with its brioche crust (much used by the *monzù*) has survived. After the shallow bottom crust is filled with some typical pizza topping ingredients, including some thinly sliced prosciutto, a top crust seals them in and the pizza is baked without allowing the dough to rise again, as in a typical pizza.

1   For the filling, heat the oil in a sauté pan and add the tomato quarters. Cook quickly over high heat to evaporate some moisture from them, but not until they disintegrate. Cool the tomatoes.

2   When you are ready to assemble the pizza, set a rack in the lowest level of the oven and preheat to 400°F.

3   Remove the dough from the refrigerator and divide it into two pieces, one slightly larger than the other. Roll the larger piece of dough to line the pan, letting the excess dough hang over the edge.

4   Arrange the tomatoes on the crust, then grind pepper over them (no salt is necessary because of the grated cheese and prosciutto); scatter on the grated cheese, then the basil. Cover with the mozzarella, then the prosciutto.

5   Roll the remaining dough for the top crust and put it in place. Press the edges of the top and bottom crust together and sever the excess dough at the rim of the pan.

6   Bake the pizza until the crust is deep golden and baked through, about 30 minutes. Unmold and slide to a platter; serve immediately.

Serving: Cut into wedges at the table and serve as a first course, or as the main course of a light meal.

Storage: You may refrigerate the pizza after it is assembled, but bake and serve it on the day it is assembled.

Note: If you only have under-ripe, out-of-season tomatoes, don't bother to peel them. Use 3 pounds of tomatoes, halve and seed them, and place them on a pan covered with oiled foil. Sprinkle the tomatoes with sugar and bake them at 350°F for 30 minutes to concentrate their flavor. Cool and arrange them on the crust as above.

10

danish pastry

Good Danish pastry isn't easy to find. Most of what's available isn't even made using the traditional method of rolling layers of butter into the dough. Though I've been making Danish pastry for years, I only recently tried a quick method—similar to the puff pastry in Chapter 4. After this yeasted Danish recipe, there's an even quicker one that is leavened with baking powder. Each recipe in this chapter is for individual Danish pastries, with plenty of variations on the fillings and toppings, and each recipe calls for a half batch of the dough (the baking powder version makes the same amount of dough) so that you can try a couple of different pastries at the same time.

quick danish pastry dough

What we know as Danish pastry probably originated in Vienna, though it's not much in evidence there today. In Denmark, these pastries are referred to as *wienerbrod,* which in English translates literally as "Vienna bread," pointing to their origin in Austria. No matter what you call it, homemade Danish is exquisite and nothing like what comes from a bakery, unless you happen to live in Scandinavia. The following method is similar to the food-processor variation for puff pastry in Chapter 4. The non-yeasted variation that follows is made the same way.

Makes about 2¼ pounds dough

3½ teaspoons (1½ envelopes) active dry yeast

¼ cup warm tap water, about 110°F

¼ cup milk, heated and cooled to 100°F

3 cups unbleached all-purpose flour (spoon into a dry-measure cup and level off)

¼ cup sugar

¾ teaspoon salt

12 ounces (3 sticks) unsalted butter, cold

2 large eggs, at room temperature

1 Whisk the yeast into the warm water. Wait a minute or two, then whisk again to make sure that all the yeast has dissolved. Whisk in the milk.

2 Combine the flour, sugar, and salt in the bowl of a food processor fitted with the metal blade. Pulse a few times to mix.

3 Cut 4 tablespoons of the butter into thin slices and add to the bowl. Pulse to a fine texture, but don't let the mixture become pasty.

4 Cut the remaining butter into $1/2$-inch cubes and add to the bowl. Pulse exactly twice for 1 second at a time to combine very roughly.

5 Transfer to a mixing bowl (A). Whisk the eggs into the yeast mixture and add it to the mixing bowl. To mix in the liquid, position a rubber spatula so its blade is flat and parallel with the bottom of the bowl and repeatedly dig down to the bottom of the bowl while turning the bowl (B). Mix until the dough comes together; it will be soft and sticky.

6 Press plastic wrap against the dough and refrigerate for 1 to 2 hours.

7 Scrape the chilled dough to a floured surface and flour the dough. Use the palms of your hands to press the dough into a rectangle about twice as long as it is wide.

8 Starting at the narrow end of the rectangle farthest from you, use a rolling pin to firmly press the dough in parallel strokes close to each other. If there are sticky pieces of butter on the surface of the dough, seal them with a large pinch of flour, making sure to clean off the rolling pin of anything stuck to it before continuing. Repeat the pressing motion from the close to farther narrow end of the dough.

9 Press the dough once in the width—it should now be a rectangle about $1/2$ inch thick. Once again, flour under and on top of the dough and roll the dough away and back toward you in the length and once in the width, without rolling over the ends, to make a rectangle about 18 inches long and 8 inches wide.

10 Fold the two 8-inch ends of the dough in toward the middle of the rectangle, leaving a 1-inch space in the middle. Fold the top down to the bottom to form 4 layers of dough. Reposition the dough so that the folded edge that resembles the spine of a book is on your left. Rolling and folding the dough is known as "giving the dough a turn."

11 Give the dough another full turn of rolling and folding.

12 Wrap the folded dough in plastic and chill for at least 2 hours or up to 12 hours before using it to prepare one of the pastries that follow.

A

B

christel's danish pastry dough

Thanks to my friend Kyra Blumberg Effren for sharing this family recipe. Named for the Blumberg family's German cook, who worked for them first in London, then outside Cape Town, this is a nonsweet version of Danish pastry that's leavened with baking powder. You may substitute an equal quantity of this dough in any of the Danish pastry recipes in this chapter; the technique is less fussy. Unlike the yeasted danish pastry dough at left, this one may be entirely mixed in a food processor.

Makes about 2¼ pounds dough

12 ounces whole-milk ricotta

2 large egg yolks, at room temperature

2¾ cups unbleached all-purpose flour
(spoon into a dry-measure cup and level off)

2½ teaspoons baking powder

¾ teaspoon salt

12 ounces (3 sticks) unsalted butter, cold,
cut into 20 pieces

1   Stir the ricotta and egg yolks together and set aside.

2   Combine the flour, baking powder, and salt in the bowl of a food processor fitted with the metal blade. Pulse several times to mix.

3   Add the butter to the bowl and pulse repeatedly until it is finely mixed into the dry ingredients. No visible pieces of butter should remain.

4   Scrape in the ricotta mixture and pulse at 1-second intervals until the dough forms a ball.

5   Invert the dough to a floured work surface and carefully remove the blade. Lightly flour the dough and form it into a rectangle about ½ inch thick. Wrap and refrigerate the dough until firm, about 1 hour.

essential tips for danish

- If the dough is very soft after mixing, develop some elasticity by pressing the dough into a rectangle on a floured surface and folding a third over the middle section and the other third over them, as in the biscuit recipe on page 180. Turn the dough 90 degrees and repeat before wrapping and chilling.

- See Essentials for Puff Pastry on page 52 for information on the rolling and folding process.

- Use the yeasted dough within 12 hours for best flavor, and let rise after pastries are formed and baked.

- Freeze the dough, double wrapped in plastic, for up to several weeks, after the rolling and folding process. Defrost the dough in the refrigerator before using it.

danish cheese pockets

This versatile Danish shape may be made with any filling that isn't runny when heated. See the variations at the end of the recipe for ideas.

Makes twelve 4-inch square pastries

½ batch Quick Danish Pastry Dough (page 108) or Christel's Danish Pastry Dough (page 109), chilled

CHEESE FILLING

8 ounces cream cheese, softened

3 tablespoons sugar

1 large egg yolk, at room temperature

½ teaspoon vanilla extract

Egg wash: 1 egg well beaten with a pinch of salt

½ cup sliced almonds

WATER ICING

¾ cup confectioners' sugar, sifted after measuring

1 tablespoon water

½ teaspoon vanilla extract

Large cookie sheet or jelly-roll pan lined with parchment paper or foil

Serving: Serve the pastries from a platter rather than a bread basket for breakfast or brunch.

Storage: Keep the pastries at room temperature, loosely covered with plastic wrap, on the day they are baked. Wrap leftovers or keep them under a cake dome.

1. For the filling, combine the cream cheese, sugar, egg yolk, and vanilla in a small bowl and use a small rubber spatula to beat them together.

2. Place the dough on a floured surface and lightly flour the dough. Use your rolling pin to press the dough in firm parallel strokes in both directions to soften it slightly. Flour the surface and the dough again if necessary and roll the dough to a 12 x 17-inch rectangle. Slide the dough to a cookie sheet or flexible cutting board and refrigerate it until firm, about 10 minutes.

3. Use a sharp pizza wheel to cut away a 1-inch-wide strip of dough from one of the 12-inch sides and reserve it. Cut the remaining dough into 12 4-inch squares.

4. Leave the squares of dough in place on the work surface and drop a heaping teaspoon of the filling in the center of each. Fold the 4 corners of the square to meet in the center over the filling, only overlapping them about ¼ inch. Place the pastries on the prepared pan.

5. Cut the reserved strip of dough into twelve 1-inch squares. Brush a little egg wash in the center of each pastry; center one of the squares of dough on each so that the sides align with the open areas of the folded-in dough. Cover the pan with a kitchen towel and let the pastries rise until they just start to puff, 20 to 30 minutes.

6. Set a rack in the middle level of the oven and preheat to 400°F.

7. Once the pastries have risen, brush them with the egg wash and sprinkle with the sliced almonds. Bake until they are deep golden and the filling is set, about 20 minutes. Transfer to a rack to cool.

8. While the pastries are cooling, prepare the water icing. Combine all ingredients in a small saucepan and stir well to mix. Place over low heat and cook until just lukewarm, about 110°F. Use a spoon to drizzle the icing in parallel lines on each pastry. Let the icing dry before serving.

variations:

Danish Poppy Seed or Walnut Pockets: Substitute the filling from Danish Poppy Seed Crescents (or the walnut variation) on page 116 for the cheese filling. Omit the sliced almonds and brush with the water icing instead of streaking it and immediately sprinkle each pastry with a pinch of poppy seeds or chopped toasted walnuts.

Danish Apricot or Prune Pockets: Use the filling from Danish Apricot Crescents (or the prune variation) on page 119, for the cheese filling above. Omit the sliced almonds and brush with Danish Apricot Glaze (see page 116) instead of the water icing.

Danish Envelopes: This is a shape variation. Only roll the dough to 12 x 16 inches. Cut into 4-inch squares and fill as above. Overlap one corner of the dough over your index finger about ½ inch over the filling. Overlap the opposite corner about ½ inch over the first. Firmly pinch the two corners together and remove your finger so that the sealed dough is centered on the filling. Fill and finish as above.

A B C

danish apricot pinwheels

Makes twelve 4-inch pastries

ALMOND FILLING

½ cup whole almonds, with or without skin, finely ground in the food processor

4 tablespoons unsalted butter, softened

⅓ cup sugar

2 large egg yolks, at room temperature

1 teaspoon finely grated lemon zest

½ teaspoon vanilla extract

3 tablespoons unbleached all-purpose flour

½ batch Quick Danish Pastry Dough (page 108) or Christel's Danish Pastry Dough (page 109)

6 fresh apricots, rinsed, halved, and pitted

Egg wash: 1 egg well beaten with a pinch of salt

Confectioners' sugar for finishing

Large cookie sheet or jelly-roll pan lined with parchment paper or foil

Possibly the most attractive Danish pastry, pinwheels are the best shape for fresh fruit Danish. If you fail to find fresh apricots, drained canned ones, especially those that are not overly sugared, make an adequate substitute. See the end of the recipe for ideas for using other fruit. Normally, this type of Danish pastry has some pastry cream under the fruit; if you intend to assemble and bake the pastries shortly before serving them and use all of them and not have leftovers, see the end of the recipe for the pastry cream filling. Don't use pastry cream if you're preparing them any more than a few hours in advance, or it might spoil. In this recipe I've substituted an almond filling that harmonizes well with the apricots.

1 For the filling, combine the almonds, butter, and sugar in a medium bowl and use a small rubber spatula to beat them together. Beat in the egg yolks, one at a time, followed by the lemon zest and vanilla. Stir in the flour.

2 Place the dough on a floured surface and lightly flour the dough. Use your rolling pin to press the dough in firm parallel strokes in both directions to soften it slightly. Flour the surface and the dough again, if necessary, and roll the dough to a 12 x 17-inch rectangle. Slide the dough to a cookie sheet or flexible cutting board and refrigerate until firm, about 10 minutes.

3 Use a pizza wheel to cut away a 1-inch-wide strip of dough from one of the 12-inch sides and reserve it. Cut the remaining dough into 12 4-inch squares (A). Make a 2-inch diagonal cut from each corner toward the center of the square (B).

4 Leave the squares of dough in place on the work surface and drop 1 heaping teaspoon of the almond filling in the center of each (C). Place one of the apricot halves cut side down on the filling.

5 Starting with the top left point, move clockwise to fold every other point into the center over the apricot (D through F). Repeat with the remaining pieces of dough. Place them on the prepared pan.

6 Use a 1-inch round cutter to cut the reserved piece of dough into 12 disks. Brush a little egg wash in the center of each pastry; center one of the disks of dough on top

D   E   F   G

of each (G). Cover the pastries with a clean kitchen towel and let rise until they just start to puff, 20 to 30 minutes.

7 Set a rack in the middle level of the oven and preheat to 400°F. Bake the pastries until they are deep golden and the filling is set, about 20 minutes. Transfer to a rack to cool.

8 Immediately before serving, generously dust the pastries with confectioners' sugar.

Serving: Serve the pastries from a platter rather than a bread basket for breakfast or brunch.

Storage: Keep the pastries at room temperature, loosely covered with plastic wrap, on the day they are baked. Wrap leftovers or keep them under a cake dome.

variations

Small prune plums or red plums may be substituted for the apricots. If they are very small, use 2 halves in each pastry.

For apple, use a tablespoon of the apple filling on page 114 in each pastry.

For pineapple, choose a small ripe pineapple and peel, halve, and core it. Cut one of the pineapple halves into 1/2-inch-thick slices and arrange them in a shallow ovenproof pan. Bake uncovered at 400°F until slightly dry, about 30 minutes, sprinkling the slices with a couple of teaspoons of sugar during the last 10 minutes. Cool, cut the half-rings in half again, and use 2 quarter-rings in each of the pastries.

For pastry cream, stir 2 tablespoons cornstarch and 3 table-spoons sugar together in a small saucepan and whisk in 3/4 cup milk. Whisk in 2 large egg yolks, and then place over medium heat. Cook, whisking constantly, until the cream thickens and comes to a full boil. Off heat, whisk in 1 teaspoon vanilla extract and then scrape into a shallow bowl. Press plastic wrap against the surface and chill until cold, 1 hour.

A

B

C

individual danish apple strudels

Makes eight 4-inch strudels

APPLE FILLING

2 tablespoons unsalted butter

3 pounds tart apples, such as Granny Smith

⅓ cup sugar

¼ teaspoon ground cinnamon

½ cup currants

½ batch Christel's Danish Pastry Dough (page 109), chilled

Egg wash: 1 egg well beaten with a pinch of salt

Granulated sugar for finishing

Cookie sheet or jelly-roll pan lined with a double thickness of parchment or heavy-duty foil

Serving: Serve the strudels for breakfast, brunch, or tea. They need no accompaniment.

Storage: Keep the strudel loosely covered at room temperature before and after serving.

This has nothing to do with the typical Viennese strudel made from dough that's stretched paper-thin, though in Vienna strudels are made from many kinds of dough, including Danish pastry dough. The apple filling here is cooked in advance and cooled to avoid a soggy bottom on the strudel.

1 For the apple filling, melt the butter in a large sauté pan with a cover or a large Dutch oven. Peel, halve, and core the apples and cut the apple halves into ½-inch dice. Add the diced apples to the pan as they are cut.

2 When all the apples have been diced, sprinkle them with the sugar and cinnamon.

3 Place the pan on high heat and wait until the butter begins to sizzle. Use a wooden spoon or silicone spatula to stir everything together. Decrease the heat to low and cover the pan. Let the apples steam and exude their liquid for 5 minutes. Uncover the pan, turn the heat to low, and stir in the currants. Continue cooking until the liquid has evaporated and the apples are tender and sizzling again. Scrape the cooked filling into a shallow bowl and allow it to cool to room temperature. To hasten cooling, place the bowl in the refrigerator or freezer and stir the filling occasionally.

4 Place the dough on a floured surface and lightly flour the dough. Use your rolling pin to press the dough in firm parallel strokes in both directions to soften it slightly. Flour the surface and the dough again, if necessary, and roll the dough to a 12 x 18-inch rectangle. Slide the dough to a cookie sheet or flexible cutting board and refrigerate it until firm, about 10 minutes.

5 Remove the dough from the refrigerator and cut it into two strips, each 6 x 18 inches. Arrange each piece of dough on a piece of parchment paper for easy transfer to the pan. Brush the long ends of both strips with egg wash and divide the filling equally between the two strips, spooning it down the center of the length (A and B). Bring the uncovered side of the dough closest to you over the filling, and then bring the opposite dough over the filling to meet and slightly overlap the first piece of dough (C and D). Quickly flip the strudel onto the pan so that the seam is on the bottom (E). (Don't be afraid; it's easy.) Repeat with the second piece of dough. Chill or freeze the strudels for 1 hour before baking them.

D   E   F   G

6 About 15 minutes before the end of the hour, set a rack in the middle level of the oven and preheat to 400°F.

7 Brush the outside of the strudel with egg wash and sprinkle generously with granulated sugar (F). Use a paring knife to make a series of ½-inch diagonal slashes every inch or so along the top of each strudel (F).

8 Bake the strudels until they are deep golden and the dough is firm, about 20 minutes.

9 Cool the strudels on the pan. Trim the ends and cut them into 4-inch lengths.

danish poppy seed crescents

Makes twelve 4-inch pastries

½ batch Quick Danish Pastry Dough (page 108) or Christel's Danish Pastry Dough (page 109)

POPPY SEED FILLING

½ cup milk

¼ cup sugar

1 tablespoon honey

1 cup ground poppy seeds

½ cup fresh bread crumbs made from firm white bread

¼ cup dark raisins

1 teaspoon finely grated lemon zest

⅛ teaspoon ground cinnamon

Egg wash: 1 egg well beaten with a pinch of salt

DANISH APRICOT GLAZE

¾ cup apricot preserves

1 tablespoon water

1 tablespoon dark rum

Whole poppy seeds for finishing

Large cookie sheet or jelly-roll pan lined with parchment paper or foil

Unlike croissants, which are often plain, Danish crescents always have a filling. Poppy seed filling is one of the most popular in Vienna, where Danish pastry originated. There are also variations with walnut, apricot, and prune fillings, as well as several variations on the shape of the crescents. Before poppy seeds can be used in a filling, they must be ground. Eastern European stores sell the seeds already ground, or you may grind them yourself in a spice grinder, but the seeds are quite hard and it takes a bit of time and a sharp blade to grind them. Note that poppy seeds and poppy seed filling do not appeal to everyone. For most Americans, it's an acquired taste, and people who are squeamish about things with "texture" don't necessarily like poppy seed pastries. The filling below makes about twice as much as you need, but you can wrap the extra filling and freeze it for a later use.

1 For the filling, bring the milk, sugar, and honey to a simmer in a medium saucepan. Add the ground poppy seeds and bread crumbs and stir until smooth. Cook, stirring constantly, until the mixture thickens, 1 to 2 minutes. Remove from the heat and stir in the raisins, lemon zest, and cinnamon. Scrape the filling into a bowl and let cool to room temperature.

2 Place the dough on a floured surface and lightly flour the dough. Use your rolling pin to press the dough in firm parallel strokes in both directions to soften it slightly. Flour the surface and the dough again if necessary and roll the dough to a 12-inch square. Use a sharp pizza wheel to cut the dough into two 6 x 12-inch rectangles. Slide the strips of dough to a cookie sheet or a flexible cutting board. Using a ruler, make a shallow mark along the bottom of each strip with your fingertip every 4 inches. Pull the top right corner and the bottom left corner of each strip at the same time to slant them slightly in opposite directions. Then mark the top of each strip every 4 inches. Use the edge of a plastic scraper or bench scraper to imprint shallow lines (do not cut through the dough) that connect the marks top to bottom on the diagonal so that each strip is marked with 6 equal triangles. Refrigerate the marked strips of dough until firm, about 10 minutes.

3 Remove the dough from the refrigerator and use a sharp pizza wheel to cut through the shallow marked lines to make 6 equal triangles. Place a heaping tablespoon of the poppy seed filling at the long base of each triangle.

4 To form a crescent, gently pull on the side corners of the base to widen it slightly, then fold and press about 1 inch of the base up over the filling. Roll up the base of the triangle of dough toward the point while gently pulling on the point to increase the height of the triangle. Pinch the point in place and position it under the formed pastry. Place each pastry as it is formed on the prepared pan, curving them into a crescent shape as you set them down.

5 Cover the pan with a clean kitchen towel and let the pastries rise until they just start to puff, 20 to 30 minutes.

6 Set a rack in the middle level of the oven and preheat to 400°F.

7 Once the pastries have risen, brush them with the egg wash and bake until they are deep golden, about 20 minutes. Transfer to a rack to cool.

8 While the pastries are cooling, prepare the apricot glaze. Combine all ingredients in a small saucepan and stir well to mix. Place on low heat and bring to a simmer. Strain into a bowl, rinse the pan, return the glaze to the pan, and bring the glaze back to a simmer. Cook until slightly thickened, about 5 minutes.

9 Brush the pastries with the glaze while it is still liquid. Sprinkle each pastry with a pinch of poppy seeds.

Serving: Serve the pastries from a platter rather than a bread basket for breakfast or brunch.

Storage: Keep the pastries at room temperature, loosely covered with plastic wrap, on the day they are baked. Wrap leftovers or keep them under a cake dome.

variations

Danish Walnut Crescents: Substitute $1^{1}/_{2}$ cups walnut pieces, finely ground in a food processor fitted with the metal blade, for the ground poppy seeds in the filling above. Decrease the milk to $1/_{3}$ cup and add 2 tablespoons unsalted butter to the milk mixture when heating it. Omit the raisins and stir 1 teaspoon each of vanilla extract and dark rum into the cooled filling. Sprinkle the glazed pastries with a pinch of chopped toasted walnuts.

Danish Apricot or Prune Crescents: Combine 1 cup diced dried apricots or pitted prunes and $1^{1}/_{4}$ cups water in a saucepan. Bring to a boil, remove from the heat, and allow to soak for 1 hour. Puree the mixture in a food processor or blender. Return the puree to the pan and add 2 tablespoons sugar. Bring to a simmer and cook, stirring frequently, until thickened to the consistency of jam, about 10 minutes. Cool the filling and stir in 1 teaspoon finely grated lemon zest. Add $1/_{4}$ teaspoon ground cinnamon to prune filling only. Substitute the apricot or prune filling for the poppy seed filling above. Omit the sprinkling of poppy seeds after the egg wash. Brush the cooled pastries with apricot glaze (see page 116) and sprinkle with a pinch of toasted sliced almonds.

essential tips for finishing danish pastries

- Real Danish pastries, whether they're made in Copenhagen or Vienna, are usually finished on the outside with a brushing of apricot glaze (see page 118) and another of thin confectioners' sugar water icing (see page 113). All the Danish pastries in this chapter may be finished that way, though I've detailed specific finishes in each recipe, too. The double brushing is especially useful if you decide to substitute Christel's Danish Dough (page 109) for the yeast-risen variety, since the non-yeasted dough contains no sugar. Remember to wait a few minutes for the coat of apricot glaze to dry before applying the sugar icing. In fact, if you brush the pastries with the apricot glaze, and then make the sugar icing afterwards, your timing will be perfect.

- If you'd like, you can add a pinch of cinnamon or cocoa powder to either a brushing or drizzling glaze. Add just enough to impart a subtle flavor but not to color the glaze too deeply.

- If the recipe calls for sprinkling on sliced almonds or other chopped nuts, make sure to do so one at a time so that you brush on the sugar glaze on one pastry and sprinkle and move one by one. If you glaze all of them first, the glaze will harden and you won't be able to sprinkle.

11
butter cakes

Aside from contributing an exquisitely delicate flavor to cake layers, butter also enhances a cake's tenderness, moisture, and keeping qualities. The recipes in this chapter follow a batter-mixing method known as the "creaming" method, named for the technique of beating (creaming) butter and sugar together until soft and light, which is the first step in the recipe. The term "creaming" has pretty much fallen from use because of the ambiguity of the phrase "combine the butter and sugar and cream until light," which sent everyone to the phone to ask how much cream to use. I refer to it as the "butter-cake method." Most butter-cake layers call for a good amount of sugar and use baking powder. Since the baking powder makes the layers rise during baking, I've eliminated folding whipped egg whites into the batter. The extra leavening from the egg whites is adequately replaced by beating the batter for a few minutes for smoothness.

white butter cake

A quintessentially American cake layer, this deserves to be better known by a wider audience. More than easy to prepare, a good butter cake is the perfect foundation for fillings and frostings, whether light or rich. And butter cake layers can't be beat if you need to mix up a birthday cake in a hurry.

Makes two 9-inch round layers, 2 inches tall

2¼ cups all-purpose flour (spoon into a dry-measure cup and level off)

2 teaspoons baking powder

¼ teaspoon salt

1¼ cups whole milk, at room temperature

4 large egg whites, at room temperature

12 tablespoons (1½ sticks) unsalted butter, softened

1½ cups sugar

2 teaspoons vanilla extract

Two 9 x 2-inch round cake pans, buttered and the bottoms lined with disks of buttered parchment or wax paper cut to fit

A

1 Set a rack in the middle level of the oven and preheat to 350°F.

2 Use a small whisk to stir together the flour, baking powder, and salt; set aside.

3 Thoroughly whisk the milk and egg whites together, then transfer to a 2-cup measure (you won't have enough room to whisk them properly in the measuring cup); set aside.

4 Combine the butter and sugar in the bowl of an electric mixer fitted with the paddle attachment. Beat on low speed until well mixed, then increase the speed to medium and beat the mixture until very light and pale in color (A), about 5 minutes. Beat in the vanilla extract.

5 Use a rubber spatula to scrape the bowl and beater. Restart the mixer on low speed and add about one quarter of the flour mixture until it is absorbed (B). Increase the speed to medium low and beat in one third of the milk mixture.

6 Repeat step 5, including the change of speed, 2 more times.

7 Stop and scrape and beat in the remaining quarter of the flour mixture. Scrape again (C). Increase the mixer's speed to medium and continuously beat the batter for 3 minutes.

8 Divide the batter equally between the prepared pans (D) and smooth the tops. Bake the layers until they are well risen, firm in the center to the touch, and lightly colored, 20 to 25 minutes.

9 Cool the baked layers in the pans on racks for 5 minutes. If necessary, use a small paring knife to loosen the layers from the side of the pans. Invert one layer to a rack or cake cardboard (don't remove the paper under the layer) and quickly re-invert to a rack. Repeat with the other layer. Cool the layers completely. Use the layers for one of the layer cakes in Chapter 15.

Storage: Wrap cooled layers in plastic wrap and keep them at room temperature if finishing the cake on the same day. Store wrapped layers in the refrigerator for up to 3 days, or freeze them for up to 3 months.

B

C

D

essential tips for the butter-cake method

- Have all your ingredients at room temperature before beginning to mix the batter. This isn't optional; it's the difference between a cake with excellent texture and a coarse-textured one.

- If you are ready to make the cake and realize you've neglected to bring the butter to room temperature, cut it into thin pats and put them on a plate. They should soften in 5 minutes or so.

- If the milk (or other liquid in different recipes) and egg whites (or whole eggs or yolks) are cold, after whisking them together stand the bowl containing them in a larger bowl of hot water in the sink. Make sure the level of the water in the lower bowl doesn't exceed the level of the milk mixture or the smaller bowl will capsize. Whisk occasionally until warmed just to room temperature, no more than 75°F.

- Alternating the flour and liquid as you add them to the batter keeps the batter smooth, resulting in a fine-textured cake. Adding too much liquid at once can make the batter separate and bake up with a coarse texture.

- When unmolding the layers, press the paring knife against the pan, not into the cake layer, or the side of the cake will tear. Use a clean sweeping motion rather than an up-and-down one, which can cut diagonally into the side of the layer and make it uneven.

- Sprinkle a large pinch of sugar on the top of the layer before inverting it to a cardboard to keep it from sticking. You may brush away the excess sugar after the layer has cooled.

- Leaving the paper stuck to the bottom of the layer makes it easy to pick up the layer once it has cooled without the danger of having it break apart. Just remember to remove the paper before assembling and filling the final cake.

- To defrost layers, unwrap them and place them back on a rack. Cover with a clean kitchen towel and defrost at room temperature. Leaving the layers in the plastic wrap as they defrost may result in condensation forming inside the package, which will make the cake's crust stick to the wrap.

moist yellow cake layers

So called because of the light yellow color whole eggs impart to the baked cake, yellow cake is an essential part of any baking repertoire. Add a simple chocolate ganache filling and frosting and you have a classic chocolate layer cake, or add whipped cream and sliced sweetened berries and you have what most retail bakeries used to call "strawberry shortcake." Many yellow cake recipes suffer from the dryness so characteristic of overly lean butter-cake layers, but this one is moist and tender.

Makes two 9-inch round layers, 2 inches tall

2 cups all-purpose flour (spoon into a dry-measure cup and level off)

1½ teaspoons baking powder

¼ teaspoon salt

3 large eggs, at room temperature

¾ cup milk

12 tablespoons (1½ sticks) unsalted butter, softened

1½ cups sugar

2 teaspoons vanilla extract

Two 9 x 2-inch round cake pans, buttered and the bottoms lined with disks of buttered parchment or wax paper cut to fit

Prepare the batter according to the master recipe for White Butter Cake on page 122, whisking the whole eggs and milk together in step 3. Mix, bake, cool, and store the same way.

chocolate butter cake layers

The rich chocolate flavor of these layers derives from unsweetened chocolate, which transforms what is basically a yellow cake batter into a chocolate one. To further enhance the flavor of the chocolate, add ¼ teaspoon of cinnamon, 2 teaspoons instant coffee granules dissolved in the milk, or the grated zest of a lemon or orange.

Makes two 9-inch round layers, 2 inches tall

2 cups all-purpose flour (spoon into a dry-measure cup and level off)

3 teaspoons baking powder

¼ teaspoon salt

12 tablespoons (1½ sticks) unsalted butter, softened

1½ cups sugar

2 teaspoons vanilla extract

3 large eggs, at room temperature

3 ounces unsweetened chocolate, melted and cooled

¾ cup whole milk, at room temperature

Two 9 x 2-inch round cake pans, buttered and the bottoms lined with disks of buttered parchment or wax paper cut to fit

Prepare the master recipe on page 122, starting with step 1, using the ingredients above, and skipping step 3. At the end of step 4, beat in the eggs one at a time, beating smooth after each addition, then beat in the melted chocolate. Finish mixing, bake, cool, and store as in the master recipe.

golden sour cream layers

Golden butter-method cakes are made with egg yolks only and are the richest and most tender of all cakes of this type. Just be careful with the baked layers; they are more fragile than the others, which have more firmness and elasticity due to the presence of egg whites.

Makes two 9-inch round layers, 2 inches tall

3 cups all-purpose flour, preferably bleached (spoon into a dry-measure cup and level off)

1 tablespoon baking powder

¼ teaspoon salt

8 large egg yolks, at room temperature

⅔ cup sour cream, at room temperature (if some whey drains from the cream, just whisk it back in)

12 tablespoons (1½ sticks) unsalted butter, softened

1¼ cups sugar

2 teaspoons vanilla extract

Two 9 x 2-inch round cake pans, buttered and the bottoms lined with disks of buttered parchment or wax paper cut to fit

Prepare the batter according to the master recipe for White Butter Cake on page 122, whisking the egg yolks and sour cream together in step 3. Mix, bake, cool, and store the same way.

butter-cake cupcakes

Butter-cake layers also make excellent cupcakes. In general, richer batters will make cupcakes with well-risen domed tops, while leaner ones tend to result in cupcakes that are more flat-topped. A standard 12-cavity muffin pan used for baking cupcakes holds a little less than ½ cup of batter. Even if you think you have standard pans, please check by measuring ½ cup water and pouring it into one of the cavities. You may certainly use any size pan you wish. If your pan has cavities that are larger or smaller, do a test run of the batter, filling one or two paper-lined cavities to within ⅜ inch of the top and seeing how they bake. Then you can adjust the amount of batter accordingly. These rich batters are not meant to be baked in free-standing aluminum foil cups, which would flatten from the weight of the batter. Since all the cake recipes in this chapter make approximately the same volume of batter, each one will make 18 to 20 individual standard-size cupcakes. When baking cupcakes, remember to spray the top of the pan with vegetable cooking spray or to brush it with some very soft butter; this will prevent cupcakes with large domed tops from sticking to the top of the pan and breaking apart when you try to unmold them. Look for signs of doneness 7 to 10 minutes before the time indicated in the cake recipe and if you're not sure, use a cake tester or the point of a paring knife to test the center of one of the cupcakes for still-unbaked batter.

12

oil-based cakes

Confirmed butter addict that I am, it took me a long time to warm up to the idea of oil-based cakes. Every time I came across a recipe that seemed interesting, I would substitute melted butter with about a 50 percent rate of success. Then I tasted a wonderful cake at a restaurant in Atlanta years ago, and when I received the requested recipe I was surprised to see that the really delicious cake had been made with oil. I became a convert, but one with reservations. I still don't use oils that have been chemically extracted from their sources. I like safflower oil because it has a neutral flavor and it's also fairly light. The one I use is expeller pressed, which means that the oil is extracted by means of pressure, not chemical processes. I've already published that original oil-based chocolate cake in another book, but I've varied that recipe to develop a few more for cakes that are just as good—devil's food, carrot, apple, pear-ginger, and pumpkin among them.

oil-based devil's food cake batter

Makes two 9-inch round layers, 2 inches tall

4 ounces unsweetened chocolate, cut into ¼-inch pieces

1 cup boiling water (boil, then measure)

1 cup granulated sugar

1½ cups all-purpose flour (spoon into a dry-measure cup and level off)

½ teaspoon salt

¾ teaspoon baking soda

1 cup light brown sugar, firmly packed

½ cup vegetable oil, such as safflower

½ cup sour cream

2 large eggs, at room temperature

1½ teaspoons vanilla extract

Two 9 x 2-inch round cake pans, buttered and the bottoms lined with disks of buttered parchment or wax paper

A

Using vegetable oil in a cake works well when the batter contains strong-flavored ingredients that would mask the flavor of butter. See the Essential Tips on page 129 if you would like to substitute butter anyway.

1 Set a rack in the middle of the oven and preheat to 350°F.

2 Place the chocolate in a large mixing bowl and pour the hot water over it. Shake the bowl to make sure all the chocolate is submerged, then let stand for a few minutes to melt the chocolate.

3 In a mixing bowl, stir together the sugar, flour, salt, and baking soda and set aside.

4 Whisk the chocolate and water smooth, then whisk in the brown sugar, oil, sour cream, eggs, and vanilla one at a time, whisking smooth after each addition.

5 Whisk in the flour mixture about one third at a time (A). The batter will be very liquid.

6 Divide the batter between the prepared pans (B). Bake until risen and firm, 30 to 35 minutes.

7 Let the cakes stand in the pans for 5 minutes, then unmold to racks, turn right side up, and cool completely. To finish as a layer cake, see Chapter 15 and use boiled icing, whipped cream, ganache, or buttercream to fill and cover the cake.

Storage: Wrap and freeze the layers for up to one month if you don't intend to use them immediately.

B

essential tips for oil-based cake batters

- The basic method for mixing these batters is to combine all the liquid ingredients and all the dry ingredients separately, then gradually whisk the dry ingredients into the liquid.

- In the batter at left, the brown sugar is added with the liquid to prevent lumps of brown sugar from forming in the baked cake.

- To substitute butter, melt about $1^1/_2$ times the equivalent of the quantity of oil in the recipe, then skim any foam from the top and discard. Pour off and measure just the clear butterfat that remains (clarified butter), leaving the watery milk solids behind.

- Alternatively, continue cooking the butter after it melts until it colors to a light brown and all the water has evaporated. Quickly pour the brown butter into a small heat-proof bowl to arrest the cooking and stop any further coloring and allow the butter to cool before measuring and adding to the batter. This is a little more difficult, but it results in butter with more flavor.

- Oil-based cakes can have a sticky top surface, which makes them a little tricky to unmold. Work quickly and sprinkle the top surface of the cake with a teaspoon of sugar to prevent sticking when inverting the cake from the pan. It will turn right side up without sticking to the cardboard or rack.

best & easiest carrot cake

Makes two 9-inch round layers,
2 inches tall

2½ cups all-purpose flour (spoon into
a dry-measure cup and level off)

1 cup granulated sugar

1 teaspoon baking powder

1 teaspoon baking soda

¾ teaspoon salt

1 tablespoon ground cinnamon

1 cup dark brown sugar, firmly packed

4 large eggs, at room temperature

1¼ cups vegetable oil, such as safflower

1 pound carrots, rinsed, trimmed, peeled,
and grated in the food processor or on the
largest holes of a box grater

¾ cup walnut or pecan pieces, coarsely
chopped

Two 9 x 2-inch round cake pans, buttered
and the bottoms lined with disks of
buttered parchment or wax paper

No cake is homier or more casual than a carrot cake, especially a carrot cake with a filling or topping of cream cheese frosting. This is loosely adapted from a recipe by Maida Heatter in her landmark *Book of Great American Desserts*.

1   Set a rack in the middle of the oven and preheat to 375°F.

2   Combine the flour, granulated sugar, baking powder, baking soda, salt, and cinnamon in a medium bowl and whisk to mix; set aside.

3   Place the brown sugar in a mixing bowl and use a large rubber spatula to work in the eggs, one at a time. Whisk in the oil.

4   Whisk in the dry ingredients about one third at a time. Use a large rubber spatula to fold in the carrots and nuts.

5   Divide the batter between the prepared pans. Bake until risen and firm, 40 to 45 minutes.

6   Let the cakes stand for 5 minutes in the pans, then unmold to racks, turn right side up, and cool completely. To finish as a layer cake, see Chapter 15 and use Cream Cheese Frosting (page 159) to fill and cover the cake.

Storage: Wrap and freeze the layers for up to one month if you don't intend to use them immediately.

Variation: Bake the batter in a 9 x 13 x 2-inch pan, prepared as above, for 45 to 50 minutes. Use a half batch of cream cheese frosting to cover the top of the cake only.

spiced pumpkin cake

Makes two 9-inch round layers,
2 inches tall

3 cups all-purpose flour (spoon into
a dry-measure cup and level off)

1 cup granulated sugar

2 teaspoons baking powder

2 teaspoons baking soda

3/4 teaspoon salt

1 tablespoon ground cinnamon

2 teaspoons ground ginger

2 teaspoons freshly grated nutmeg

1 cup light brown sugar, firmly packed

2 cups canned pumpkin puree

5 large eggs, at room temperature

1 1/4 cups vegetable oil

Two 9 x 2-inch round cake pans, buttered
and the bottoms lined with disks of
buttered parchment or wax paper

Pureed pumpkin makes a wonderfully moist cake, and I particularly love this version of pumpkin cake because it echoes the flavors of a pumpkin pie, near the top of my list of favorite desserts. It has become stylish to use fresh pumpkin for pies and cakes, but unless you use an orange-fleshed pie pumpkin, you'll get a watery puree that's low in pumpkin flavor. For this reason, I prefer to use canned pumpkin, which also makes it possible to prepare this cake when fresh pumpkins aren't in season. If you absolutely have to use a fresh vegetable, then use cooked, pureed winter squash (but not spaghetti squash) or cooked sweet potatoes as on page 19. Thanks to my dear friend, baking teacher and author Carole Walter, for allowing me to adapt this recipe from her book *Great Cakes*, for which I wrote the preface.

1 Set a rack in the middle of the oven and preheat to 350°F.

2 Combine the flour, granulated sugar, baking powder, baking soda, salt, and spices in a medium bowl and whisk to mix; set aside.

3 Place the brown sugar in a mixing bowl and use a large rubber spatula to work in about one third of the pumpkin a little at a time, until there are no lumps of brown sugar. Use a whisk to incorporate the remaining pumpkin, the eggs, and the oil, adding them one at a time and stirring to combine between additions.

4 Whisk in the dry ingredients a third at a time.

5 Divide the batter between the prepared pans. Bake until risen and firm, 40 to 45 minutes.

6 Let the cakes stand in the pans for 5 minutes, then unmold to racks, turn right side up, and cool completely. To finish as a layer cake, see Chapter 15 and use the larger amount of Cream Cheese Frosting (page 159) to fill and cover the cake.

Storage: Wrap and freeze the layers for up to one month if you don't intend to use them immediately.

variations

Bake the batter in a 9 x 13 x 2-inch pan, prepared as above, for 45 to 50 minutes. Use the lesser amount of cream cheese frosting to cover the top of the cake only.

Add 1 1/2 cups coarsely chopped walnut or pecan pieces and/or 1 cup dark or golden raisins (or a combination of the two) to the batter after the dry ingredients, if you wish.

pear & ginger cake

Makes one 10-inch tube or Bundt cake, about 16 servings

3 cups all-purpose flour (spoon into a dry-measure cup and level off)

1½ cups sugar

1½ teaspoons baking soda

½ teaspoon salt

2 teaspoons ground ginger

1 teaspoon ground cinnamon

½ teaspoon freshly grated nutmeg

¼ teaspoon ground cloves

5 large eggs, at room temperature

1 tablespoon vanilla extract

1½ cups vegetable oil (see Note)

⅓ cup finely minced crystallized ginger

4 cups peeled and chopped or grated Bartlett pears, about 2 pounds or 4 medium pears

One 10-inch (16-cup) tube or Bundt pan, buttered, coated with fine dry bread crumbs, and sprayed with vegetable cooking spray

Use firm-ripe Bartlett pears for this cake. When you press the blossom end of the pear with your thumb, it should yield to gentle pressure. Softer pears will immediately turn to a watery puree if you try to grate them. This cake, and the apple variation that follow it, utilize the grated fruit as a means of retaining moisture in the baked cake. While each contributes a dimension of flavor to the cake, it's one that successfully blends with the seasonings to create a moist harmonious finished product. Neither is anything like biting into a ripe pear or apple.

1 Set a rack in the lower third of the oven and preheat to 350°F.

2 In a medium bowl, combine the flour, sugar, baking soda, salt, and spices and whisk well to combine.

3 In a large mixing bowl, whisk the eggs with the vanilla. Whisk in the oil followed by the crystallized ginger.

4 Use a large rubber spatula to stir in all the grated pears, followed by the dry ingredients, a third at a time.

5 Pour the batter into the prepared pan and bake the cake until it is well risen and firm and the point of a paring knife inserted halfway between the side of the pan and the central tube emerges clean, about 65 to 75 minutes.

6 Cool the cake in the pan for 5 minutes, then invert it to a rack to cool completely.

Serving: Serve the cake with some lightly sweetened whipped cream.

Storage: Keep the cake under a cake dome or covered with plastic wrap at room temperature. Double wrap and freeze for longer storage. Defrost and bring to room temperature before serving.

Note: You may replace half of the vegetable oil with melted butter for both this recipe and the apple variation that follows.

variation

Apple Spice Cake: Replace the pears with peeled and grated Granny Smith apples. Omit the ginger and crystallized ginger and fold in 1 cup each of coarsely chopped walnut or pecan pieces and dark or golden raisins after the last of the dry ingredients.

individual coconut cakes

Makes 24 individual cakes

¾ cup sugar

½ cup all-purpose flour (spoon into a dry-measure cup and level off)

1½ cups unsweetened dried coconut

4 large egg whites, at room temperature

Pinch of salt

2 teaspoons finely grated lemon zest

8 tablespoons (1 stick) unsalted butter, melted and slightly cooled

2 tablespoons sweetened shredded coconut, or unsweetened ground or shredded coconut, for topping the cakes before baking

Two 12-cavity mini muffin pans, buttered and floured

These snow-white little cakes are as delicious as any coconut candy I've ever tasted. It's not necessary to clarify the butter for these. Unsweetened coconut is available both as long shreds (like the sweetened coconut you can buy in the supermarket) or more finely ground. The shreds retain more moisture than the ground coconut does. Either may be used in this recipe, but if you use the shredded variety, pulse it in the food processor half a dozen times, not to grind it to a powder, but to reduce the shreds in size to about ⅛ inch. Obviously this isn't an oil-based batter but it's grouped here because it's mixed the same way.

1   Set a rack in the middle level of the oven and preheat to 375°F.

2   In a medium mixing bowl, combine the sugar, flour, and unsweetened dried coconut; set aside.

3   In another bowl, whisk the egg whites with the salt until smooth, then whisk in the lemon zest and butter. Whisk in about half the dry ingredients, then use a rubber spatula to fold in the remainder.

4   Spoon the batter into the prepared pans, filling them about two-thirds full. Sprinkle the top of each cake with a pinch of shredded coconut.

5   Bake the cakes until they are well risen and deep golden and they are firm when pressed with a fingertip, about 15 minutes. Invert them to a rack, then immediately turn them right side up and let them cool completely.

Serving: Serve these after dessert with coffee, or as part of an assortment of desserts.

Storage: Keep the cakes loosely covered with plastic wrap on the day they are made. Arrange them in a tin or plastic container with a tight-fitting cover in one layer and refrigerate them for longer storage. Bring to room temperature before serving.

variations

Substitute ground blanched almonds or a combination of ground hazelnuts and ground almonds for the coconut.

Before baking, sprinkle the top of each little cake with a pinch of chopped almonds or hazelnuts.

Bake the batter in a buttered and paper-lined 8 x 2-inch round cake pan. It will take about 5 minutes longer to bake; test for doneness with the point of a paring knife in the center of the cake. Unmold, cool, and serve in wedges.

13

pound cakes & coffee cakes

Though there isn't anything uninteresting about this type of cake, it is frequently referred to as a "plain" cake. Pound cakes and coffee cakes are usually not iced, except for perhaps a drizzle of glaze, so they depend on their intrinsic flavor and texture rather than on a rich accompaniment such as ganache or buttercream. The cakes in this chapter are all mixed according to a fairly recent innovation called the high-ratio method. The name refers to the high ratio of sugar to flour. Developed in the late 1940s by American food chemists for commercial and industrial bakeries, the method ensures a perfectly smooth and emulsified batter—essential when hundreds or thousands of pounds of batter are being mixed at the same time. Fortunately, the method works well even in a recipe for a single cake and results in a moist and tender crumb.

A   B

high-ratio pound cake

Makes one 9 x 5 x 5-inch cake, about
16 slices

2 cups bleached all-purpose flour (spoon
into a dry-measure cup and level off)

1 cup sugar

1 teaspoon baking powder

¼ teaspoon salt

8 ounces (2 sticks) unsalted butter,
very soft

5 large eggs, at room temperature

2 teaspoons vanilla extract

2 teaspoons finely grated lemon zest,
optional

One 9 x 5 x 3-inch (7-cup) loaf pan,
buttered and the bottom lined with a
rectangle of parchment or buttered
wax paper

The "pound" in the title refers to the quantity of the three main ingredients in the batter. There are also many variations on the original recipe that include milk or another dairy product such as sour cream. See the variations at the end of the recipe for some of the more popular twists on the classic pound cake.

1   Set a rack in the middle level of the oven and preheat to 325°F.

2   Combine the flour, sugar, baking powder, and salt in the bowl of an electric mixer fitted with the paddle attachment. Mix on the lowest speed for 30 seconds.

3   Stop the mixer, add the butter, and continue mixing on the lowest speed until the butter is absorbed and no visible pieces remain (A). Stop the mixer and use a rubber spatula to scrape down the bowl and beater.

4   In a small bowl, whisk the eggs with the vanilla and lemon zest, if using.

5   Start the mixer on the lowest speed and add about one third of the egg mixture to the bowl. Beat for 1 minute on medium speed; stop and scrape the bowl and beater (B). Repeat two more times. Then beat the batter for 2 minutes continuously on medium speed (C).

6   Scrape the batter into the prepared pan (D) and smooth the top.

7   Bake the cake until it is well risen and deep golden and the point of a paring knife inserted in the center emerges clean, about 60 minutes.

8   Cool the cake on a rack for 10 minutes. Unmold and cool completely right side up.

Serving: Serve slices of the cake with coffee or tea, or use a slice of pound cake as the base for a simple dessert, topping it with some whipped cream and lightly sweetened berries or soft fruit.

Storage: Keep the baked cake under a cake dome or wrapped in plastic at room temperature. Double wrap and freeze for longer storage. Defrost and bring back to room temperature before serving.

C   D

variations

Vanilla Bean Pound Cake: Split a plump vanilla bean and scrape the seeds from the inside instead of using vanilla extract in the cake batter.

New Orleans Praline Pound Cake: Use light brown sugar for half the sugar; add 1/4 teaspoon ground cinnamon along with the other dry ingredients. Add 2 tablespoons dark rum or bourbon to the egg mixture. Fold in 1 cup coarsely chopped pecan pieces tossed with 1 tablespoon flour after taking the batter off the mixer.

Chocolate Chip Pound Cake: Add 1 cup semisweet, bittersweet, or milk chocolate chips, or a combination, using a rubber spatula to fold them in after taking the batter off the mixer.

Lemon Pound Cake: Increase the lemon zest to 4 teaspoons and add 2 tablespoons lemon juice, strained before measuring, to the batter.

Le "Cake" (French Pound Cake): Fold in 1/3 cup each of 1/4-inch dice candied orange peel and quartered candied cherries after taking the batter off the mixer.

"Le Weekend" (French Lemon Pound Cake): Prepare Lemon Pound Cake. While the cake is baking, bring 1/2 cup water and 1/3 cup sugar to a boil, stirring to dissolve the sugar. Cool and stir in 2 tablespoons strained lemon juice. After unmolding the cake, place the rack over a platter or jelly-roll pan and paint the uncooled cake repeatedly with the cooled syrup, using all of it and scooping up and reusing any that drips off the cake, until all the syrup is absorbed.

essential tips for high-ratio cakes

- Make sure the butter is as soft as mayonnaise or it will not be easily absorbed by the batter.

- Make sure the eggs and any liquid are both at room temperature—not cold—or they will make the batter separate.

- Follow the timing instructions exactly when mixing, or the batter will not be as smooth as necessary. If adding liquid of any kind as a flavoring, as in the lemon pound cake, be sure to whisk it into the eggs so that they are added together.

- Try using a 7- to 8-cup tube pan instead of the loaf pan. The baking time will be about 10 minutes shorter.

- The pound cake and the almond cake in this chapter are better when served the day after they are baked. Freshly baked and cooled, they can sometimes have a slightly rubbery texture.

torta di mandorle: ligurian almond cake

Makes one 9-inch tube or Bundt cake, about 16 slices

2½ cups blanched almonds, very lightly toasted

1½ cups sugar

2¼ cups all-purpose flour (spoon into a dry-measure cup and level off)

1 teaspoon baking powder

¼ teaspoon ground cinnamon

12 ounces (3 sticks) unsalted butter, very soft

1 tablespoon grated lemon zest

5 large eggs, at room temperature

One 9-inch (10-cup) tube or Bundt pan, buttered, coated with fine dry bread crumbs, and sprayed with vegetable cooking spray

In the Italian region of Liguria, of which Genoa is the capital, almond trees thrive, though Sicily is the largest almond-growing area of the country. The cooking of the two regions is even similar, due to the fact that they are separated only by the Tyrrhenian Sea. Though they may look far apart on a map, when travel by boat was easier than overland travel, there was frequent contact between the two areas. Slightly reminiscent of a French *gâteau breton*, this dense cake is perfect with a glass of sweet wine or a cup of tea. As a dessert, it would need to be dressed up with some fruit or berries.

1 Set a rack in the middle level of the oven and preheat to 325°F.

2 Combine the almonds and sugar in the bowl of a food processor fitted with the metal blade and pulse repeatedly until the mixture is a fine powder. Invert the work bowl to the bowl of an electric mixer fitted with the paddle attachment.

3 Add the flour, baking powder, and cinnamon and mix on the lowest speed for 1 minute.

4 Add the butter and mix until absorbed.

5 Add the lemon zest and 2 eggs and mix until absorbed. Increase the speed to medium and beat for 1 minute. Add another 2 eggs and repeat, beating for 1 minute after they are absorbed. Add the last egg and repeat.

6 Scrape the batter into the prepared pan and bake the cake until it is well risen and deep golden and the point of a thin knife inserted midway between the side of the pan and the central tube emerges clean, 45 to 50 minutes.

7 Cool the cake in the pan for 5 minutes, then unmold and cool completely.

Serving: This is best as a tea cake. Serve thin slices; a spoonful of lemon curd to accompany it wouldn't be bad, either.

Storage: Keep the baked cake under a cake dome or wrapped in plastic at room temperature. Double wrap and freeze for longer storage. Defrost and bring back to room temperature before serving.

maida's chocolate bourbon pound cake

Makes one short 9-inch tube or Bundt cake, about 16 slices

5 ounces unsweetened chocolate, cut into ¼-inch pieces

1½ cups hot brewed coffee

½ cup best bourbon

2 cups all-purpose flour (spoon into a dry-measure cup and level off)

2 cups sugar

1 teaspoon baking soda

¼ teaspoon salt

8 ounces (2 sticks) unsalted butter, softened

3 large eggs, at room temperature

2 teaspoons vanilla extract

One 9-inch (10-cup) tube or Bundt pan, buttered, coated with fine dry bread crumbs, and sprayed with vegetable cooking spray

This recipe from my friend and mentor Maida Heatter is adapted from one called 86-Proof Chocolate Cake in her *Book of Great Chocolate Desserts*. The original recipe calls for dissolving ¼ cup instant espresso or regular instant coffee granules in boiling water before proceeding. I prefer to use strong brewed coffee.

1   Set a rack in the lower third of the oven and preheat to 325°F.

2   Place the chocolate in a medium mixing bowl and pour the hot coffee over it. Gently shake the bowl a couple of times to immerse the chocolate, then wait 1 to 2 minutes; whisk smooth.

3   Whisk in the bourbon.

4   Combine the flour, sugar, baking soda, and salt in the bowl of an electric mixer fitted with the paddle attachment. Mix on the lowest speed for 30 seconds.

5   Stop the mixer, add the butter, and continue mixing on the lowest speed until no visible pieces of butter remain. Stop the mixer and use a rubber spatula to scrape down the bowl and beater.

6   Start the mixer on the lowest speed and add the eggs and vanilla. Beat for 1 minute on medium speed; stop and scrape the bowl and beater. Add half the chocolate mixture and beat 1 minute. Add the remaining chocolate mixture and beat on medium speed for 2 minutes. The batter will be very liquid.

7   Pour the batter into the prepared pan and bake the cake until it is well risen and firm and the point of a thin knife inserted midway between the side of the pan and the central tube emerges clean, 60 to 70 minutes.

8   Cool the cake in the pan for 15 minutes, then unmold and cool completely.

Serving: Serve thick slices with some lightly sweetened whipped cream.

Storage: Keep the baked cake under a cake dome or wrapped in plastic at room temperature. Double wrap and freeze for longer storage. Defrost and bring back to room temperature before serving.

banana coconut crumb cake

Makes one 9-inch cake, 8 to 10 servings

1¼ cups all-purpose flour (spoon into a dry-measure cup and level off)

¾ cup sugar

½ teaspoons baking powder

¼ teaspoon salt

8 tablespoons (1 stick) unsalted butter, softened

2 large eggs, at room temperature

1 large egg yolk, at room temperature

1 teaspoon vanilla extract

1 pound (3 medium) bananas, peeled and sliced about ½ inch thick

Almond Crumb Topping (see page 46), unbaked, substitute ½ cup sweetened, shredded coconut for the almonds

One 9-inch springform pan, buttered and the bottom lined with a disk of parchment or buttered wax paper

Sliced bananas make a perfect crumb cake because they're safely insulated between the cake batter and crumb topping and baked to a moist jam-like consistency. See the Variations for suggestions for using other fruit in this cake or other nuts in the crumb topping.

1   Set a rack in the middle level of the oven and preheat to 350°F.

2   For the batter, combine the flour, sugar, baking powder, and salt in the bowl of an electric mixer fitted with the paddle attachment. Mix on the lowest speed for 30 seconds.

3   Stop the mixer, add the butter, and continue mixing on the lowest speed until no visible pieces of butter remain. Stop the mixer and use a rubber spatula to scrape down the bowl and beater.

4   In a small bowl, whisk the eggs, yolk, and vanilla together.

5   Start the mixer on the lowest speed and add about one third of the egg mixture to the bowl. Beat for 1 minute on medium speed; stop and scrape the bowl and beater. Repeat two times. Then beat the batter for 2 minutes continuously on medium speed.

6   Scrape the batter into the prepared pan and smooth the top. Arrange the banana slices on top of the batter, leaving a clear ¼-inch margin near the side of the pan. Evenly scatter on the crumb topping.

7   Bake the cake until it is well risen and deep golden and the point of a paring knife inserted in the center of the cake emerges clean, about 50 to 60 minutes.

8   Cool the cake on a rack for 10 minutes. Unbuckle the side of the pan and let the cake cool on the springform base. Once the cake has cooled completely, use a wide spatula slipped between the cake and the paper to ease it off the pan base and transfer it to a platter.

Serving: Serve wedges of this cake for tea or brunch or as dessert after a light meal.

Storage: Keep the baked cake under a cake dome or wrapped in plastic at room temperature. Double wrap and freeze for longer storage. Defrost and bring back to room temperature before serving.

variations

Use 3 cups of fruit, such as peeled, cored, and sliced pineapple, pitted prune plums, pitted fresh apricots, pitted sour cherries, or blueberries, in place of the dried apricots.

Substitute any nut you wish for the almonds in the base recipe on page 46 instead of adding the coconut. Or omit and nuts or coconut from the crumb topping.

14

sponge &
meringue
layers

This chapter is about how eggs, or just egg whites, can absorb and trap air and use steam during baking to create leavening. Genoise is the classic French sponge cake, made with whole eggs, enriched with extra yolks warmed with sugar, and whipped to a dramatic increase in volume before the dry ingredients are added. Nut sponge cakes are made with separated eggs, and a portion of the sugar is separately whipped with the yolks and whites before they're combined and the ground nuts and flour are added. Finally, meringue layers are made from egg whites warmed with part of the sugar, the rest being incorporated later—my new technique that guarantees crisp, but never hard, results.

A   B

> ESSENTIAL TECHNIQUE

genoise sponge cake

Makes one 9-inch layer about 2½ inches tall

4 large eggs

2 large egg yolks (save the whites for buttercream or meringue)

⅔ cup sugar

Pinch of salt

2 teaspoons vanilla extract

¾ cup all-purpose flour (spoon into a dry-measure cup and level off)

⅓ cup cornstarch

One 2½- to 3-inch deep 9-inch-round springform pan or 9-inch-round cake pan, buttered and the bottom lined with a disk of parchment or buttered wax paper

Many recipes call for folding melted butter into genoise after the flour has been added to the batter. While the butter does produce a more delicate cake, its presence is not very noticeable once the layer is split, moistened with flavored syrup, and finished with a rich buttercream, ganache, or other filling. I stopped adding butter to genoise years ago and have never regretted it, because the lack of butter makes the batter easier to prepare and ensures a successful outcome on the first try.

1   Set a rack in the middle level of the oven and preheat to 350°F.

2   Whisk the eggs, yolks, sugar, salt, and vanilla together by hand in the bowl of an electric mixer.

3   Set the bowl over a saucepan of gently boiling water and slowly whisk until the egg mixture is warm, around 120°F, about 30 seconds. Don't overheat or the eggs won't whip well.

4   Place the bowl on a mixer fitted with the whisk attachment and whip on medium-high speed until the egg foam is light in color and increased in volume and the bowl no longer feels warm, about 3 minutes. When the eggs are ready, they'll hold their shape on the whisk and you'll be able to draw a line through them (A and B).

5   While the eggs are whipping, stir the flour and cornstarch together. Use a strainer with open mesh to sift the flour mixture once onto a piece of paper.

6   Remove the bowl from the mixer and sift about one third of the flour mixture over the egg foam, using a large rubber spatula to fold it in (C). Dig down to the bottom of the bowl and cut through the batter with the flat side of the spatula parallel to the

C

D

bottom of the bowl to prevent the flour from accumulating there. Repeat with the last two batches of the flour.

7 Scrape the batter into the prepared pan (D). Tilt the pan in a circular motion to bring the batter about $3/4$ inch from the top of the pan; this prevents the batter from doming in the center so that the baked layer has a flat, even top. Bake until it is well risen and firm in the center and the point of a paring knife inserted in the center of the cake emerges clean, about 30 minutes.

8 Immediately use a small paring knife to loosen the cake from the side of the pan if it is at all stuck and invert it to a rack. Remove the pan, but leave the paper on the cake layer. Cover with another rack and invert the stack, removing the top rack. Cool the cake completely on the rack.

Storage: Wrap the cooled cake in plastic wrap and refrigerate it for 3 days, or double wrap and freeze for up to a month. Unwrap and defrost before using.

variation

For cocoa genoise, use $2/3$ cup flour, $1/4$ cup cornstarch, and 3 tablespoons akalized (Dutch process) cocoa. After measuring the cocoa, force it through a fine mesh strainer to eliminate any lumps. Then mix it with the flour and cornstarch, but use a strainer with more open mesh to sift the mixture into the batter, as it will go more quickly.

essential tips for genoise

- Fill a saucepan halfway with water and begin to heat it as soon as you start measuring the ingredients.

- It's not necessary to whisk the egg mixture furiously while it's heating; just keep it in motion so it doesn't begin to set in the bottom of the bowl.

- Don't overheat the eggs; they won't whip up to the necessary volume afterward if you do.

- You can test the egg foam for the right degree of expansion by drawing a line about $1/4$ inch deep on top of it with a fingertip. If the line holds and the two sides don't flow back together, the egg foam is ready.

- You can decrease the speed on a stand mixer to lowest once the egg foam is ready, sift the flour onto a piece of paper, and then slowly shake the flour over the egg foam. After you take the bowl off, use a large rubber spatula to dig down to the bottom to make sure there is no flour hiding there. This only works in a stand mixer.

- Unmold the genoise immediately or it will shrink and fall if left in the pan. Work quickly once you have inverted the layer to the first rack or it will stick there.

- Always chill the genoise overnight before cutting if possible; it makes cutting through it easier.

kyra's hot milk sponge cake

Makes two 9-inch round layers, each about 1½ inches tall

4 tablespoons unsalted butter

½ cup whole milk

1½ cups all-purpose flour (spoon into a dry-measure cup and level off)

2 teaspoons baking powder

3 large eggs, at room temperature

¼ teaspoon salt

1 cup sugar

1 teaspoon vanilla extract

Two 1½- to 2-inch-deep x 9-inch-round cake pans, buttered and the bottoms lined with disks of parchment paper or buttered wax paper

This is the easiest and best-tasting sponge layer you can imagine, and since it's baked in two pans, you won't need to slice through it to make a layer cake. Thanks to my friend Kyra Effren, one of the world's great bakers, for sharing this recipe. Kyra often serves this as a tea cake with a thin layer of raspberry preserves between the layers and a light dusting of confectioners' sugar on top; it is elegant simplicity at its best. Though a hot milk sponge is not quite as light and delicate as a genoise layer, you may easily substitute these layers in recipes that call for genoise. In fact, they can often substitute for white or yellow cake layers, too.

1 Set a rack in the middle level of the oven and preheat to 350°F.

2 Combine the butter and milk in a small saucepan and cook over low heat until the butter is completely melted. Set aside in the pan.

3 Stir the flour and baking powder together and sift onto a piece of wax paper.

4 In the bowl of an electric mixer, whisk the eggs by hand to break them up, then whisk in the salt. Whisk in the sugar in a stream, then whisk in the vanilla. Place on the mixer fitted with the whisk attachment and whip on medium-high speed until very light, about 3 minutes.

5 Gently whisk in the warm milk mixture by hand. Use the whisk to fold the flour mixture into the liquid in 4 additions, again gently whisking to incorporate between additions. Using the whisk helps to prevent lumps from forming. Handle the whisk exactly as though you were using a rubber spatula for the folding.

6 Evenly divide the batter between the prepared pans and smooth the tops.

7 Bake the layers until they are well risen and golden and feel firm when touched in the center with a fingertip, about 20 minutes.

8 Use a sharp paring knife to loosen the layers from the sides of the pans, then invert to racks. Immediately re-invert the layers so that they cool with the paper on the bottom. Cool completely.

Storage: Wrap and store as for Genoise Sponge Cake (page 146).

almond sponge cake layer

Makes one 9-inch round layer, 2 inches tall

¾ cup whole or slivered blanched almonds, lightly toasted

¾ cup sugar, divided use

5 large eggs, at room temperature, separated

1 teaspoon finely grated lemon zest

¼ teaspoon almond extract

Pinch of salt

1 cup all-purpose flour (spoon into a dry-measure cup and level off)

One 2½- or 3-inch deep x 9-inch-round springform pan or one 3-inch-deep x 9-inch-round cake pan, buttered and the bottom lined with a disk of parchment or buttered wax paper, see Note below

Storage: Wrap the layer in plastic and reserve at room temperature until needed, up to 24 hours. Double wrap and freeze for longer storage. Defrost at room temperature for several hours before using.

Note: If you prefer to bake the cake in two pans, use two 1½- or 2–inch-deep x 9-inch-round cake pans, prepared as above. Check for doneness after about 20 minutes.

Use this as a model for all sponge cake layers made with the addition of ground nuts. Quantities for different kinds of nuts follow in the variations. I like to bake this as a single layer and split it afterward (instructions are in the cake recipes that use the layer), but you may also bake it in two separate pans; see the Note at bottom left.

1 Set a rack in the middle level of the oven and preheat to 350°F.

2 Combine the almonds and 1 tablespoon of the sugar in the bowl of a food processor fitted with the metal blade and pulse repeatedly until the mixture is finely ground. Use a thin metal spatula to scrape away any of the mixture caked up in the corner where the bottom meets the side of the bowl. Set aside.

3 Whisk half the remaining sugar into the egg yolks in the bowl of an electric mixer fitted with the whisk attachment. Whip the yolk mixture on medium speed until lightened, about 3 minutes. Whip in the lemon zest and almond extract.

4 In a clean dry mixer bowl (if you only have one bowl and whisk attachment, scrape the yolk mixture into a mixing bowl and wash the bowl and whisk attachment in hot soapy water, rinse well, and dry) combine the egg whites and salt. Whip on medium speed until white and beginning to hold their shape. Increase speed to medium-high and whip in the remaining sugar 1 tablespoon at a time, continuing to whip until the egg whites hold a firm peak (A).

5 Use a large rubber spatula to fold the yolk mixture into the whipped whites (B). Then scatter the ground almond mixture over the egg mixture and sift the flour over that. Use a large rubber spatula to fold everything together (C). Work quickly but gently to avoid deflating the batter.

6 Scrape the batter into the prepared pan and use the spatula to spread it evenly and smooth the top.

7 Bake the layer until it is well risen, deep golden, and firm in the center, about 30 minutes. Immediately invert the layer to a rack, leaving the paper on the bottom; place another rack on the layer and invert the whole stack, removing the top rack, so that the layer cools right side up. Cool completely.

variations

Pistachio Sponge: Use ¾ cup blanched unsalted pistachios in place of the almonds. To blanch the nuts, cover with water in a saucepan and bring to a full boil. Drain, rub in a clean kitchen towel, and separate the nutmeats from the skins. Place the nuts on a jelly-roll pan and bake them at 300°F until just dry but not coloring, 7 to 8 minutes.

Hazelnut Sponge: Use ¾ cup unblanched hazelnuts instead of almonds. Don't bother to remove the skins from the hazelnuts before grinding; the flecks of skin in the baked cake look appealing. Use 1 teaspoon vanilla extract instead of almond extract.

Walnut or Pecan Sponge: Use 1 cup nutmeats or weigh 4 ounces before grinding. Use 1 teaspoon vanilla extract instead of the almond extract. Stir ¼ teaspoon ground cinnamon into the flour before sifting and folding it in.

A

B

C

baked meringue & nut meringue layers

Makes two or three meringue layers, depending on the size you choose to make them

4 large egg whites, at room temperature

Pinch of salt

½ teaspoon distilled white vinegar or strained lemon juice

2 teaspoons vanilla extract

1⅓ cups sugar, divided use

2 cookie sheets or jelly-roll pans lined with parchment paper or silicone pan liners and one 20-inch pastry bag fitted with a ½-inch plain tube (Ateco #806)

Crunchy, sweet meringue layers may be used to make a festive dessert on their own or may be coupled with sponge or butter-cake layers for a truly extravagant presentation. There are three types of meringue. Making ordinary meringue, also known as French meringue, involves whipping egg whites with part of the sugar used and folding in the rest. Swiss meringue calls for combining the egg whites with all the sugar and heating the mixture over simmering water until hot, dissolving the sugar at the same time, and whipping afterward. Italian meringue is made from whipped egg whites that have hot sugar syrup poured over them while they are whipping. The method below is a personal combination of the first two methods and results in meringue that holds its shape perfectly and bakes to a fragile texture. Meringue layers are piped out, which makes them easier to form, not more complex. If you've never tried piping before, meringue is a great place to start because unlike some other mixtures that are piped out, meringue won't flow from your pastry bag of its own accord.

1 Half fill a saucepan with water and bring it to a boil. Decrease the heat so that the water boils gently.

2 Combine the egg whites, salt, vinegar, vanilla, and ⅔ cup (half of) the sugar in the bowl of an electric mixer and whisk by hand to mix.

3 Set the bowl over the pan of simmering water and whisk constantly but slowly to keep the mixture in motion, but not to incorporate air, until the egg whites are hot, about 140°F, and the sugar has dissolved, about 3 minutes.

4 Place the bowl on a mixer fitted with the whisk attachment and whip on medium-high speed until cooled and increased in volume.

5 Once you can touch the bowl and feel that it has completely cooled, decrease the speed to medium and add the remaining sugar about 2 tablespoons at a time, continuing to whip until all the sugar has been added.

6 Remove the bowl from the mixer and follow the instructions for shaping and baking below.

variation

Nut Meringue: Grind 1 cup almonds, hazelnuts, or a combination in the food processor until medium fine; you may still have pieces of nuts as large as ⅛ inch across, but no larger or they will clog the end of the piping tube. Pour the ground nuts onto the surface of the whipped meringue and sprinkle on 1 tablespoon cornstarch or potato starch. Fold the nuts and starch into the meringue (A).

A   B   C

piping meringue layers

1. Use a dark pencil to trace the shape you want, either a circle or square, onto a piece of parchment paper, then invert the paper onto the prepared pan. If you're using a silicone mat, have a plate or a cardboard pattern the same size and shape you wish to make nearby to compare to the layer to gauge the correct size.

2. Fold back one third of the pastry bag and stand it in a jar or large measuring cup to fill. Spoon in one third to one half the meringue, unfold the bag, and twist the top of the bag closed behind the meringue.

3. For a disk of meringue, start piping in the center of the circle, holding the pastry bag perpendicular to the pan and about 1 inch above it. Spiral the meringue around, moving from your waist up, and holding the bag fairly stationary while squeezing the top, closed end of the bag (B and C). When you come to the end of your traced pattern, just stop squeezing and pull the tube away. You don't have to worry if the outside edge isn't perfect, it's always trimmed before use.

4. For a square or other angular-shaped layer, hold the bag at a 45-degree angle to the pan with the tube touching the surface of the paper. Start at the far side of your pattern and, while squeezing, pull the bag toward the side closer to you. Repeat, making a series of lines with the meringue that are almost touching (they'll puff a little and join while baking).

5. Squeeze out a few blobs of meringue the same height as your layers, which you'll be able to press to determine the degree of doneness later on.

baking meringue layers

1. Set racks in the upper and lower thirds of the oven and preheat to 200°F for plain meringue and 300°F for nut meringue.

2. Bake plain meringue until it is almost completely dry, which can take up to 2 hours, watching carefully that the meringue takes on no color or as little color as possible. After $1^1/2$ hours, press one of the extra pieces of meringue; there should only be $^1/2$ inch in the center that is still soft. For nut meringue, the degree of doneness is the same, but at the higher temperature it should only take about 30 minutes. Test as above, but only continue baking another 10 minutes before testing again if it's still too soft when you press.

3. Cool the meringues on the pans on racks. Stack them on a cake cardboard with parchment paper between them and slide them into a plastic bag for storage. If the weather is very humid, they will soften. Crisp plain or nut meringues at 200°F for about 20 minutes, cool, and use immediately.

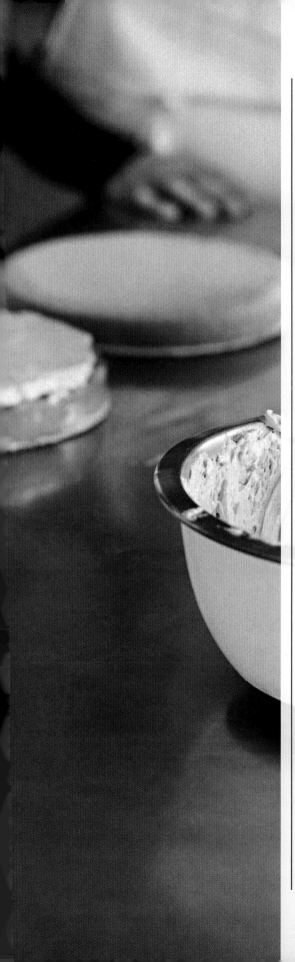

15

layer &
molded cakes

In this chapter we'll use the butter-based, genoise, and meringue layers to create cakes both homey and elegant. Organized a little differently, the chapter starts by taking a look at the fillings and frostings most common in layer cakes and then outlines the essential techniques for assembling a layer cake. The subsequent recipes presume that the layer is baked and ready to go, so you can follow the instructions for assembly, only having to look up the recipe for the frosting earlier in this chapter. The recipes for molded cakes stand alone and only reference the separate cake layer. Making a slick layer cake isn't difficult, but it requires a little practice and the right tools. A sharp serrated knife for splitting layers is a requirement. A tiny and a medium offset spatula make spreading fillings and frostings a breeze. And cardboard cake circles are essential.

perfect meringue buttercream

Real buttercream—not the kind made with vegetable shortening—is light and rich at the same time and perfectly complements delicate cake layers. Meringue buttercream is on the sweet side, so it pairs well with strong flavorings such as lemon, unsweetened berries, bittersweet chocolate, and coffee. This recipe is particularly easy to prepare, but please be patient and observe all the temperature guidelines for both ingredients and mixing. I promise if you do you'll achieve a perfectly smooth and delicious buttercream.

Makes about 1½ pounds unflavored buttercream, enough to fill and finish a 9-inch 2- or 3-layer cake

4 large egg whites

Pinch of salt

1¼ cups sugar

12 ounces (3 sticks) unsalted butter, very soft

Flavoring suggestions (at right)

1 Half fill a saucepan big enough to fit your mixer bowl a couple of inches. Bring the water to a boil over medium heat and decrease the heat so that the water boils gently.

2 Whisk the egg whites, salt, and sugar together by hand in the bowl of an electric mixer. Place over the boiling water and whisk constantly but not furiously until the egg whites are hot (about 140°F) and the sugar is dissolved, 3 to 4 minutes. Test a little by withdrawing the whisk and letting a little of the mixture flow onto a fingertip; it should be a smooth liquid with no sugar grit.

3 Place the bowl on the mixer fitted with the whisk attachment and whip on medium speed until the meringue is very risen in volume and beginning to cool. The outside of the bowl should feel just slightly warm.

4 Switch to the paddle attachment and beat on the lowest speed until the meringue is completely cooled and the bowl no longer feels at all warm. This is critical; if you add the butter when the meringue is still warm it will melt and ruin the buttercream.

5 Add the butter in 6 or 8 additions immediately following each other, still mixing on the lowest speed. Scrape the bowl and beater and increase the speed to medium; beat the buttercream until it is smooth, thick, and shiny, about 5 minutes. Don't be concerned if the buttercream appears separated a little while after adding the butter; it's normal. Just continue beating and it will smooth out as soon as the fat in the butter and the water in the meringue emulsify completely.

6 Once the buttercream is perfectly smooth, add flavorings as suggested at right. Add liquid flavorings such as lemon juice or coffee 1 tablespoon at a time, beating smooth after each addition. Thicker flavorings such as melted chocolate or reduced berry puree may be added in larger amounts, provided that they are neither chilled not warm.

flavoring the buttercream

Lemon or Lime: Beat in ⅓ cup freshly squeezed lemon or lime juice, strained before measuring. Add a tablespoon of kirsch or white rum if you wish.

Raspberry: Beat ½ cup thick, cooled raspberry puree into the buttercream. Add a tablespoon of raspberry liqueur or eau-de-vie if you wish. To make the raspberry puree, combine 1 to 1¼ pounds fresh or frozen raspberries with ½ cup water. Bring to a boil over medium heat, stirring to crush the berries. Pour the crushed mixture into a bowl, rinse the pan, and press the berries through a fine strainer back into the pan. Return to a simmer and cook, stirring occasionally, until thickened, 5 to 10 minutes. Cool completely. If you can only buy raspberries that have been frozen with a small amount of sugar added, don't be concerned; it won't oversweeten the buttercream.

Coffee: Dissolve 2 tablespoons instant espresso coffee granules in ⅓ cup warm brewed coffee. Cool completely before adding.

Chocolate: Cut 8 ounces bittersweet chocolate (65–70%) into ¼-inch pieces. Combine it with ⅓ cup milk or water in a small saucepan and cook over low heat, stirring constantly, until melted. Scrape into a small bowl and cool completely before adding to the buttercream. Add 1 tablespoon dark rum or 2 teaspoons vanilla extract, if you wish.

Vanilla: Beat in 1½ tablespoons vanilla extract or vanilla bean paste, or 1 tablespoon vanilla extract mixed with the seeds scraped from the inside of one plump vanilla bean, into the buttercream.

essential tips for meringue buttercream

- Make sure the egg whites are free of any traces of yolk or the meringue won't whip firm.

- Cool the meringue completely. If the butter melts when it's added it might be impossible to rescue the buttercream.

- The butter has to be very soft—the consistency of mayonnaise—or it won't combine smoothly with the meringue.

- When adding a liquid, add no more than 1 tablespoon at a time. The buttercream will separate slightly, sliding away from the side of the mixer bowl. Keep beating until the liquid is absorbed and the buttercream adheres firmly to the side of the bowl again before adding more.

- If the buttercream separates after liquid has been added too quickly or too soon, try beating on medium speed for at least 5 minutes. If it remains separated, scrape the buttercream into another bowl and beat 8 tablespoons of butter in the bowl with the paddle on medium speed until it is very soft and light, about 5 minutes. Beat the separated buttercream a little at a time into the butter, beating smooth after each addition.

- For advance preparation, cover and chill unflavored buttercream. Let it come to room temperature before using, then beat smooth with the paddle on medium before adding flavoring.

ganache for filling & frosting

A rich filling made principally from chocolate and cream, ganache goes well with every cake layer. Semi-sweet or bittersweet chocolate with 50 to 62% cocoa-solid content works best for ganache, but bittersweets with a higher cocoa-solid content can make the ganache too bitter in contrast with a sweet cake layer. Ganache should be used as soon as it's thick enough to spread or it can be whipped to lighten it. Recipes that call for it as a filling specify which way to use it.

Makes about 1½ pounds ganache, enough to fill and finish a 9-inch cake

1 cup heavy whipping cream

2 tablespoons light corn syrup

14 ounces bittersweet (65 to 70% cocoa solids) or semisweet (55 to 65%) chocolate, cut into ¼-inch pieces

4 tablespoons unsalted butter, very soft

1 Whisk the cream and corn syrup together in a saucepan. Bring to a simmer over low heat, about 180°F.

2 Place the chocolate in bowl and pour the cream over it. Gently shake the bowl a couple of times to submerge all the chocolate. Let melt for 2 to 3 minutes, then whisk smooth.

essential tips for ganache

- Always use a premium brand of chocolate. Chocolate chips or baking chocolate won't make a fine-flavored ganache.

- Only whisk enough to mix the chocolate and cream mixture. Overmixing can cause separation. In ganache for glazing, too much mixing will make a glaze riddled with air bubbles.

- Before you fill a cake with ganache, it should have the consistency of room-temperature peanut butter. If it's too soft, refrigerate for a few minutes only and then stir smooth with a rubber spatula. Chilling too long can harden the ganache and it will tear through the cake layers if you try to spread it.

- If you wish to lighten the ganache more than hand whisking allows, beat it on medium-low speed with the paddle for 1 minute. Work quickly when finishing, because beating air into ganache encourages it to set quickly.

- Keep ganache overnight at a cool room temperature.

3 Cool the ganache to room temperature (about 65°F) and quickly whisk in the butter all at once. Use immediately or whisk by hand for 30 seconds to lighten.

variations

Ganache for Glazing: Reduce the amount of chocolate to 8 ounces and omit the butter. Cool to about 80°F so that it's still pourable before using.

pastry cream

A starch-thickened custard cream, pastry cream is a versatile and delicate filling for cakes and pastries of many types. The recipe here is thickened with cornstarch because it allows the pastry cream to be whisked smooth before spreading, which might liquefy a pastry cream thickened with flour. Be careful to bring the pastry cream to a full boil when cooking it (no, it won't make the egg yolks scramble; the starch prevents this) or the pastry cream won't be thick enough to spread.

Makes about 2½ cups, enough to fill a 9-inch cake

1½ cups whole milk, divided use

½ cup heavy whipping cream

⅓ cup sugar

¼ cup cornstarch

5 large egg yolks

2 teaspoons vanilla extract

3 tablespoons unsalted butter, cut into 6 pieces

1 Set aside ½ cup of the milk in a medium, heatproof bowl.

2 Combine the remaining 1 cup milk with the cream and sugar in a medium nonreactive saucepan and whisk to mix. Place on low heat and bring to a full boil.

3 Meanwhile whisk the cornstarch into the reserved ½ cup milk and whisk in the egg yolks.

4 Once the milk boils, whisk about a third of it into the yolk mixture. Return the remaining milk to a full boil. Beginning to whisk before pouring, pour in the yolk mixture in a quick stream, continuing to whisk constantly.

5 Cook, whisking constantly, until the pastry cream thickens and comes to a full boil. Cook, whisking, for 30 seconds longer.

6 Off heat, whisk in the vanilla and butter. Pour the pastry cream into a shallow bowl so that it cools quickly and press plastic wrap directly against the surface. Refrigerate immediately. Use the pastry cream within 36 hours.

variations

Crème Mousseline: A cross between pastry cream and buttercream, crème mousseline is a delicate cake filling and, unlike buttercream, it pairs well with fresh fruit. Make crème mousseline immediately before spreading it.

Omit the butter from the pastry cream. Beat 12 tablespoons soft unsalted butter with the paddle on medium speed until soft and light. Beat in the whole batch of pastry cream all at once and beat until well mixed, about 1 minute. Scrape the bowl and beater, increase the speed to medium high, and continue beating until the cream is smooth and fluffy, about 5 minutes longer. If you wish, add a tablespoon of kirsch or light or dark rum right after scraping the bowl.

meringue frosting

Egg white–based frostings have always been popular for American-style layer cakes. This variation is of a classic that used to be called "seven-minute frosting" because it was whipped with a rotary egg beater in the top of a double boiler. With the heavy-duty mixers of today, it's just a question of heating the ingredients first and then whipping them by machine.

Makes about 3 cups, enough to fill and finish a 9-inch cake

4 large egg whites

Pinch of salt

1⅓ cups sugar

½ cup light corn syrup

1 Put all the ingredients in the bowl of an electric mixer and whisk by hand to mix.

2 Heat and whip as for the Perfect Meringue Buttercream, page 156.

3 Use the frosting immediately after it's whipped up; it might still be a little warm, but that's okay.

sweetened whipped cream

Making perfect whipped cream and finishing a cake with it isn't difficult, but you have to remember a few basic rules: Keep everything cold, and don't over-whip. Softly whipped cream holds its shape well and doesn't disintegrate on the outside of a cake.

Makes about 5 cups, enough to fill and finish a 9-inch cake

3 cups heavy whipping cream, ice cold

⅓ cup sugar

2 teaspoons vanilla extract

1 About 30 minutes before whipping the cream, chill the mixer bowl and whisk in the refrigerator. Take out and put the cream, sugar, and vanilla in the bowl and whisk once by hand to mix. Place on the mixer fitted with the whisk attachment and whip on medium high until you see traces of the whisk holding in the cream.

2 Decrease the speed to medium and continue whipping until the cream holds a soft peak on the end of a rubber spatula.

3 Cover the bowl and chill the cream until you need it. Before using the refrigerated whipped cream, re-whip it briefly by hand to a soft peak again.

essential tips for...
...pastry cream

- A pointed whisk gets into the corners of the pan when cooking.

- Make sure to bring the pastry cream to a full boil—large bubbles that slowly burst on the surface —or it won't thicken and will have a strong starchy flavor.

- Use as soon as possible after cooking, and refrigerate any cake filled with it.

...meringue frosting

- When heating the mixture, make sure the sugar fully dissolves or the frosting will be gritty.

- Frost the outside of the cake with swirled strokes, but don't go back once you have applied; it crusts almost immediately and the surface will look rough if you go back over it.

- Adding corn syrup makes the frosting smooth and soft instead of hardening.

...whipped cream

- Remember to have everything ice cold. If it's hot in the kitchen, pour the cream into a bowl and freeze it for 15 minutes.

- Whipped cream always melts a little in the refrigerator; don't over-whip when re-whipping it.

- Keep the finished cake at a cool room temperature for only a few hours before serving. Refrigerate for longer, but no more than half a day; whipped cream rapidly acquires a stale taste. Wrap leftovers tightly in plastic and serve no later than the next day.

cream cheese frosting

Traditional with carrot cake or another spiced layer cake, cream cheese frosting is also perfect on cupcakes. Both the cream cheese and butter should be only slightly softened; let your mixer complete the softening while beating in some air to lighten the frosting and give it a more appealing texture.

Makes about 3 cups, enough to fill and cover a 2-layer 9-inch cake

12 ounces cream cheese, slightly softened

6 tablespoons unsalted butter, slightly softened

3 cups confectioners' sugar, sifted

2 teaspoons vanilla extract

1 Put the butter and cream cheese in the bowl of an electric mixer and beat with the paddle on medium speed until completely mixed, about 3 minutes, stopping and scraping the bowl and beater several times.

2 Decrease the speed to low and add the confectioners' sugar a cup at a time, beating until absorbed after each addition. After the last cup, the frosting might look dry.

3 Beat in the vanilla and increase the speed to low-medium until the mixture is no longer dry looking, about 2 minutes.

4 Increase the speed to medium and beat until smooth and light, 4 to 5 minutes. Use soon after mixing.

A

assembling layer cakes

The general directions at right pertain no matter which of the fillings and/or frostings outlined in the previous recipes you are using.

1   To prepare a layer, invert the cake onto the work surface and peel off any parchment paper. Turn the cake right side up again.

2   With a sharp serrated knife, trim the top of the cake flat. If a dome has formed in the center, trim it off.

3   If you need to cut one layer into more layers, hold the serrated knife perpendicular to the side of the cake about one third of the way down from the top if you are making three layers and about halfway down if you are making two layers. Use the blade of the knife to mark a shallow line all the way around the cake, turning the cake so it presses against the knife (A). Turn the cake again, cutting a little deeper this time (B). After two turns, you should have cut all the way through. If not, repeat a third time. Slide a cake cardboard under the cut layer and remove it. Repeat if you are cutting three layers (C).

4   Invert what was the top of the cake onto a cake cardboard. Dip a pastry brush into any syrup and sprinkle it on the layer. (Do not brush.)

5   Spread on any filling, using a medium offset spatula; the filling should be about 1/4 inch thick. If you're using some jam or chocolate filling under the principal filling, use a small offset spatula to spread it on before the principal filling.

6   Slide what was the middle layer of the cake to the edge of the cardboard it's on so that it hangs 1 inch over the edge. Hold that edge of the cake to the far end of the previous layer at about a 30-degree angle, pull away the cardboard, and let the layer fall into place. Moisten and spread with filling. Place the top layer (the former bottom of the cake) on next with its smooth side up. Moisten with syrup, if using.

7   Before frosting the outside of the cake, clean the work surface. Any crumbs lying around tend to get stuck to the outside of the cake, marring its appearance.

B C

8   Hold the cake in your left hand (assuming you are right handed) and use a metal offset spatula to "mask" the side of the cake. Use about 1 tablespoon of filling at a time, and press it onto the cake, holding the offset spatula at a right angle. Pat it on; do not spread smooth.

9   Place the cake on the work surface and spread the frosting over the top using the metal offset spatula. (Reserve some frosting if you are planning to decorate the finished cake.) If any crumbs appear on the spatula, wash and dry it carefully.

10 Again hold the cake in your left hand and use the offset spatula to smooth the side of the cake, holding the spatula steady and turning the cake.

11 Return the cake to the work surface and smooth the top, working any frosting that has accumulated on the edge of the cake in toward the center.

12 If you are using ground nuts, hold the cake in your left hand, over the work surface, and use your right hand to press the nuts into the side of the cake, allowing the excess to fall away. If you are decorating with chocolate shavings, use a metal spatula rather than your hand, which will melt the chocolate. Always do this before refrigerating the cake.

13 To decorate a cake, place the remaining frosting in a pastry bag and pipe a border around the perimeter.

14 To glaze the cake, refrigerate it after spreading the frosting smooth but before piping on a border or pressing anything against the side of the cake. Chill until the outside is set, then place the cake on a rack set over a pan and pour the glaze evenly and slowly over the cake in a spiral from the center outward. Refrigerate the cake to set the glaze, then loosen the bottom edge with a small paring knife and transfer the cake to a serving platter.

essential tips for assembling & glazing

- If the outside of your cake isn't perfectly straight, apply a crumb coat to the outside to hide the imperfection. Spread a thin layer of buttercream all over the outside of the cake as thinly as you would spread butter on toast. Chill for 30 minutes before continuing, which prevents any crumbs from mixing into the buttercream as you spread them onto the outside of the cake.

- When glazing a cake with ganache, if you see any bubbles in the glaze before pouring it, put the glaze through the finest strainer you have a couple of times, which will help to eliminate the bubbles.

hazelnut meringue dacquoise

Makes one 8- or 9-inch 3-layer cake, 12 to 16 servings

Three 8- or 9-inch layers of hazelnut meringue (see page 152), baked until still moist within and cooled

1 batch coffee meringue buttercream (see page 156)

Toasted chopped hazelnuts or crumbled meringue scraps for finishing

Confectioners' sugar for serving

Serving: A dacquoise is always a little difficult to slice and if you don't use a really sharp knife it will look as though you used a hammer to cut it. Use a long, sharp serrated knife held perpendicular to the top of the dacquoise and saw back and forth, cutting across the diameter of and through the top layer only. Wipe any buttercream off the blade (with the sharp edge held away from your hand) and repeat at a 90-degree angle to the first cut—you now have 4 wedges. Continue cutting through the top layer to make as many wedges as you need, always cutting across the entire top of the cake at the same time. After the top layer is cut, go back and follow the initial cuts in the same order, cutting through the remaining layers to the bottom and wiping the knife after each cut. A final hint: It's easier to cut the dacquoise when it's chilled, then let the slices come to room temperature before serving.

Storage: Wrap and chill leftovers and bring to room temperature before serving again.

One of the signature desserts developed by then-executive pastry chef Albert Kumin for the opening of Windows on the World in 1976, dacquoise took New York by storm and was one of the most popular desserts on restaurant menus for years afterward. James Beard, who loved the dessert and had first introduced it to the United States after he tasted it in Paris in the early 1960s, was acting as consultant to Joe Baum, the owner of the company that installed all the food-service facilities in the newly opened World Trade Center. It's my guess that this is how the confection of hazelnut meringue layers and coffee-flavored buttercream made it onto the restaurant's dessert menu, where it remained until the restaurant closed after the parking garage bombing in 1993. Dacquoise always makes me remember the early days of Windows, as we all called it, and the thrill of (over)working in the world's most talked-about restaurant right at the beginning of my career.

1 Using a plate or cardboard cake circle as a guide, trim the meringue layers to an even 9-inch diameter. Save the one that has the best spiral pattern for the top.

2 Put a dab of the buttercream on a cardboard cake circle or platter and place one of the layers flat (bottom) side down on it. Save the trimmed-away scraps for finishing the cake if you wish.

3 Use a medium offset spatula to spread a little more than a third of the buttercream on the layer.

4 Place the second trimmed layer on top and spread on the same amount of buttercream.

5 Place the last layer on top. If you don't have a really nice spiraled layer for the top, then place it on flat side up and cover it with buttercream and meringue crumbs or chopped hazelnuts.

6 Spread the remaining buttercream to cover the side of the cake; crumble or chop the meringue scraps left from trimming the layers (use the chopped hazelnuts if you don't have enough scraps) and press them against the buttercream.

7 Lightly dust the top with confectioners' sugar immediately before serving.

variations

Use ganache (see page 157), whipped or unwhipped, rather than coffee meringue buttercream to finish the dacquoise. Substitute chocolate shavings instead of the meringue crumbs or chopped hazelnuts.

Substitute plain white meringue layers and use coffee meringue buttercream or ganache to finish.

strawberry chantilly cake

Yellow cake, whipped cream, and strawberries make a simple yet elegant cake that always has everyone hoping that seconds will be offered. When I was a child, retail bakeries referred to this as strawberry shortcake, but real shortcake is made with rich baking-powder biscuit dough that has sugar and eggs added to it. I make this a couple of times a year and only when really sweet local berries are in season or it just doesn't have enough flavor.

Makes one 2-layer 9-inch cake, about 10 servings

1½ pints height-of-season strawberries, rinsed

2 9-inch layers yellow or gold cake (see page 124 or 126), baked and cooled

1 batch Sweetened Whipped Cream (page 159)

1 Select six of the best-looking strawberries and reserve them. Hull and slice the remaining strawberries.

2 Place one of the cake layers on a cardboard or platter smooth side down. Spread with 1 cup of the whipped cream. Arrange the sliced berries on the cream evenly.

3 Spread another cup of cream on the berries—spread gently or all the strawberry slices will go flying.

4 Top with the other cake layer, smooth side up. Spread the outside and top of the cake with the whipped cream and evenly smooth the top.

5 Slice through 5 of the reserved berries, hull and all, and arrange them cut side up perpendicular to the edges of the cake and evenly spaced apart from each other. Place the last whole berry in the center of the cake. Refrigerate until serving.

Serving: Cut wedges of the cake at the table; it needs no accompaniment.

Storage: Wrap leftovers in plastic and refrigerate them. Plan on serving all the leftovers within 24 hours.

variations

Substitute sweet raspberries or blackberries for the strawberries, leaving them whole.

Victoria Sandwich: Use the yellow cake on page 124, or the hot milk sponge on page 149. Stack the layers with ½ cup strawberry preserves between them and sprinkle the top of the cake with confectioners' sugar. You can also add a layer of whipped cream (made with 1 cup cream, 2 tablespoons sugar, 1 teaspoon vanilla extract) between the cake layers, and even a few sliced strawberries.

Black Forest Cake: A real Black Forest cake is made from cocoa sponge cake layers soaked with kirsch syrup and filled with whipped cream and preserved sour cherries. Bad versions turn the cherries into something that resembles canned cherry pie filling. I like to use *amarene*, Italian sour cherries in a thick syrup that are used as a gelato topping in Italy. Failing that, sour cherry preserves are a good substitute.

Slice the cocoa genoise layer (see page 147) into 3 and place the top layer on a cardboard, crust side down. Sprinkle it with a third of the rum syrup from the Russian Punch Cake (page 165), substituting 2 tablespoons kirsch for the rum. Spread with ¾ cup sweetened whipped cream and top the cream with ⅔ cup *amarene* (if using jam, spread on first, then top with 1½ cups whipped cream). Spread another ¾ cup whipped cream on the cherries. Place the middle layer on and repeat syrup, whipped cream, cherries, whipped cream. Place the last layer on, smooth side up, and sprinkle with the last of the syrup. Spread the outside of the cake with the remaining whipped cream. Press milk chocolate shavings all over the cake using a metal spatula. Lightly dust with confectioners' sugar right before serving.

Some versions of the cake add a layer of chocolate whipped cream under the cherries: Melt 4 ounces bittersweet chocolate with 2 ounces heavy whipping cream and cool to room temperature before assembling. Whisk half the chocolate mixture into the ¾ cup whipped cream to be spread on the first layer, then repeat with the remaining chocolate mixture and another ¾ cup whipped cream for the second layer; if you mix for both layers at the same time, it might harden before you get to the second layer.

russian punch cake

Makes one 3-layer 9-inch cake, about 12 servings

RUM SYRUP

⅓ cup water

¼ cup sugar

¼ cup dark rum

One 9-inch plain genoise cake (page 146)

1 batch Pastry Cream (page 158), chilled

VIENNESE MERINGUE FROSTING

5 large egg whites, at room temperature

1 cup granulated sugar

1 cup confectioners' sugar, sifted after measuring

Cookie sheet or jelly-roll pan

Serving: Serve wedges of this rich cake at the table; it needs no accompaniment.

Storage: Loosely wrap leftovers in plastic and serve within 24 hours.

This is a specialty of Demel, the great Viennese pastry shop, arguably one of the top half dozen in the world. I learned the recipe when I visited in the spring of 2008, to write an article about the shop for *Saveur* magazine, and this was one of the recipes that Dietmar Muthenthaler, the head pastry chef, had given us for the story. The elements in the cake are so simple that I was surprised at the delicate and delicious result when they were combined. The "punch" in the name indicates the use of rum for moistening and flavoring the layers; I think calling it Russian is just a way of distinguishing it from the classic Viennese punch cake, which is filled with a mixture similar to what we would call rum balls—cake scraps, apricot jam, rum, a little chocolate—and covered with pink sugar icing.

1 For the syrup, stir the water and sugar together in a small pan over low heat. Stir until the sugar is dissolved. Pour into a heat-proof bowl and cool. Stir in the rum.

2 To assemble the cake, use a long, sharp serrated knife to split the genoise cake into 3 equal layers. Place the former top of the cake, crust side down, on a cake cardboard. Sprinkle with a third of the rum syrup.

3 Whisk the pastry cream to smooth it out and use a medium offset spatula to spread half on the layer.

4 Place the middle layer on the pastry cream and sprinkle with another third of the rum syrup; spread with the remaining pastry cream.

5 Place the last layer on top, smooth side up, and sprinkle with the remaining syrup. Slide the cake to a cookie sheet or the back of a jelly-roll pan and chill it while preparing the meringue.

6 Place the egg whites and granulated sugar in the bowl of an electric mixer and whisk by hand to mix. Place over a pan of gently boiling water (see Meringue Frosting, page 158) and whisk gently until hot (140°F) and the sugar is dissolved, about 3 minutes. Place on the mixer with the whisk attachment and whip on medium until increased in volume and almost cooled, 4 to 5 minutes. Decrease the speed to low and whip in the confectioners' sugar ¼ cup at a time. Increase the speed back to medium and whip until the meringue has completely cooled.

7 Set a rack in the lower third of the oven and preheat to 400°F.

8 Remove the cake from the pan it's resting on and spread a thick layer of the meringue all over the outside of the cake. Use a ½-inch plain tube (Ateco #806) to pipe a border of overlapping spheres at the top edge of the cake. Pipe any remaining meringue onto the side of the cake.

9 Replace the cake on the pan and bake it until the meringue is light golden, checking after about 20 seconds. If necessary, turn the cake from back to front and continue until the meringue colors sufficiently.

10 Slide the cake to a platter and refrigerate, uncovered, until serving time.

devil's food bombe

Makes one 8- to 9-inch dome-shaped cake, depending on the size of the bowl used

2 layers Devil's Food Cake (page 128)

Whipped cream (page 159), made with 4 cups cream and ½ cup sugar

¼ cup dark rum for sprinkling, optional

½ pint fresh raspberries, optional

Chocolate shavings or fine devil's food cake crumbs for finishing

One 1½- to 2-quart round-bottomed bowl, buttered and lined with plastic wrap

This is an original and amusing presentation for plain old devil's food cake. It's sliced vertically and layered in a bowl with whipped cream. You can even sprinkle on a little dark rum and/or a handful of raspberries along the way. After spreading the outside of the unmolded cake with whipped cream, you may press chocolate shavings against the cream or crumble any bits of leftover cake and use them instead.

1 Cut the devil's food layers into 1/4-inch-thick vertical slices.

2 Line the bowl with a single layer of the slices, patching them together if necessary. Sprinkle the slices with rum.

3 Spread a large spoonful of whipped cream on top of the layer.

4 Trim 2 or 3 cake slices to the diameter of the bottom of the bowl and arrange them on the cream. Sprinkle with rum and spread with more cream. If you're using raspberries, sprinkle a few on each layer.

5 Repeat, cutting enough cake slices to fit the changing diameter of the bowl as you build up higher and so that they cover the previous layer of cream, until the bowl is full. Finish with a layer of cake.

6 Wrap and chill the bowl at least 4 hours or overnight. If chilling the cake overnight, only whip 3 cups of the cream as in the recipe on page 159 and whip the rest for covering the cake soon before you're going to serve it.

7 Place a cardboard or platter on the bowl and invert, then lift off the bowl. If the cake is stuck, wring out a clean kitchen towel in hot water and place on the bowl. This will melt the layer of butter between the bowl and the plastic wrap, then you can lift off the bowl and carefully peel off the plastic.

8 Spread the outside of the cake with the remaining whipped cream and sprinkle with chocolate shavings or fine devil's food cake crumbs.

Serving: Since the cake is tall, it's difficult to serve even wedges. Use a sharp thin knife to cut them and use a wide cake server or other spatula to transfer them to plates.

Storage: Tightly wrap leftovers with plastic and refrigerate and plan on serving all of them within 24 hours for best flavor.

variations

Substitute a batch of ganache (see page 157) for the cream inside the bowl. Cover the cake on the outside with Meringue Frosting (see page 158) or if you want a golden meringue, use the Viennese Meringue Frosting in the recipe for Russian Punch Cake on page 165, and bake the cake briefly as in that recipe.

chocolate pistachio orange cake

Makes one 2-layer 9-inch cake, about 12 servings

ORANGE GANACHE FILLING

1 cup heavy whipping cream

2 tablespoons light corn syrup

1 tablespoon grated orange zest

12 ounces semisweet chocolate (55 to 65% cocoa solids), cut into ¼-inch pieces

2 tablespoons unsalted butter, very soft

1 tablespoon orange liqueur, such as Triple Sec

½ cup candied orange peel cut into ¼-inch dice

ORANGE SYRUP

⅔ cup water

⅓ cup sugar

2 tablespoons orange liqueur

2 teaspoons vanilla extract

1 batch whipped cream, made with 1½ cups cream, 2 tablespoons sugar, and 1 teaspoon vanilla extract

1 Pistachio Sponge cake layer (see page 150), baked and cooled (when you bake the cake layer, blanch an extra ¼ cup of pistachios for finishing the cake)

FINISHING

Milk chocolate shavings

Candied orange peel

¼ cup blanched pistachios, finely chopped

This is one of my favorite cakes, bar none. I first prepared it for a lunch cooked by my friend Ann Amendolara Nurse at the James Beard House in New York in the fall of 1988. A restaurant chef had canceled at the last minute, and Ann was called in to replace him for one in a series of Italian lunches. The first thing Ann did was to phone and ask me to make a dessert, and this cake was the result.

1 For the ganache, combine the cream, corn syrup, and orange zest in a saucepan and bring to a boil over low heat, whisking occasionally. Meanwhile place the chocolate in a heat-proof bowl. Once the cream mixture boils, pour it through a fine-mesh strainer (discard the orange zest) over the chocolate. Wait for 1 minute, then whisk smooth. Cool to room temperature and whisk in the butter, then the liqueur. About 1 hour before you intend to finish the cake, refrigerate the ganache briefly until it reaches spreading consistency.

2 Meanwhile, for the syrup, stir the water and sugar together in a small saucepan and place over low heat. Bring to a boil, stirring occasionally. Pour the syrup into a heat-proof bowl, cool to room temperature, and stir in the liqueur and vanilla.

3 When you are ready to assemble the cake, whip the cream by hand or by machine with the sugar and vanilla until it holds a soft peak. Chill in the refrigerator.

4 To assemble the cake, use a sharp serrated knife to split the pistachio sponge cake layer horizontally into 2 equal layers. Invert the top of the cake to a cardboard or platter and use a brush to moisten it with half the syrup. Whisk half the ganache by hand until lightened and spread it on the layer. Scatter the diced candied orange peel over the ganache. Remove the whipped cream from the refrigerator and re-whisk it if necessary. Spread about a cup of the cream over the candied peel.

5 Invert the other layer onto the cream and peel off the paper. Moisten with the remaining syrup. Spread the top and side of the cake with the remaining whipped cream.

6 Use a metal spatula to adhere the chocolate shavings to the side of the cake. Whisk up the remaining ganache and place it in a pastry bag fitted with a 1/2-inch star tip (Ateco #824). Pipe 12 rosettes around the top edge of the cake. Decorate each rosette with a small disk or shred of candied orange peel. Scatter the chopped pistachios all over the top of the cake.

Serving: Serve thin wedges of this rich cake.

Storage: If you are serving the cake within a few hours, keep it at a cool room temperature. Or cover loosely with plastic wrap and refrigerate. Bring to room temperature for a couple of hours so that the ganache inside the cake isn't hard when it's served.

mocha walnut cake

Makes one 9-inch 3-layer cake,
about 12 servings

COFFEE SYRUP

3 tablespoons sugar

**½ cup hot brewed coffee (don't heat
cold coffee; it will turn bitter)**

2 teaspoons vanilla extract

**One 9-inch Walnut Sponge cake layer
(page 150), baked and cooled**

**1 batch Perfect Meringue Buttercream
(page 156), coffee flavored**

**1¼ cups walnut pieces, lightly toasted,
cooled and finely chopped, but not ground**

Coffee and walnuts make an excellent combination of flavors, and I like to intensify it by using a vanilla and coffee syrup on the walnut cake layers. See the variations at the end of the recipe for adding a note of chocolate to this cake.

1 For the syrup, stir the sugar into the coffee until it dissolves, let cool, and stir in the vanilla.

2 Use a sharp serrated knife to cut the cake layer into 3 thin layers. Place the top layer of the cake crust side down on a cardboard and sprinkle it with a third of the syrup. Use a medium offset spatula to spread about 1 cup of the buttercream on top.

3 Place the middle layer on top and repeat with another third of the syrup and another cup of the buttercream.

4 Place the last layer on the cake, smooth side up, and sprinkle with the remaining syrup.

5 Spread the outside of the cake with the remaining buttercream. Press the chopped walnuts all over the side of the cake, then sprinkle the remaining walnuts on top. Use a medium offset spatula to sweep across the top of the cake to even it off, letting the excess walnuts fall onto the work surface.

Serving: Cut the cake into wedges at the table; this rich cake needs no accompaniment.

Storage: Keep the cake at a cool room temperature until serving. If it's cool indoors, you can keep leftovers under a cake dome or loosely wrapped in plastic. Or wrap and refrigerate the cake and bring it to room temperature before serving again.

variations

Chocolate Mocha Walnut Cake: Prepare 1½ times the recipe for ganache glaze on page 157. Refrigerate a third of the glaze until it's thick enough to spread, 10 to 20 minutes. Spread half the chilled ganache on the bottom layer after the syrup, then spread with the buttercream. Repeat with the middle layer. Top with the last layer and sprinkle with syrup. When spreading the outside of the cake with the buttercream, reserve ½ cup for decorating the cake. After spreading the outside of the cake, chill it for an hour. If necessary, gently reheat the glaze until it is pourable, but not above 90°F or it will melt the buttercream. Place the chilled cake on a rack over a clean pan and pour the glaze over it in a spiral, starting at the center of the cake and ending at the top edge (A and B). Quickly sweep across the top of the cake using a medium offset spatula to remove excess glaze (C); quickly check to see that the sides are evenly covered. If not, use some of the glaze that has dripped into the pan to patch. Let the glaze set, then pipe the reserved ½ cup buttercream into a dozen or so rosettes with a ½-inch star tip (Ateco #824) at the top edge of the cake. Dust 12 walnut halves with confectioners' sugar and arrange them on the rosettes and tilted toward the center of the cake.

If you wish, use a plain or cocoa genoise (see page 146) for the cake in either variation above and omit the walnuts. If using a cocoa genoise and not glazing the cake, press chocolate shavings against the side of the cake.

A

B

raspberry meringue wedge

Makes one 9 x 9 x 13-inch triangular cake, about 16 to 20 servings

Two 9-inch square meringue layers, plus the rest of the meringue piped into a rectangle on another pan (page 152), baked and cooled

1 batch raspberry meringue buttercream (page 156)

Multicolored curling ribbon, optional

In the fall of 1986, I was teaching my first career-training intensive baking course at Peter Kump's New York Cooking School when I learned that Peter's birthday was a few days away. I asked Gaynor Grant, our registrar, what kind of cake I should make for Peter, and she told me that he absolutely adored the raspberry meringue cake from Maurice Bonté's patisserie, then the best pastry shop in Manhattan. So I took a walk over after class and with the pretext of buying a few pounds of cake yeast, which they were always happy to sell to us, I asked Mme. Bonté about the unusual triangular cake covered with chunks of broken meringue with a bright pink buttercream showing through beneath, and two narrow corners festooned with thin multicolored curling ribbons. Yes, it was all meringue layers, and yes, it was raspberry buttercream, were her answers. Leaving with the three pounds of yeast (she charged only a dollar a pound!), I returned to the school to start preparations, happy that the recipe had cost me so little. I was very flattered when Peter refused to believe we hadn't bought the cake from Bonté.

C

D

1. Trim each of the meringue layers to an even 9-inch square, then carefully cut through each diagonally with a sawing motion to make 4 triangles; only 3 will be used to assemble the cake (A).

2. Use a chef's knife to chop the least even of the triangles and the extra rectangle into 1/4- to 1/2-inch pieces.

3. Cut a cardboard that will fit under one of the layers and use a dab of the buttercream to secure a layer in place, flat (bottom) side down. Spread the layer with a third of the buttercream.

4. Place the second triangle on top, flat side down, and spread with another third of the buttercream (B).

5. Place the last layer on top, again flat side down, and gently press into place (C). Spread the entire outside of the triangle with the remaining buttercream.

6. Press the broken meringue chunks against the buttercream all over the top and sides of the triangle (D).

7. If you want to decorate the triangle with ribbon, cut about twelve 16-inch lengths and bunch six together. Tie them around one of the narrow corners of the triangle, then scrape a table knife or a single blade of a pair of scissors against them to curl. Repeat with the remaining ribbon on the opposite narrow angle. Chill the cake to set the buttercream.

Serving: Snip the ribbons away and cut slices from either narrow end of the cake inward. Once the slices are very long, cut the remaining cake in half lengthwise to make more manageable slices.

Storage: Keep the cake refrigerated, but bring it to room temperature for 1 to 2 hours before serving. Wrap and refrigerate leftovers and bring to room temperature again before serving.

variations

This will work well with any flavor of buttercream as well as with ganache. For a triangle filled with ganache, dust the meringue shards on the outside of the cake with a very light coating of cocoa powder.

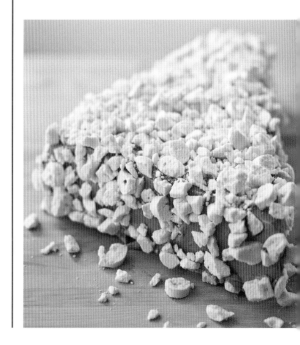

assembling molded cakes

Some of the molded cakes in this chapter have a cake layer as a base under the bottom of the fillings, as in the case of the cheesecake.

1 To prepare the layer, invert onto a clean work surface and peel away any parchment paper. With a sharp serrated knife, trim the crust and any domed portions from the cake so that it is flat.

2 To cut one layer into two or three, see page 160.

3 The pan used for molding the cake should be 1 inch wider in diameter than the cake layer so that when the filling is added it automatically finishes the side of the cake.

4 Place a trimmed layer in the bottom of the pan to be used as a mold. Dab on about half the syrup, if using, with a pastry brush.

5 Pour on about half of the filling and smooth it with a small metal offset spatula, making sure that some of it fills in the gap between the side of the pan and the side of the cake layer.

6 If there is a second layer, place it on top of the first. Again, moisten it by dabbing with syrup. (If the cake just has one layer, skip to the next step.)

7 Scrape the rest of the filling onto the top layer and use the same small spatula to spread it over the top, again making sure that it fills in the gap between the side of the pan and the side of the layer. To finish off the top of the cake, use a metal spatula or the back of a knife whose blade is longer than the diameter of the mold to scrape across the top of the mold and make the filling perfectly even.

8 Refrigerate the cake, uncovered, until the filling starts to set on the outside, about a couple of hours. After that, loosely cover the mold with plastic wrap and keep the cake refrigerated until it's completely set, at least 4 hours (overnight works best).

9 To unmold a cake, warm the side of the pan/mold with a cloth dipped in hot water and wrung out. Run the tip of a sharp, thin knife between the side of the cake and the pan, pushing against the pan. Then unbuckle the outside of the springform and carefully lift it away without touching the cake. Leave the cake on the bottom of the springform pan, but transfer to a platter to serve.

10 If you like, you can finish the sides of the cake, once unmolded, with nuts or chocolate shavings. You can also decorate the top with slices of fruit, meringue, or piped whipped cream.

no-bake cheesecake

The only baking involved in this cheesecake recipe is for the cake base. You can shave a thin layer from a genoise you're using for a layer cake or from almost any other plain cake layer you wish. If you make one of the other molded cakes in this chapter, you'll automatically have a single thin genoise layer left over; just wrap and freeze it until you want to make this. The filling here is a cream cheese mousse, but its flavor and texture are that of an incredibly light and delicate cheesecake.

Makes one 9- or 10-inch cheesecake, about 16 servings

One ¼-inch-thick 9-inch layer of plain genoise (see page 146), or any other firm cake layer in Chapter 11

CHEESECAKE

1½ pounds cream cheese, very soft

1 cup sour cream or plain low-fat yogurt

1 tablespoon lemon juice, strained

2 teaspoons vanilla extract

⅓ cup water

4 teaspoons (1½ envelopes) unflavored powdered gelatin

4 large egg whites

Pinch of salt

¾ cup sugar

One 9- or 10-inch springform pan, 2½ to 3 inches deep

1. Arrange the cake layer in the bottom of the pan and set aside.

2. Beat the cream cheese in the bowl of an electric mixer fitted with the paddle attachment on medium speed until smooth, about 1 minute. Scrape the bowl and beater and beat again, then scrape again.

3. Beat in the sour cream, lemon juice, and vanilla until smooth. Stop, scrape, and beat again until lightened, about 2 minutes. Scrape the cream cheese mixture into a large bowl and wash the mixer bowl in hot, soapy water, then rinse and dry it.

4. Pour the water into a small shallow bowl and use a fork to stir in the gelatin, making sure that all the granules are moistened. Set aside so that the gelatin evenly absorbs all the water.

5. Half fill a small saucepan to fit your mixer bowl without being too deep in the pan and bring the water to a boil. Decrease the heat so that the water boils gently.

6. By hand, whisk the egg whites, salt, and sugar together in the mixer bowl. Set the bowl on the pan of boiling water and whisk gently until the egg whites are hot (140°F) and the sugar is dissolved, about 2 minutes. Scrape the gelatin into the egg whites and whisk it in. Continue to heat for 30 seconds longer to melt the gelatin.

7. Place the meringue on the mixer with the whisk attachment and whip on medium-high speed until white and fluffy but not completely cooled, 4 to 5 minutes.

8. Vigorously whisk a third of the meringue into the cream cheese mixture, then whisk the cream cheese mixture, more gently this time, back into the remaining meringue in the mixer bowl.

9. Pour the cheese mixture into the prepared pan and refrigerate immediately.

10. After the mixture has set in the pan, 2 to 3 hours, loosely wrap the pan in plastic and chill until you wish to unmold the cake, up to 2 days.

11. To unmold the cake, insert a thin paring knife between the side of the cake and the side of the pan and, pressing it against the pan, loosen the cake. Unbuckle the side of the pan and lift it off. Use a wide spatula to slide the cake from the springform base to a platter. Keep the cake chilled until serving.

Serving: Cut the cake into wedges at the table, wiping the knife after each cut. Serve with some crushed sweetened strawberries or mixed berries.

Storage: Keep the cheesecake refrigerated, loosely covered with plastic wrap.

variations:

Chocolate Cheesecake: Omit the lemon juice. Add 8 ounces semisweet chocolate, melted with ⅓ cup water or milk and cooled, to the cream cheese mixture, whisking it in by hand, then pick up the recipe above at step 4.

Devil's Food Cheesecake: Cut one layer devil's food cake, page 128, horizontally into two layers. Put one in the springform pan and make sure it's tight. Omit the lemon juice and divide the cream cheese mixture into two bowls, one with slightly more. Melt 4 ounces semisweet chocolate with 3 tablespoons water and cool; whisk into the bowl with slightly less cream cheese. Prepare the gelatin and meringue as above, then whisk half into each of the mixtures. Pour the chocolate mxture into the prepared pan and set the other cake layer on it. Pour the plain mixture over and chill and unmold.

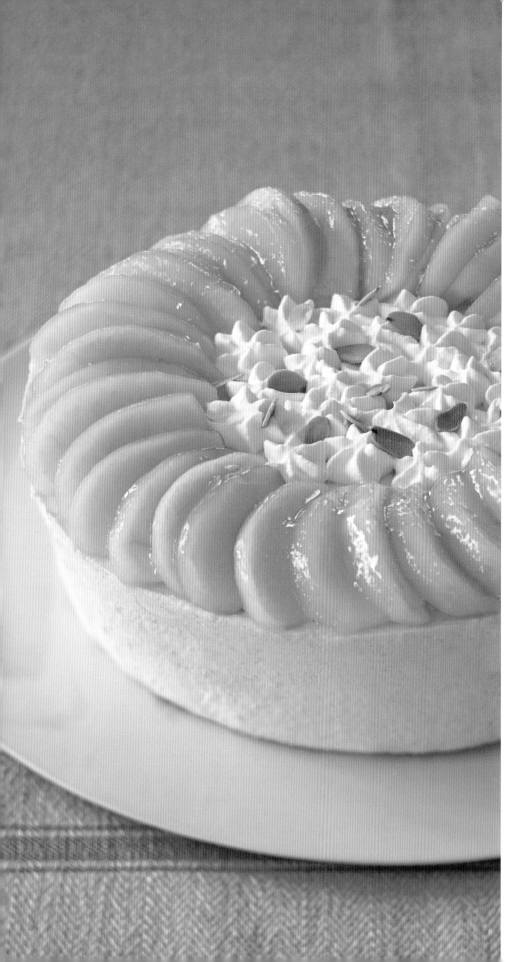

apple & calvados bavarian cake

Makes one 10-inch cake, about 16 servings

APPLE PUREE

2½ pounds McIntosh or Golden Delicious apples, peeled, cored, and diced

½ cup water

1 cup sugar

CALVADOS SYRUP

⅓ cup water

¼ cup sugar

¼ cup Calvados

1 teaspoon vanilla extract

POACHED APPLE WEDGES

2 cups dry white wine or cider

½ cup sugar

2 3-inch-long pieces lemon zest

4 large (about 2 pounds) Golden Delicious apples

One 9-inch plain genoise cake layer (page 146), baked and cooled

APPLE BAVARIAN CREAM

2½ cups apple puree, above

¼ cup Calvados

¼ cup poaching liquid from the apple wedges

4½ teaspoons (2 envelopes) unflavored powdered gelatin

2½ cups heavy whipping cream, whipped to a soft peak and refrigerated

APRICOT GLAZE

¾ cup apricot jam

2 tablespoons water

FINISHING

½ cup heavy whipping cream, whipped to a soft peak

2 tablespoons toasted sliced almonds

One 10-inch springform pan and one 12-inch pastry bag fitted with a ½-inch star tip (Ateco #824)

Calvados, or aged French apple brandy, is produced in Normandy, one of the world's great centers of apple cultivation. Sweet, tart, and bitter apples are first pressed and fermented into hard (alcoholic) cider, then the cider is distilled into Calvados that's aged in oak barrels for a minimum of two years, often much longer for premium brands. Two-year-old Calvados is fine for making desserts, as is American applejack, which is made in a similar manner. This cake is for a special fall or winter occasion; it's not only delicious, but beautiful as well. Crowned with a ring of apple wedges poached in white wine and glazed with apricot jam, it's so impressive that everyone will ask you for the recipe. *Plan ahead:* This dessert has a lot of elements, all of which can be prepared in advance. Bake the cake layer and refrigerate it for up to five days. Make the syrup and refrigerate it in a covered jar, and prepare the apple puree several days in advance. Cook the apple wedges the day before and leave them in their syrup, covered, in the refrigerator. You can even assemble the cake in its mold beforehand, but only unmold and decorate it the day you intend to serve it.

1   For the apple puree, combine the apples, water, and sugar in a large saucepan or enameled iron Dutch oven with a tight-fitting lid. Place on medium heat and bring to a boil. Decrease the heat, cover the pan, and let the apples cook, uncovering and stirring occasionally, until they have completely disintegrated. Cool the apples and puree them in a food processor or blender. Pack the apple puree into a plastic container, cover, and refrigerate. Remember to remove the apple puree from the refrigerator 1 to 2 hours before preparing the filling from it.

2   For the syrup, bring the water and sugar to a boil in a small saucepan, stirring occasionally to dissolve the sugar. Pour into a small bowl, cool, and stir in the Calvados and vanilla. Cover and refrigerate if not using on the same day.

3   For the poached apple wedges, combine the wine, sugar, and lemon zest in a wide, shallow sauté pan. Bring to a simmer and remove from the heat. Peel, halve, and core the apples and cut each half into 6 wedges, adding them to the syrup as soon as they are cut. When all the apple wedges are in the pan, jostle them around so that they are in a single layer and add water to cover. Cut a piece of parchment paper the same diameter as the inside of the pan and cut a hole in the center. Press the paper into the liquid so that it is completely submerged and will in turn keep the apple wedges submerged. Bring the liquid to a simmer and cook until the apple wedges are tender when pierced with a fork. Use a slotted spoon to remove them from the hot liquid and cool them on a plate. Refrigerate the leftover liquid in a shallow bowl to cool quickly, then store the apple wedges covered in the cold liquid until you need them. Drain thoroughly on a pan covered with paper towels before finishing the cake.

4   To assemble, cut the genoise layer into 3 layers. Wrap and freeze one of the layers for another use, such as a base for the No-Bake Cheesecake on page 175. Place one of the layers in the bottom of a springform pan and use a brush to sprinkle it with less than half of the Calvados syrup.

5   For the apple Bavarian cream, put the apple puree into a large mixing bowl. Put the Calvados and poaching liquid into a small heat-proof bowl and use a fork to stir in the gelatin. Half fill a small saucepan or sauté pan with water and place over low heat. Once the gelatin has absorbed all the liquid and is wet looking, place the bowl in the water and let the gelatin melt. Once the gelatin has melted, remove the bowl from the hot water. Quickly re-whip the cream. Whisk 1 cup of the apple puree into the dissolved gelatin to cool it and whisk the gelatin mixture into the bowl of apple puree. Quickly use a large rubber spatula to fold in the whipped cream.

6   Pour half the Bavarian cream over the cake layer in the springform pan, spreading it with a medium offset spatula and making sure it also covers the side of the layer. Quickly place the second layer on top and sprinkle on the remaining syrup. Pour the remaining Bavarian cream over the layer and spread smooth. Cover with plastic and refrigerate until set, preferably overnight.

7   To finish the cake, insert a thin paring knife between the side of the cake and the side of the pan and, pressing against the pan, loosen the cake. Unbuckle the side of the pan and lift it off. Use a wide spatula to slide the cake from the springform base to a platter. **>**

8 For the glaze, stir the jam and water together in a small pan and bring to a simmer over low heat. Strain into a bowl, rinse out the pan, and return the glaze in the pan to low heat to reduce slightly, about 5 minutes.

9 Arrange the drained apple wedges around the top edge of the cake and brush them with the apricot glaze. Re-whip the decorating cream and use the pastry bag to pipe a series of stars into the center area of the cake top not covered by the apples. Sprinkle with a few pieces of sliced almonds. Refrigerate until ready to serve.

Serving: Use a sharp knife to cut the cake into wedges. Serve a sparkling cider or slightly fizzy Moscato d'Asti with the cake.

Storage: Wrap and refrigerate leftovers.

variations:

Apricot Bavarian Cake: Really sweet, perfect apricots would make a perfect substitute for the apples. For the top of the cake, poach unpeeled apricot halves and cool them. If the skin slips off easily, remove it; if not, don't be concerned. You'll need about 2 pounds of apricots rinsed and pitted for the puree and a dozen medium apricots to ring the border of the cake. Substitute white rum for the Calvados.

Raspberry or Strawberry Bavarian Cake: Use 1 1/2 pounds fresh or frozen raspberries or 2 1/2 pints strawberries for the puree (rinse and hull strawberries). Use sweetened raspberry liqueur in place of the Calvados for raspberries and 2 tablespoons kirsch for strawberries. For both, use water in place of the poaching liquid. Decorate the top of the cake with perfect berries, uncooked, of course; they don't need to be glazed.

suggestions for pairing cake layers, fillings, and frostings

- Though butter- and oil-based cake layers are richer in general than sponge and meringue layers, they may still pair successfully with rich fillings such as buttercream or ganache, as long as the filling is used with restraint. This is why in the past these types of cake layers were almost always finished with meringue frosting.

- When using a neutral-flavored cake layer such as a plain genoise or a white or yellow cake, choose a filling and frosting that will impart both color and flavor to the finished cake. Vanilla buttercream and plain whipped cream are both excellent fillings, but using them to finish a yellow cake doesn't bring out the best qualities of either.

- The addition of fruit can make a simple presentation more colorful and appealing. Remember that fresh fruit pairs best with pastry cream and whipped cream, which have a texture that better serves as a backdrop than the richness of buttercream or ganache.

- There's nothing wrong with choosing a filling that's different from the frosting. Just remember when preparing the filling and frosting that you'll need only half of the quantities stated in the recipes.

- Liqueurs and brandies make excellent flavorings or adjuncts to flavorings in fillings, frostings, and syrups used for moistening sponge layers. It's better not to mix and match here, and if you're using a particular liqueur or alcohol in one element of the cake, use the same one throughout. No matter which element of the cake it appears in, liqueur should be used with restraint and should have a subtle flavor, and you should never be able to detect the bitterness of alcohol as a result.

- Spreading the outside of a cake smoothly takes a little practice to master. Covering the outside of a cake by adhering toasted sliced almonds, chocolate shavings, or even shredded coconut camouflages any little imperfections in the frosting beneath. Just make sure that whatever you choose to press against the outside of the cake harmonizes with what's inside.

16

baking powder biscuits & scones

Quick breads became popular during the 19th century due to the invention of baking powder. Primitive baking powders caused aeration in doughs by combining an acid, usually cream of tartar, with bicarbonate of soda, a strong alkali. Acids and alkalis throw off carbon dioxide gas in the presence of water, thus causing a leavening somewhat similar to what takes place in a yeast-risen dough. Baking powder biscuits originated in the American South, while scones have a British origin. Each area of the United Kingdom has a particular native version of scones, some of them baked on griddles like pancakes. The biscuits and scones in the chapter are made in a manner very similar to a pastry dough and are easy to prepare in the food processor or by hand.

A   B   C

baking powder biscuits

Biscuits and scones are prepared in a similar manner, though contemporary versions of the latter are quite a bit sweeter. They both require careful handling, but as long as it's cool in the kitchen and you don't over-knead the dough, it's easy to turn out excellent versions of both.

Makes about 12 biscuits, depending on the size of the cutter used

3 cups all-purpose flour (spoon into a dry-measure cup and level off)

2 tablespoons baking powder

1 teaspoon salt

14 tablespoons (1¾ sticks) unsalted butter, cold and cut into 12 pieces

1¼ cups whole milk

2 cookie sheets or jelly-roll pans lined with parchment or foil

Serving: Serve the biscuits in a napkin-lined basket with butter, honey, and your favorite jam or marmalade.

Storage: Biscuits are a little like a soufflé—they have to be served immediately and are less delicate once they've cooled. Leftover biscuits become a little hard, but you can split and lightly toast them instead of throwing them away. Since the biscuits made from this recipe contain a large amount of butter, they reheat more successfully than biscuits normally do. I reheat them in a toaster oven for a couple of minutes on the lowest toaster setting.

1   Set a rack in the middle level of the oven and preheat to 425°F.

2   Combine the flour, baking powder, and salt in the bowl of a food processor fitted with the metal blade and pulse several times to mix.

3   Add the butter and pulse again repeatedly until no visible pieces of butter remain and the mixture is still cool and powdery, but not pasty.

4   Invert to a mixing bowl and carefully remove the blade. Add the milk and use a rubber spatula to scrape upward from the bottom of the bowl and moisten the dough as evenly as possible.

5   Invert the contents of the bowl to a floured work surface (A). Press the dough into a 6- to 7-inch square (B), then fold it in three: Fold the bottom third of the dough closest to you up over the middle third (C), then fold the top third down over that. Press it out again a little longer in the length and repeat the folding into thirds, this time from the short ends (D through F). Press the dough back out into a 6- to 7-inch square (G).

6   Use a 2- to 2½-inch plain round cutter, flouring it before each cut, to cut out the biscuits (H). Cut straight down and don't twist the cutter or the biscuits won't bake straight-sided. Cut them close together to avoid generating too many scraps.

7   Press the scraps together into a rectangle only as wide as your cutter and three times as long. Cut out three more biscuits and discard the remaining scraps

8   Arrange the biscuits about 1 inch apart on the prepared pans. For advance preparation, cover the pans with plastic wrap and chill the biscuits for up to 2 hours before baking, then bake them straight from the refrigerator, without returning them to room temperature. If you intend to prepare the biscuits in advance, preheat the oven only about 20 minutes before baking.

9   Bake the biscuits until they are deep golden and well risen, 15 to 20 minutes. Let the baked biscuits cool for a couple of minutes on the pan before serving.

variations

Buttermilk Biscuits: Substitute buttermilk for the milk, adding ½ teaspoon baking soda to the dry ingredients.

Drop Biscuits: Increase the milk to 1¾ cups. Use a 2-inch-diameter ice cream scoop or a large soup spoon to drop mounds of the dough on the prepared pan and bake immediately as for the biscuits above. Some Southern cooks like to bake these in

D   E   F

G   H

- Biscuit and scone doughs need to be made slightly smoother and a little elastic before being cut, but don't overdo the folding too much or they'll be tough and chewy after baking.

- Biscuit and scone doughs respond well to a gentle patting out to the right thickness. Only use a rolling pin to smooth out the top of the dough if necessary.

- As with all doughs, use pinches of flour on the work surface and on the dough. You can add as many pinches as you need without adding too much flour to the dough. Flouring with handfuls, rather than pinches, will make the dough absorb so much flour it will increase the proportion of flour in the dough and make the results dry after baking.

- Baking powder biscuits are best hot from the oven, but the recipes here can stand to be cooled and filled, or even reheated, without becoming dry.

- Don't twist: Dip your cutter into a small bowl of flour before each cut, then cut straight down without twisting the cutter for attractive straight-sided biscuits that rise well in the oven.

- All the scone recipes included here may be served after cooling; they're the cakey variety and don't need to be served immediately after baking.

a round cake pan, positioning them close together, so they have soft sides when pulled apart after baking. This amount of dough will fill two 8- or 9-inch round pans. You can accomplish the same soft sides by arranging the mounds of dough close together on a cookie sheet, and that way you can make some soft and some crusty biscuits too.

Old-Fashioned Southern Biscuits: Substitute good-quality lard for the butter in the recipe. Don't even think of using vegetable shortening.

Potato or Sweet Potato Biscuits: Bake a large (8- to 12-ounce) baking potato or sweet potato at 400°F until it is tender, about 1 hour. (To minimize last-minute fuss, it's better to do this the day before.) Cool, peel, and coarsely mash the potato. Measure 2/3 cup mashed potato for the recipe. Start by pureeing the potato in a food processor fitted with the metal blade, scraping and pulsing several times. Mix the flour with the baking powder and salt in a bowl and add the dry ingredients and butter to the food-processor bowl at the same time. Resume the recipe at step 3.

Cheese Biscuits: Before adding the butter, add 2/3 cup coarsely grated sharp cheddar, aged Gouda, or Gruyère to the work bowl. Pulse until finely mixed into the dry ingredients before adding the butter. Cheese biscuits are great split and filled with some thick-sliced baked ham.

cream cheese scones

Cream cheese adds a note of richness and some flakiness to these simple scones.

Makes sixteen 2½ x 3-inch triangular scones

3 cups bleached all-purpose flour
(spoon into a dry-measure cup and level off)

¼ cup sugar

1 tablespoon baking powder

¾ teaspoon salt

4 ounces cream cheese, cold and cut into 20 pieces

6 tablespoons unsalted butter, cold and cut into 12 pieces

2 large eggs, cold

⅓ cup milk, cold

Cookie sheet or jelly-roll pan lined with parchment or foil

1 Set a rack in the middle level of the oven and preheat to 425°F.

2 In a bowl, mix the flour, sugar, baking powder, and salt and set aside.

3 Place the cream cheese, butter, and eggs in the bowl of a food processor fitted with the metal blade and pulse 6 to 8 times to combine; the mixture will look a little curdled.

4 Use a thin metal spatula to scrape down the bowl. Add the dry ingredients and milk. Pulse 3 times and scrape again.

5 Pulse 3 more times and invert the dough to a floured work surface. Carefully remove the blade. Fold the dough over on itself several times to make it smoother.

6 Divide the dough into 2 equal pieces and press each piece into a 6-inch disk. Arrange the disks of dough on the prepared pan about 3 inches apart.

7 Use a bench scraper or a large knife to mark each square of dough into 8 triangles, cutting about halfway through .

8 Bake the scones until they are well risen and deep golden, about 15 minutes.

9 Cool the baked scones on the pan for a few minutes, then use a knife to separate them at the marked divisions.

Serving: Serve immediately with jam or marmalade; these don't need any cream or butter.

Storage: These keep better than biscuits because of the tenderness imparted by the sugar and the higher fat content. Wrap and freeze for up to 1 month. Defrost and reheat for 7 to 8 minutes at 375°F and serve immediately.

milk chocolate scones

Reducing the milk and dark chocolates to a powder before adding the remaining dry ingredients eliminates the need to melt the chocolate separately. Orange marmalade, raspberry preserves, or sour cherry jam are great when paired with a chocolate scone like this one.

Makes sixteen 2 ½ x 3-inch triangular scones

3 cups bleached all-purpose flour
(spoon into a dry-measure cup and level off)

1 tablespoon baking powder

½ teaspoon salt

¼ teaspoon ground cinnamon

4 ounces milk chocolate, cut into ¼-inch pieces and chilled for 20 minutes

4 ounces bittersweet (65 to 70% cocoa solids) chocolate, cut into ¼-inch pieces and chilled for 20 minutes

½ cup slivered almonds

4 tablespoons unsalted butter, cold and cut into 12 pieces

1 large egg, cold

1 cup milk, cold

Cookie sheet or jelly-roll pan lined with parchment or foil

1 Set a rack in the middle level of the oven and preheat to 425°F.

2 In a bowl, mix the flour, baking powder, salt, and cinnamon and set aside.

3 Place the chocolate and almonds in the bowl of a food processor fitted with the metal blade and pulse to grind fine. Stop if you see any signs of the chocolate melting.

4 Add the dry ingredients to the work bowl and pulse again to combine. Add the butter and pulse to mix in fine.

5 Quickly whisk the egg and milk together and add to the food-processor bowl.

6 Pulse 3 times and then invert the contents of the bowl to a floured work surface. Carefully remove the blade. Press the dough together and fold it over on itself several times to make it smoother.

7 Divide the dough into 2 equal pieces and press each into a 6-inch disk. Arrange them on the prepared pan about 3 inches apart. ❯

8   Use a bench scraper or a large knife to mark each square of dough into 8 triangles, cutting about halfway through the dough.

9   Bake the scones until they are well risen, firm, and dull rather than shiny, about 15 minutes.

10 Cool the baked scones on the pan for a few minutes, then use a knife to separate them at the marked divisions. Cool them completely on a rack.

Serving: Serve the scones in a napkin-lined basket; they need no accompaniment.

Storage: Use immediately or wrap and freeze for up to 1 month. Defrost and reheat for 7 to 8 minutes at 375°F and serve immediately.

variation

If you'd like to add some chocolate chips, invert the contents of the work bowl to a mixing bowl at the end of step 4, add the chips, use a rubber spatula to quickly mix them through the dry ingredients, and then use the same spatula to mix in the egg and milk mixture by hand.

orange & almond scones

Almond paste adds richness and an elusive flavor to these sweet scones. If you only have marzipan, which has about a third more sugar in it than almond paste, decrease the sugar in the recipe by 2 tablespoons.

Makes sixteen 2½ x 3-inch triangular scones

3 cups bleached all-purpose flour (spoon into a dry-measure cup and level off)

¼ cup sugar

1 tablespoon baking powder

½ teaspoon salt

4 ounces almond paste (or marzipan), cut into ½-inch cubes

6 tablespoons unsalted butter, cold and cut into 12 pieces

1 large egg

²/₃ cup milk

1 tablespoon finely grated orange zest

Egg wash: 1 egg well beaten with a pinch of salt

½ cup whole unblanched almonds, coarsely chopped

Cookie sheet or jelly-roll pan lined with parchment paper or foil

1   Set a rack in the middle level of the oven and preheat to 425°F.

2   Place the flour, sugar, baking powder, and salt in the bowl of a food processor fitted with the metal blade and pulse to mix. Add the almond paste and pulse again until the mixture is powdery looking.

3   Add the butter and pulse again until finely mixed in.

4   In a small bowl, whisk the egg with the milk and orange zest and add to the food-processor bowl. Pulse 3 times and invert the contents of the bowl to a floured work surface. Carefully remove the blade. Press the dough together and fold it over on itself several times to make it smoother.

5   Divide the dough into 2 equal pieces and press each into a 6-inch disk. Arrange them on the prepared pan 3 inches apart.

6   Use a bench scraper or a large knife to mark each square of dough into 8 triangles, cutting about halfway through the dough. Brush the tops with the egg wash and sprinkle with the chopped almonds, then gently press in the almonds.

7   Bake the scones until they are well risen, firm, and deep golden, about 15 minutes.

8   Cool the baked scones on the pan for a few minutes, then use a knife to separate them at the marked divisions. Cool them completely on a rack.

Serving: Serve the scones in a napkin-lined basket; they need no accompaniment.

Storage: Use immediately or wrap and freeze for up to 1 month. Defrost and reheat for 7 to 8 minutes at 375°F and serve immediately.

17
quick breads & muffins

Quick breads, minimally sweet loaves leavened with baking powder, deserve to be more popular again. A mainstay of home baking of the last century, they're now neglected in favor of richer, sweeter cakes. Perfect with a thin spread of cream cheese or butter, quick breads can pass from the I-feel-like-baking-something stage to the table in a little more than an hour. And nothing is better than a homemade muffin. As a veteran of more airport breakfasts than I care to remember, I can attest to the fact that commercially and industrially made muffins often taste as though they've been made with recycled frying oil. Muffins mix up quickly and are ready for the table before you know it. They also freeze beautifully, so you can get them ready in advance for a breakfast or brunch when you might need to be concentrating on cooking or baking other things.

old-fashioned cornbread

Makes one 9-inch round cornbread, about 8 servings

1 cup all-purpose flour (spoon into a dry-measure cup and level off)

1 cup stone-ground white or yellow cornmeal

3 tablespoons sugar

1 tablespoon baking powder

1 teaspoon salt

2 large eggs

¾ cup whole milk

8 tablespoons (1 stick) unsalted butter, melted

One 9 x 2-inch round pan, buttered and the bottom lined with a disk of parchment or buttered wax paper

essential tips for quick breads & muffins

- Easy does it. Overmixing the batter could make the results tough and chewy after baking.

- Check for doneness at the three-quarter point in the baking time; a lean batter doesn't tolerate any overbaking without becoming much too dry.

- For best results, use standard size (½-cup-cavity) muffin pans—not the aluminum-foil reinforced papers, which may flatten out.

- Brush the top of the muffin pan with some butter or grease with vegetable cooking spray. That way, even if the muffins rise over the top of the cavity, they won't stick to the top of the pan.

The only thing to use for cornbread is stone-ground cornmeal. Industrially milled cornmeal that you find in the supermarket has been degerminated. The small sprouting end of the corn kernel has been removed, because it contains some fat and there's a remote possibility that it could make the cornmeal turn rancid. Unfortunately, a lot of flavor is in the corn germ and it's lost after removal. Use either yellow or white cornmeal; they taste exactly the same, but some Southern and New England cooks prefer the white variety.

1 Set a rack in the middle level of the oven and preheat to 400°F.

2 Stir the flour, cornmeal, sugar, baking powder, and salt together in a large bowl.

3 In another bowl, smoothly whisk together the eggs, milk, and melted butter.

4 Add the liquid to the bowl of dry ingredients and use a large rubber spatula to quickly fold everything together. Scrape the batter into the prepared pan and smooth the top.

5 Bake the cornbread until it is well risen and light golden on top, it feels firm in the center, and the point of a paring knife inserted in the center emerges clean, about 25 minutes.

6 Cool in the pan on a rack for 5 minutes, then loosen the cornbread from the side of the pan with a small paring knife if necessary and invert it to another rack. Peel off the paper and replace it with a platter. Invert the whole stack, lift off the rack, and serve immediately.

Serving: Serve warm with butter and honey for breakfast, brunch, or tea.

Storage: Best as soon as it comes out of the oven, leftover cornbread may be reheated or toasted.

variations

Corn Muffins: Bake the batter in a standard muffin pan, lining the cavities with paper cases. Divide the batter evenly among the 12 cavities in the pan and bake as above, for about 20 minutes. These are best immediately after they're baked.

Buttermilk Cornbread: Omit 1 egg and substitute 1 cup buttermilk for the milk. Add ¼ teaspoon baking soda to the dry ingredients.

Savory Cornbread: To serve the cornbread with a meal of Southern-style food (like barbecued ribs or fried chicken), reduce the sugar to 1 tablespoon or omit it entirely. If you're making cornbread for a crowd, double the recipe and bake the cornbread in a 9 x 13 x 2-inch pan—the baking time is approximately the same. Cut the cornbread into 2- or 3-inch squares in the pan and use a wide spatula to lift them out.

Cornbread for Turkey Dressing: When I cook Thanksgiving dinner, I always bake a cornbread dressing alongside the bird. To make the cornbread for that, use the Savory Cornbread variation and add 1 tablespoon each of rubbed sage and poultry seasoning directly to the dry ingredients. Visit my Web site for the dressing recipe.

perfect banana walnut bread

Makes one 9 x 5 x 4-inch loaf, about 16 slices

2⅓ cups all-purpose flour (spoon into a dry-measure cup and level off)

¾ cup sugar

2½ teaspoons baking powder

½ teaspoon salt

2 large eggs

1½ cups mashed bananas (use a potato masher or a fork), about 3 medium

8 tablespoons (1 stick) unsalted butter, melted

2 teaspoons vanilla extract

1 cup walnut pieces, coarsely chopped and tossed with 1 tablespoon flour

One 9 x 5 x 3-inch (7-cup) loaf pan, buttered and the bottom lined with a parchment or buttered wax paper

There are only two secrets to making perfect banana bread: Use very ripe bananas with spotted or darkened skin and measure the quantity of mashed banana. All too often, home bakers mash a couple of bananas and just throw the resulting quantity into a batter—and usually it's either too much or too little. I like to add some chopped walnuts for texture; you could add raisins, currants, or even shredded sweetened coconut.

1   Set a rack in the middle level of the oven and preheat to 350°F.

2   In a large mixing bowl, stir together the flour, sugar, baking powder, and salt.

3   In another bowl whisk the eggs to break them up, then whisk in the bananas, butter, and vanilla one at a time, whisking smooth between additions.

4   Pour the liquids into the bowl of dry ingredients and use a large rubber spatula to fold them in. Fold in the floured walnuts.

5   Scrape the batter into the prepared pan and smooth the top.

6   Bake the bread until it is well risen and golden in color and the point of a paring knife inserted in the center emerges clean, 55 to 60 minutes.

7   Cool in the pan on a rack for 10 minutes, then unmold, remove the paper, and cool the loaf right side up.

Serving: Serve the bread plain with tea or coffee, or add a little butter or cream cheese.

Storage: Wrap the loaf in plastic after it has cooled completely and store it that way. For advance preparation, double wrap and freeze, then unwrap and bring to room temperature before serving.

lemon coconut tea bread

Makes one 9 x 5 x 4-inch loaf, about 16 slices

2 cups all-purpose flour (spoon into a dry-measure cup and level off)

⅔ cup sugar

2½ teaspoons baking powder

½ teaspoon salt

1⅔ cups unsweetened finely shredded coconut

2 large eggs

½ cup milk

6 tablespoons unsalted butter, melted

2 tablespoons lemon juice, strained before measuring

1 tablespoon finely grated lemon zest

One 9 x 5 x 3-inch (7-cup) loaf pan, buttered and the bottom lined with parchment or buttered wax paper

Unsweetened finely shredded coconut imparts both sweetness and richness to this easy quick bread. If you can only find sweetened coconut in large shreds, reduce the sugar in the recipe by 2 tablespoons and pulse the coconut in the food processor to make it finer.

1   Set a rack in the middle level of the oven and preheat to 350°F.

2   In a large bowl, stir together the flour, sugar, baking powder, salt, and coconut.

3   In another bowl, whisk the eggs to break them up, then whisk in the milk, butter, lemon juice, and zest one at a time, whisking to combine between additions.

4   Pour the liquids into the bowl of dry ingredients and use a large rubber spatula to fold them in.

5   Scrape the batter into the prepared pan and smooth the top.

6   Bake the bread until it is well risen and golden in color and the point of a paring knife inserted in the center emerges clean, 55 to 60 minutes.

7   Cool the pan on a rack for 10 minutes, then unmold, remove the paper, and cool the loaf right side up.

Storage: Wrap the loaf in plastic after it has cooled and store it that way. For advance preparation, double wrap and freeze, then bring to room temperature before serving.

molasses gingerbread

Makes one 9-inch round gingerbread,
about 8 servings

2 cups all-purpose flour (spoon into
a dry-measure cup and level off)

2 teaspoons ground ginger

½ teaspoon ground cinnamon

¼ teaspoon ground cloves

8 tablespoons (1 stick) unsalted butter,
cut into 8 pieces

⅔ cup dark brown sugar, firmly packed

¼ cup molasses

1 cup water

1 teaspoon baking soda

One 9 x 2-inch round pan, buttered and
the bottom lined with parchment or
buttered wax paper

Gingerbread's long history pretty much concludes in the British Isles, where it is a standard. This is an adaptation of a 1940s British recipe. As soon as spices became commonly available in Europe in the late Middle Ages, all sorts of spiced honey cakes, the most common example of which is probably the *Lebkuchen* of German-speaking countries, began to appear. Gingerbread is both a descendant and a variation of those kinds of cakes, most of which are more like what we would call cookies. This type of gingerbread is about 1½ inches thick after baking, and it certainly qualifies a little bit more as a cake than a bread due to its sweetness. You can masquerade it as a dessert by serving some whipped cream with it, or you can serve it with butter for breakfast or brunch.

1　Set a rack in the middle level of the oven and preheat to 350°F.

2　Stir the flour and spices together in a large bowl.

3　Melt the butter in a medium saucepan over low heat, then (still on low heat) stir in the brown sugar, molasses, and most of the water, leaving a couple of tablespoons in the measuring cup. Stir together to combine and increase the heat to medium. Bring to a simmer, stirring occasionally.

4　Stir the baking soda into the remaining water. Remove the butter mixture from the heat and pour the baking soda mixture into it.

5　Add the liquid to the bowl of dry ingredients and use a large rubber spatula to quickly fold everything together.

6　Scrape the batter into the prepared pan and smooth the top.

7　Bake the gingerbread until it is well risen and feels firm in the center and the point of a paring knife inserted in the center emerges clean, 25 to 30 minutes.

8　Cool in the pan on a rack for 5 minutes, then loosen the gingerbread from the side of the pan with a small paring knife if necessary, and invert it to another rack. Peel off the paper and replace it with a rack, then invert the stack and remove the top rack. Cool completely before serving.

Serving: Serve gingerbread for breakfast, brunch, or tea.

Storage: This is a good keeper well wrapped at room temperature.

all-purpose muffins

I love a recipe, like this one, that can be varied in infinite ways. Here the basic muffin batter can be altered to make a dozen different types of easy-to-prepare muffins. Thanks to my dear friend Cara Tannenbaum for sharing her recipe. The recipe that follows is the basis for making muffins with the flavorings and other enhancements listed in the variations below it; this recipe is not meant to be made plain.

Makes 12 standard-size muffins

2 cups all-purpose flour (spoon into a dry-measure cup and level off)

½ cup sugar

1 tablespoon baking powder

¼ teaspoon salt

8 tablespoons (1 stick) unsalted butter, melted and slightly cooled

1 large egg

1 cup milk

Other ingredients as per the variations below

One 12-cavity, standard-size muffin pan with paper liners

1 Set a rack in the middle level of the oven and preheat to 375°F.

2 In a medium bowl, mix the flour, sugar, baking powder, and salt and set aside.

3 Pour the butter into a mixing bowl (scrape out the pan with a rubber spatula) and thoroughly whisk in the egg; whisk in the milk.

4 Whisk about one third of the flour mixture into the liquid until the liquid is absorbed. Whisk in another third, again until the liquid is absorbed. Use a rubber spatula to fold in the last of the flour mixture.

5 Gently fold in any solid enhancements to the batter and distribute the batter into the muffin pan.

6 Bake the muffins until they are well risen and golden and the point of a knife inserted in the center of one emerges dry, about 20 minutes.

7 Cool the muffins in the pan on a rack and lift them out only after they have cooled completely.

Serving: This style of sweet, cake-like muffin needs no accompaniments.

Storage: Wrap the muffins individually in plastic wrap and freeze after the day they're baked. Defrost and bring to room temperature before serving.

variations

Blueberry Muffins: Add 1 teaspoon grated lemon zest to the liquids. After mixing the batter, fold in 1 ½ cups rinsed, dried, and picked-over blueberries. Sprinkle the tops of the muffins with 2 tablespoons sugar mixed with ¼ teaspoon ground cinnamon right before baking.

Lemon Poppy Seed Muffins: Add 2 tablespoons poppy seeds to the flour mixture, and add 1 tablespoon of finely grated lemon zest to the liquids.

Apple Raisin Muffins: Peel 1 large (8-ounce) Golden Delicious apple and grate it on the largest holes of a box grater. Turn the shreds into a strainer and place the strainer over a bowl to drain. Press plastic wrap against the surface of the apple so that it doesn't darken too much. Add ½ teaspoon ground cinnamon to the dry ingredients. After mixing the batter, fold in the grated apple along with ¾ cup dark raisins. Sprinkle the tops of the muffins before baking with cinnamon sugar as in Blueberry Muffins, above.

Chocolate Chip Muffins: Add 2 teaspoons vanilla extract to the liquids. After mixing the batter, fold in one 6-ounce (1-cup) package milk, semisweet, or bittersweet chocolate chips. Sprinkle the tops of the muffins before baking with 2 tablespoons unflavored sugar.

Old-Fashioned Jam Muffins: Add 2 teaspoons vanilla extract and 2 teaspoons finely grated lemon zest to the liquids. Half fill the cavities in the muffin pans and drop 1 (measuring) teaspoon of your favorite jam or preserves in the center of the batter. Add the rest of the batter, being careful to cover the jam completely.

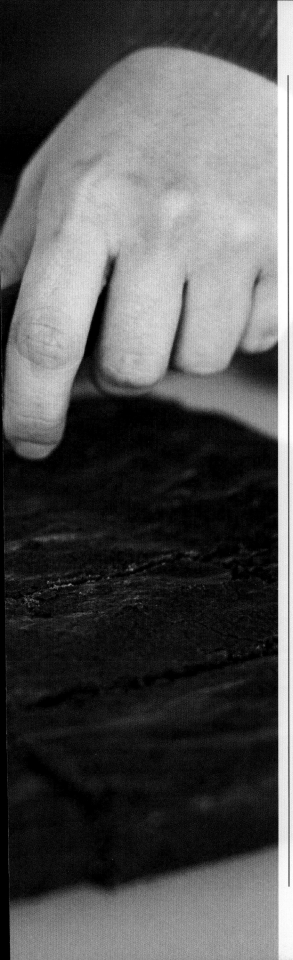

18

bar cookies &brownies

If you ever have to make a lot of cookies in a hurry, turn to bar cookies, a slab of baked cookie dough, often with a topping or filling, that's easy to cut into squares—and even very small squares if you really need to stretch the quantity. Bar cookies are great for rounding out the holiday cookie assortment, too: You can wrap and freeze the whole slab and then cut them after they're defrosted. Brownies are the quintessential bar cookie—a square of moist, fudgy indulgence that has you wondering by the time you're halfway through one whether you're eating a bar cookie or a candy bar. Some people like cakey brownies, I consider them totally inedible; a brownie is all about chocolate and richness, and that's good enough for me.

A   B   C   D   E

golden almond bars

I know I say it about far too many recipes, but these are a real favorite. In fact, I seldom bake them much in advance of serving them because I can't be trusted around them—they are that addictively good. This is loosely based on a recipe shared by my old friend Jayne Sutton, who's been attending my classes for over thirty years. Light toasting brings out the flavor in almonds. Just be careful to toast them very lightly; they'll be in the oven again and will continue to toast then.

Makes 24 square cookies

1 batch Sweet Pastry Dough (page 14), chilled

ALMOND TOPPING

10 tablespoons (1¼ sticks) unsalted butter

⅓ cup granulated sugar

⅓ cup light brown sugar

3 tablespoons dark corn syrup or golden syrup

⅛ teaspoon salt

¼ cup heavy whipping cream

3½ cups slivered almonds, lightly toasted

One 9 x 13 x 2-inch pan lined with buttered parchment paper

variations

Pecan pieces, crushed skinned hazelnuts, or coarsely chopped honey-roasted peanuts are all wonderful in place of the almonds. I once made a batch of these bars with odds and ends of nuts I had in the freezer and they were delicious. Whatever type of nut or combination you choose, just make sure they are in ½- to ¼-inch pieces or they won't cover the dough evenly enough.

1 Place the dough on a floured surface and gently knead it until it is pliable and slightly softened. Form the dough into a rectangle and flour the work surface and the dough again. Roll the dough, occasionally adding pinches of flour under and on it, to a 12 x 16-inch rectangle. Gently fold the dough into quarters and line up the folded corner with the center of the pan. Unfold the dough into the pan and gently ease it down into the pan. Use your fingertips to make sure that the dough molds to the angle between the bottom and side of the pan and into the corners. Trim away all but about 1½ inches of dough on the sides of the pan. Chill.

2 For the topping, melt the butter in a large saucepan over medium heat. Stir in the sugar, brown sugar, and corn syrup one at a time, stirring to combine between additions. Add the salt and bring the mixture to a full boil, stirring occasionally. At the boil, add the cream a little at a time (the mixture will bubble up). Continue cooking for 1 minute, stirring frequently. Most of the water in the cream should evaporate. Stir in the almonds and scrape the mixture into a buttered bowl to cool slightly.

3 Set a rack in the lower third of the oven; preheat to 350°F.

4 Use a large kitchen spoon to deposit mounds of the topping all over the chilled crust. Then use the point of a spoon to join the mounds and make a fairly even layer of topping. Concentrate on distributing the almonds evenly; the syrupy part of the topping will come to a boil while the bars are baking and even itself out.

5 Bake until the dough is baked through and the topping is gently bubbling, 25 to 35 minutes.

6 Cool on a rack for at least 1 hour.

7 To unmold and cut the bars, cover the pan with another rack and invert (A). Lift off the pan and peel away the paper (B). Place a cutting board on the back of the bars and invert the whole stack (C). Lift off the top rack. Neatly trim away the sides of the bars (D) and use a ruler to mark (E), then cut, 2-inch squares.

essential tips for bar cookies & brownies

Pastry-Based Bars

- I like to use a 9 x 13 x 2-inch pan for bar cookies. If you want to double any of the recipes in this chapter you can use an 11 x 17 x 1-inch pan, or a standard commercial 12 x 16 x 1-inch half-sheet pan.

- Here's a quick way to line a deep pan with aluminum foil that I learned from Maida Heatter: Tear off a sheet of foil that's equal to the base of the pan plus the sides and mold it over the back of the pan. Invert the pan. The foil, which now has sharp corners, will press into place.

- Always line part of the pan's side to keep toppings from sticking to it or running under the crust.

- Chill bars with a topping before cutting to minimize breakage.

- Always use a really sharp knife and a ruler for cutting; nothing looks worse than a platter of bar cookies that are different sizes.

Brownies and Cakey Bars

- These are best left uncut until shortly before serving because the exposed sides dry out easily. For advance preparation, cut the whole baked slab in half, wrap in plastic, and freeze until needed (the stacked halves take up less room and are less likely to break). Defrost and cut while still cold.

- Dust unglazed bars and brownies with a little confectioners' sugar before serving.

lemon crumb bars

This is possibly the most popular non-brownie bar cookie ever. I wanted to experiment with adding a crumb topping to the tart lemon filling and I love the result, but it does add some extra work. Feel free to omit the crumbs if you're pressed for time.

Makes 24 squares

1 batch Sweet Pastry Dough (page 14), chilled

CRUMB TOPPING

1¼ cups all-purpose flour (spoon into a dry-measure cup and level off)

½ cup sugar

1 teaspoon baking powder

Pinch of salt

8 tablespoons (1 stick) unsalted butter, melted

LEMON TOPPING

3 large eggs

1 tablespoon finely grated lemon zest

4 tablespoons fresh lemon juice, strained before measuring

1¼ cups sugar

One 9 x 13 x 2-inch pan lined with buttered foil for the bars and one jelly-roll pan lined with parchment paper or foil for baking the crumb topping

1 Set racks in the upper and lower thirds of the oven and preheat to 350°F.

2 Line the pan with the dough as in the recipe for Golden Almond Bars on page 194. Cut away all but ½ inch of the dough on the sides of the pan. Chill the crust while preparing the crumb topping.

3 For the topping, in a medium mixing bowl, stir together the flour, sugar, baking powder, and salt. Use a rubber spatula to stir in the butter. Let the mixture stand for a few minutes, then use your fingertips to break the mixture into ¼- to ½-inch crumbs. Scatter the crumbs on the prepared pan.

4 Press a rectangular sheet of parchment paper into the crust and weigh down with dried beans. (See page 29 for more on blind baking a crust.)

5 Bake the crust in the lower third of the oven and the crumb topping in the upper third. After 10 minutes, remove the paper and beans from the crust and place it on the upper rack and the crumbs on the lower one.

6 Continue baking the crust until it is dry and light golden, about another 5 minutes. Bake the crumb topping until it is deep golden and firm, 10 to 15 additional minutes.

7 Cool the crust and the topping on racks. If the crumbs have grown together during baking, let them cool completely and then use a bench scraper or table knife to coarsely chop them.

8 Reset the rack to the middle level of the oven.

9 For the lemon topping, whisk the eggs and lemon zest in a mixing bowl. In a small bowl, stir the lemon juice and sugar together to dissolve the sugar as much as possible. Add the juice mixture to the egg mixture and use a rubber spatula to gently stir them together.

10 Pour the lemon topping into the crust and bake until the topping is set, 15 to 20 minutes.

11 Remove the pan from the oven and scatter on the crumb topping. Bake another 5 minutes.

12 Cool the bars on a rack in the pan for 15 minutes. If you have someone to help you do this, each lift 2 corners of the foil on the wide ends of the pan and quickly transfer the bars to a cutting board; let them cool completely. Then use a ruler to mark, then cut the bars into 2-inch squares. If you're on your own, let the bars cool completely in the pan and mark and cut them there, then lift them out with a wide spatula.

Serving: Arrange the bars on a platter to serve; these aren't good to stack up because of the soft lemon filling.

Storage: Store in a tin or plastic container with a tight-fitting lid. They don't need to be refrigerated because the acidity of the lemon juice prevents the eggs from spoiling.

lemon ginger bars

Makes 24 bars—see page 198 for photo

GINGER BARS

2½ cups all-purpose flour (spoon into a dry-measure cup and level off)

¾ cup sugar

2 tablespoons ground ginger

2 teaspoons baking powder

8 ounces (2 sticks) unsalted butter

1 large egg, lightly beaten

¼ cup finely chopped crystallized ginger

2 tablespoons honey

2 teaspoons finely grated lemon zest

LEMON GLAZE

2 cups confectioners' sugar, sifted after measuring

3 tablespoons lemon juice, strained before measuring

One 9 x 13 x 2-inch pan lined with buttered foil

These are about as gingery as you can get, so consider yourself forewarned if you're not a ginger lover. Actually these bar cookies make a lot of converts to the pleasures of ginger, because they have a strong ginger flavor but, since they're made with dried ground ginger and crystallized ginger, they have little of the burning spiciness that fresh ginger can impart. Lemon zest in the bars and lemon juice in the glaze add a note of contrast.

1 Set a rack in the middle level of the oven and preheat to 375°F.

2 Mix the flour, sugar, ground ginger, and baking powder in a medium bowl.

3 Melt the butter over medium heat and immediately add to the dry ingredients; use a large rubber spatula to stir to a smooth, shiny dough. Add the egg, crystallized ginger, honey, and lemon zest and beat vigorously to make a smooth dough.

4 Scrape the dough into the prepared pan and use the palm of your hand to press it evenly over the bottom of the pan. Don't be concerned if the dough looks greasy, as though some of the butter has separated out.

5 Bake the bars until well risen, firm, and lightly golden, 20 to 25 minutes.

6 While the bars are baking, use a small rubber spatula to beat the confectioners' sugar and lemon juice together. If it's too thick to spread, thin by adding ½ teaspoon water at a time until it's right.

7 As soon as the bars are baked, place a cutting board on the pan and use oven mitts to invert the hot bars to the board. Remove the pan and foil and replace with another board. Turn right side up and remove the top board. Immediately brush the lemon glaze on the bars so that it sets as the bars cool.

8 Use a ruler to mark, then cut 2-inch squares.

Serving: Arrange the bars on a platter; the icing is dry, so they can be stacked.

Storage: Keep the bars in a tin or plastic container with a tight-fitting lid between sheets of wax paper.

florida brownies

This is my take on a famous Maida Heatter recipe called Palm Beach Brownies. Once when we taught a class together Maida added a layer of miniature chocolate mint patties between two halves of this batter. I cringed when I saw her do it, but I have to admit they were delicious.

Makes 24 square brownies

8 ounces (2 sticks) unsalted butter

8 ounces premium unsweetened chocolate, cut into ¼-inch pieces

5 large eggs, at room temperature

1 tablespoon vanilla extract

¼ teaspoon salt

3¾ cups sugar

1⅔ cups all-purpose flour (spoon into a dry-measure cup and level off)

One 9 x 13 x 2-inch pan lined with buttered foil

1 Set a rack in the middle level of the oven and preheat to 375°F.

2 Melt the butter in a medium saucepan over medium heat. Let the butter get hot and start to sizzle after it's melted. Remove the pan from the heat and add the chocolate all at once. Gently shake the pan to submerge all the chocolate in the butter. Set aside.

3 Combine the eggs, vanilla, and salt in the bowl of an electric mixer fitted with the whisk attachment. First whisk by hand to mix. Whisk in the sugar by hand.

4 Whip on medium-high speed for 10 minutes, until very light.

5   Whisk the butter and chocolate smooth and scrape into the mixer bowl. Whip on lowest speed just until smooth, then stop the mixer.

6   Sift the flour onto a piece of paper, bend the paper, and slide the flour into the bowl. Mix again on lowest speed until the flour is absorbed—no longer.

7   Remove the bowl from the mixer and use a large rubber spatula to give a final mixing to the batter.

8   Scrape the batter into the prepared pan and smooth the top.

9   Bake the brownies until they are firm, but not dry, and the point of a paring knife inserted in the center of the pan emerges with moist crumbs clinging to it, about 35 minutes.

10 Cool in a pan on a rack. Unmold the brownies to a cutting board and remove the pan and paper. Cover with another board and invert the whole stack. Remove the top board and wrap the brownies on their board in a double thickness of plastic wrap. Keep the brownies at a cool room temperature or in the refrigerator overnight before cutting. Use a ruler to mark, then cut the brownies into 2-inch squares.

Serving: Pile the brownies on a platter to serve.

Storage: If you don't intend to serve the brownies all at once, only cut what you need; the whole slab will keep better wrapped in the refrigerator. Individual brownies tend to dry out quickly if they're not wrapped in plastic.

truffle brownies

These are so named because they're almost as rich as chocolate truffles. They are best cut the day after being baked so they have time to firm up.

Makes 24 square brownies—see photo opposite

8 ounces (2 sticks) unsalted butter

10 ounces bittersweet chocolate (65 to 70% cocoa solids), cut into ¼-inch pieces

2 cups light brown sugar, firmly packed

1 cup all-purpose flour (spoon into a dry-measure cup and level off)

¼ teaspoon salt

4 large eggs

2 teaspoons vanilla extract

One 9 x 13 x 2-inch pan lined with buttered parchment paper or foil

1   Set a rack in the middle level of the oven; preheat to 350°F.

2   Melt the butter in a medium saucepan over medium heat. Let the butter get hot and start to sizzle after it's melted. Add the chocolate all at once and gently shake the pan to submerge all the chocolate in the butter. Set aside.

3   Combine the brown sugar, flour, and salt in the bowl of an electric mixer fitted with the paddle. Beat with the paddle on lowest speed until evenly mixed together.

4   Add 2 eggs to the mixer and continue to beat just until they are absorbed. Stop and scrape the bowl and beater. Repeat with the remaining 2 eggs.

5   Remove the bowl from the mixer and stir in the vanilla.

6   Whisk the butter and chocolate smooth and scrape it into the bowl. Use a large rubber spatula to mix it in thoroughly.

7   Scrape the batter into the prepared pan and smooth the top.

8   Bake the brownies until they are firm, but not dry, and the point of a paring knife inserted in the center of the pan emerges with moist crumbs clinging to it, about 30 minutes.

9   Cool in a pan on a rack. Invert the brownies to a cutting board and remove the pan and paper. Cover with another board and invert the whole stack. Remove the top board and wrap the brownies on their board in a double thickness of plastic wrap. Keep the brownies at a cool room temperature or in the refrigerator overnight before cutting.

10 Using a ruler, cut the brownies into 2-inch squares.

variations

Walnut Crunch Brownies: Place 1¼ cups coarsely chopped walnut pieces in a bowl. Whisk an egg white until it's just beginning to foam and add 2 teaspoons to the bowl. Rub the walnuts between the palms of your hands to coat them all over with the egg white. Use a large rubber spatula to toss the moistened walnuts with ⅓ cup sugar. Scatter the walnut crunch on top of the brownie batter before baking. Gently press the walnuts in with the palm of your hand. Bake, cool, and cut.

Walnut or Pecan Brownies: Fold 2 cups coarsely chopped walnut or pecan pieces into the batter right before scraping it into the pan.

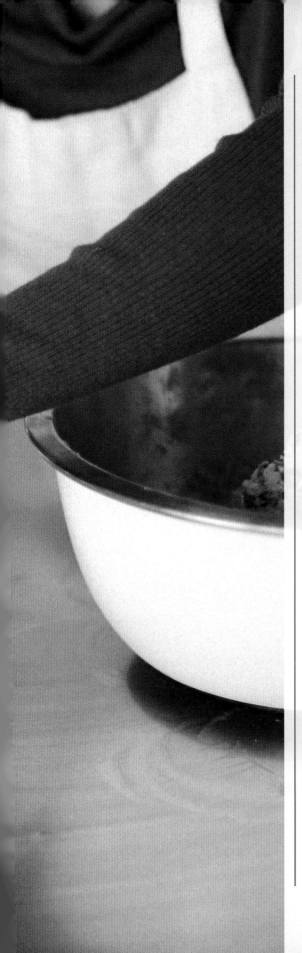

19

piped & drop cookies

Drop cookies are among the simplest to prepare. As their name implies, you just drop the dough from a spoon onto a pan and you're finished shaping. Piped cookies take the method a small step further and drop the dough onto the pan through a plain or decorative tip fitted in a pastry bag. Piping cookies isn't difficult, but like any new technique, it takes a bit of practice to master. Besides the information and photos here, we have a video about piping on my Web site, www.nickmalgieri.com, so you can easily see the steps and motions involved.

butter rosettes

Makes about 30 to 40 cookies, depending on the size you pipe them

8 ounces (2 sticks) unsalted butter, very soft

⅓ cup sugar

2 teaspoons vanilla extract

1 large egg

2¼ cups all-purpose flour (spoon into a dry-measure cup and level off)

2 cookie sheets or jelly-roll pans lined with parchment paper or foil

These are fragile and buttery and easy to pipe because the dough is rather firm. The dough is also fine for putting through a cookie press if you have one. These cookies don't need to be finished off with anything before or after baking, but there are a few suggestions after the recipe if you're so inclined.

1 Set racks in the upper and lower thirds of the oven and preheat to 350°F.

2 Combine the butter, sugar, and vanilla extract in the bowl of an electric mixer fitted with the paddle attachment. Beat on medium speed until just combined.

3 Stop the mixer, add the egg, and scrape down the bowl and beater. Beat again on medium speed until smooth.

4 Stop and scrape again, then beat in the flour on lowest speed. Remove the bowl from the mixer and use a large rubber spatula to give a final mixing to the dough.

5 Pipe the dough (full instructions at right) onto the prepared pans using a ½-inch star tip (Ateco #824), leaving about 1 inch between the cookies in all directions.

6 Bake the cookies until they are light golden, 10 to 12 minutes. The best test for doneness is to turn one of the cookies upside down: If it's light golden on the bottom too, they're ready. Since the baking time is so short, it's not necessary to change racks midway through baking, but stack 2 pans together for the bottom rack if you know your oven gives strong bottom heat to prevent the cookies from burning.

Storage: Keep the cookies between sheets of wax paper in a tin or plastic container with a tight-fitting lid. These last well for a week or so, after which the buttery flavor starts to go stale. Freeze for longer storage.

variations

Very lightly dust the outside of the cookies with cocoa powder before baking.

Sprinkle the tops of the cookies with some crushed sliced almonds or plain or multicolored chocolate sprinkles.

Place a chocolate chip flat side up or a quarter of a candied cherry in the center of each.

Use a floured fingertip to make a small cavity in the center of each cookie, bake, and cool. Carefully spoon in some strained reduced raspberry or apricot preserves (see page 118) after the cookies have cooled.

> ESSENTIAL TECHNIQUE
piping cookies

1. Piped cookies are formed using a pastry bag with a metal tip. Fold back the cuff of the bag and spoon a third of the dough into the bag (A). It can be useful to place the bag in a jar or glass to hold it steady. Twist the bag above the dough to force the dough down toward the tip. You want the dough to be a single smooth mass so that it will pipe neatly.

2. Hold the bag directly behind the dough with the hand you use to write. Press your other index finger against the side of the bag to steady and guide it. Use your writing hand to squeeze the bag and force the dough through the tip.

3. For most shapes, you will be holding the tip perpendicular to the surface and about 1 inch above it. To pipe a rosette, start with the tube only about 1/4 inch above the pan and at a 60-degree angle. Begin squeezing, and when the dough touches the pan, keep the pressure steady and curl around to the left as if writing a cursive letter C (B). Once you've completed the movement, stop squeezing and pull away parallel to the pan instead of lifting the bag straight up, which would leave a point.

4. If using a nylon or cloth bag, wash it immediately in hot soapy water when you are finished. Pastry bags can also be cleaned in the top rack of a dishwasher or in a washing machine with other kitchen laundry.

A

B

chocolate meringue "s" cookies

Makes about 40 to 50 cookies, depending on the size they're piped

4 large egg whites

Pinch of salt

1¼ cups sugar

5 ounces bittersweet chocolate (70 to 75% cocoa solids), melted and slightly cooled

2 cookie sheets or jelly-roll pans lined with parchment paper

Storage: Keep the cookies between sheets of wax paper in a tin or plastic container with a tight-fitting lid. They last indefinitely, but will only be moist inside on the day they're baked.

These are a mainstay of almost every pastry shop in Switzerland. These are a sweet cookie, as anything meringue-based tends to be. In the past I always used unsweetened chocolate to make them, but I once accidentally substituted some premium bittersweet chocolate and the cookies were already in the oven before I realized my mistake. Though still sweet (the sugar in the chocolate didn't really make them appreciably sweeter), they had a much more complex flavor because of the superior quality of the chocolate. An S shape is traditional for these, but of course you may pipe them in any shape you wish.

1 Half-fill a saucepan that will fit your mixer bowl with water. Bring the water to a boil over low heat.

2 Place the egg whites in the bowl of an electric mixer and whisk by hand to break them up. Whisk in the salt and sugar.

3 Set the bowl over the pan of water so only a small part of the bottom is submerged and whisk gently to keep the mixture moving so that it doesn't set on the bottom; whisking too vigorously can tighten the mixture and prevent the sugar from melting. Continue whisking until the egg whites are hot (130°F) and the sugar has dissolved. Lift the whisk and let a little of the mixture run over a fingertip to test the temperature and smoothness. While heating the mixture, occasionally scrape the side of the bowl with a rubber spatula to keep sugar from accumulating there.

4 Place the bowl on the mixer and whip with the whisk attachment on medium-high speed until the meringue is very increased in volume and looks like marshmallow, about 3 minutes. Stop whipping when the side of the bowl feels just slightly warm.

5 Use a large rubber spatula to fold the chocolate into the meringue. Be careful not to fold so much that the meringue liquefies from contact with the fat in the chocolate. If there are a few streaks of white remaining, ignore them.

6 Half-fill a pastry bag fitted with a ½-inch star tip (Ateco #824) and pipe the meringue onto the pans in "S" shapes: Hold the bag almost perpendicular to the pan and inclined slightly toward you, with the end of the tube close to the pan. Start to squeeze out an "S" shape; when you come to the end, pull away parallel to the pan, not straight upward, to avoid leaving a point.

7 After piping the cookies, let them dry at room temperature for a couple of hours so they retain their shape better and they form the characteristic "foot" at the bottom (see the photograph on page 205).

8 About 20 minutes before you're ready to bake the cookies, set racks in the upper and lower thirds of the oven and preheat to 350°F.

9 Bake the cookies until they are matte looking but still a little moist within (press one with a fingertip), 8 to 10 minutes. Cool on the pans on racks.

french lemon disks

Makes about 35 to 40 cookies

COOKIE BATTER

8 tablespoons (1 stick) unsalted butter, softened

½ cup sugar

2 teaspoons finely grated lemon zest

1 teaspoon vanilla extract, or ¼ teaspoon seeds scraped from a split vanilla bean

2 large eggs, at room temperature

1 cup all-purpose flour (spoon into a dry-measure cup and level off)

1 batch Lemon Glaze (page 197)

2 cookie sheets or jelly-roll pans lined with parchment paper or foil

The French name for these cookies, *palets des dames*, is one I've always translated as "ladies' disks," not really knowing what the name referred to. After close to forty years of making these cookies, I decided to look up *palet* in a dictionary; I found that it refers to a discus, the flat round object thrown by an athlete. Does the French name mean that ladies throw cookies as a competitive sport? In any case, these are much better when inserted into the mouth than when thrown at a target. Currants are often added to the batter (they distort the shape of the baked cookies) or three are arranged in a little triangle atop each cookie. If you want to add currants in or on, go ahead; you'll need about ⅔ cup for the batch below. If the currants are in the dough, you'll have to spoon it onto the pan neatly rather than pipe it because the currants will clog the tip.

1   Set racks in the upper and lower thirds of the oven and preheat to 350°F.

2   Combine the butter, sugar, lemon zest, and vanilla in the bowl of an electric mixer fitted with the paddle attachment. Beat on medium speed until lightened, 3 to 4 minutes.

3   Add the eggs, one at a time, beating smooth between additions.

4   Scrape down the bowl and beater and beat for an additional 30 seconds. Scrape again and add the flour.

5   Restart the mixer on lowest speed and mix only until the flour is absorbed.

6   Use a large rubber spatula to give a final mixing to the batter. (Add the currants, if using.)

7   Use a pastry bag fitted with a ½-inch plain tip (Ateco #806) to pipe the batter in ¾-inch mounds, keeping them about 2 inches apart all around to allow for spreading.

8   Bake the cookies until they have spread and are golden and firm, about 12 minutes. If your oven gives strong bottom heat, bake the cookies on the lower rack stacked on a second pan for insulation.

9   While the cookies are baking, make the glaze if you haven't already.

10   Immediately after taking the cookies out of the oven, set the pans on racks and brush the glaze over the hot cookies so that it sets as they cool. Let the cookies cool completely.

Serving: These are very good with tea or with a custardy dessert.

Storage: Keep the cooled cookies between sheets of wax paper in a tin or plastic container with a tight-fitting lid.

the original chocolate chip cookie

Makes about 40 cookies

2¼ cups all-purpose flour (spoon into a dry-measure cup and level off)

1 teaspoon baking soda

1 teaspoon salt

8 ounces (2 sticks) unsalted butter, slightly softened (see Note)

¾ cup granulated sugar

¾ cup light brown sugar, firmly packed

1 teaspoon vanilla extract

2 large eggs, at room temperature

2 cups coarsely chopped walnut pieces

1 12-ounce bag semisweet chocolate chips

3 cookie sheets or jelly-roll pans lined with parchment paper or foil

Note: If the butter is too soft, the cookies will spread too flat.

Chocolate chip cookies were first made by a New England dietician, Ruth Wakefield, some time in the late 1920s. Wakefield and her husband were the proprietors of an inn that had originally been a way station between Boston and New Bedford, and that's how both the inn and the cookies came to bear the Toll House name. The story goes that Wakefield added cut-up chunks of chocolate to a brown sugar–based cookie dough, expecting the chocolate to melt into the dough resulting in a chocolate cookie. The rest is history. This is the recipe from Ruth Wakefield's book with two differences: The baking soda is added to the flour and not dissolved in water (as it makes absolutely no difference), and chips are now ready-made, so you don't have to cut up bars of chocolate unless you want to. Chocolate chip cookies are like fried eggs: Everyone has a preferred version. Ruth Wakefield's cookies are fairly thin and crisp; if you like them chewy, bake a couple first as a test. Take them out when they're still soft and slide the paper off the pan to cool them. If they're as chewy as you like, bake the rest for the same amount of time. Chilling the dough first will also help. If you want thicker cookies, add another ⅓ cup flour. Increase the chips, leave out the walnuts, add raisins, or do anything you like as it won't affect the texture. Finally, don't overmix. Beating air into this cookie will make it rise to great heights, then fall into a wrinkled wafer, not unlike a gingersnap.

1 Set racks in the upper and lower thirds of the oven and preheat to 375°F.

2 Stir the flour together with the baking soda and salt; set aside.

3 Combine the butter, granulated sugar, brown sugar, and vanilla in the bowl of an electric mixer fitted with the paddle attachment. Beat on medium speed until just combined. Add the eggs, one at a time, beating smooth between additions.

4 Stop and scrape the bowl and beater and start the mixer again on lowest speed. Beat in the flour mixture. Once absorbed, beat in the walnuts and chocolate chips.

5 Use a large rubber spatula to give a final mixing to the batter and drop it by tablespoon onto the prepared pans, keeping the mounds of dough about 3 inches apart in all directions.

6 Bake the cookies until they are deep golden all over, 12 to 14 minutes. Cool the cookies on the pans on racks.

Storage: Keep the cooled cookies between sheets of wax paper in a tin or an airtight plastic container.

A   B

almond lace
cookies

Makes about 30 cookies

4 tablespoons unsalted butter, very soft

½ cup sugar

1 teaspoon vanilla extract

⅛ teaspoon salt

1 large egg

3 tablespoons all-purpose flour

⅓ cup finely ground blanched almonds

3 cookie sheets or jelly-roll pans,
buttered with soft butter

Fragile and delicate in the extreme, these cookies are a labor of love to make because you need to bake them one pan at a time on the middle rack of the oven. If you have a double oven, start to bake another pan a couple of minutes before the first pan is ready to come out. These spread best on a bare buttered pan; brush the pans with very soft but not melted butter. If you don't mind cookies that are a little thicker, you may use silicone mats to bake them.

1 Set a rack in the middle level of the oven and preheat to 350°F.

2 In a small mixing bowl, use a medium rubber spatula to stir together the butter, sugar, vanilla, and salt. Add the egg and beat until smooth.

3 Add the flour and almonds and stir smooth.

4 To save time, deposit all the batter on the pans right away. Drop level measuring teaspoons of the batter onto the pans at least 3 inches apart in all directions (A). Put 10 to 12 mounds of batter on each pan.

5 Bake one pan of cookies until they have spread, come to a simmer on the pan, and are deep golden in color, 5 to 7 minutes.

6 Remove the pan from the oven and immediately place another pan in to bake.

7 Let the cookies cool for about 20 seconds, then slide a wide thin-bladed spatula under the edge of the cookie closest to you and gently work the spatula back and forth to pry the cookie off the pan and move it to a parchment-covered pan or wire rack to cool (B). Repeat with remaining cookies. Don't get nervous, but you have to do this quickly while the cookies are still warm or they'll shatter when you try to lift them from the pan.

Serving: Plan on serving the cookies the day you bake them; they are too fragile to try to store. These are perfect to accompany any elegant mousse or custard dessert, or serve them with after-dinner coffee.

peanut drops

Makes about 40 cookies

1 cup all-purpose flour (spoon into
a dry-measure cup and level off)

1 teaspoon baking powder

¼ teaspoon salt

10 tablespoons (1¼ sticks) unsalted
butter, softened

⅓ cup granulated sugar

⅓ cup light brown sugar, firmly packed

1 teaspoon vanilla extract

1 large egg, at room temperature

1 cup honey-roasted peanuts, coarsely
chopped, plus more for sprinkling

2 cookie sheets or jelly-roll pans
lined with parchment paper or foil

Honey-roasted peanuts are the secret to the intense flavor of this cookie. Ordinary peanuts just don't do the trick. These are addictively good, though sometimes I'm not sure whether they're really a candy or a cookie. It's always best to purchase a fresh jar of peanuts if you want to prepare these. Unless you store your honey-roasted peanuts in the freezer, they become stale-tasting pretty quickly and would ruin the delicate sweetness of these cookies.

1 Set racks in the upper and lower thirds of the oven and preheat to 375°F.

2 Mix the flour with the baking powder and salt and set aside.

3 Combine the butter, sugars, and vanilla in the bowl of an electric mixer fitted with the paddle attachment. Beat on medium speed until soft and light, 3 to 4 minutes.

4 Beat in the egg and continue beating until smooth.

5 Stop the mixer and scrape down the bowl and beater. Beat on lowest speed and add the flour about a third at a time, beating to incorporate between additions, followed by the cup of chopped peanuts.

6 Use a large rubber spatula to give a final mixing to the batter. Set a small bowl of water near your work surface.

7 Drop the batter by heaping teaspoon onto the prepared pans, keeping them 2 or 3 inches apart in all directions. After all the batter is on the pans, moisten your fingertips and flatten the cookies slightly. Sprinkle the tops with more chopped peanuts.

8 Bake the cookies until they have spread and are deep golden, 12 to 15 minutes. Slide the papers from the pans to racks to cool the cookies.

Storage: Keep the cookies between sheets of wax paper in a tin or plastic container with a tight-fitting lid.

variation

Melt 4 ounces milk chocolate, let it cool, and then sandwich the cookies bottom to bottom with it.

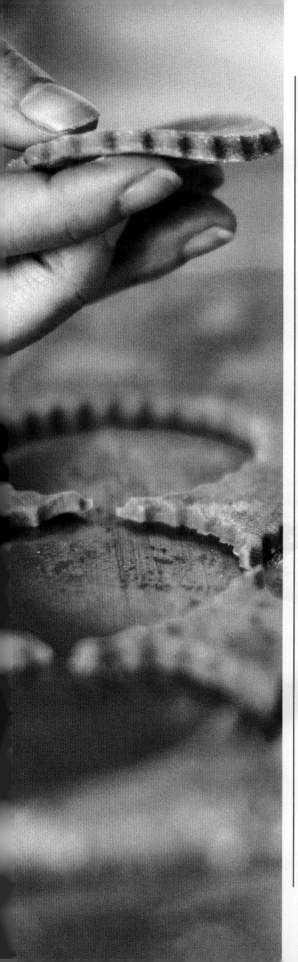

20

rolled &
sandwich
cookies

Nothing can make you look more like an
accomplished baker than a beautiful—and
symmetrical—assortment of rolled cookies.
The little cutter does all the work and we get
to take all the credit. Rolling is even easy, once
you know the essential secret of rolling out soft
doughs: rolling small pieces of dough at a time
so it never gets a chance to soften too much
before you've got those perfectly shaped cookies
safely on your baking pan. Sandwich cookies
are the cookie lover's dream—the politest way
to eat two cookies at the same time without
appearing greedy (well, not too greedy).

A

B

C

crisp brown sugar wafers

All good cookies are addictive, but these are particularly dangerous. As if their shatteringly crisp texture weren't enough, their buttery flavor is accentuated and deepened by brown sugar. Unlike most cutout cookies, these spread quite a bit while they're baking.

Makes about 40 cookies

2¼ cups all-purpose flour (spoon into a dry-measure cup and level off)

½ teaspoon baking soda

¼ teaspoon salt

12 tablespoons (1½ sticks) unsalted butter, softened

1½ cups light brown sugar, firmly packed

2 teaspoons vanilla extract

1 large egg

1 large egg yolk

2 to 3 cookie sheets or jelly-roll pans lined with parchment paper or foil

1 Stir the flour, baking soda, and salt together and set aside.

2 Beat the butter, brown sugar, and vanilla with the paddle attachment of an electric mixer on medium speed until well mixed, about 1 minute. Beat in the egg and yolk one at a time, beating smooth between additions. Scrape the bowl and beater and beat again for 30 seconds.

3 Stop the mixer, add the flour mixture, and beat on lowest speed to incorporate. Remove the bowl and use a large rubber spatula to give a final mixing to the dough.

4 Scrape the dough onto a large piece of plastic wrap, fold the wrap over it, and press the dough to about ½ inch thick. Refrigerate until ready for baking, up to 2 days.

5 When you are ready to bake the cookies, set racks in the upper and lower thirds of the oven and preheat to 350°F.

6 Remove the dough from the refrigerator and cut it into quarters. Return three of the pieces to the refrigerator. Place the piece of dough on a floured work surface and use a rolling pin to press the dough firmly in close parallel strokes (A) until it is slightly softened and malleable.

7 Flour the dough again and gently roll it out to ¼ inch thick (B). Use a 2- to 2 ½-inch round cutter to cut cookies, placing them on one of the prepared pans about 3 inches apart in all directions to allow for spreading (C).

8 Repeat with the next piece of dough, incorporating the scraps from the previous piece as you knead it. Continue cutting out cookies and repeat adding the scraps with the remaining pieces of dough. When you have nothing but scraps left to roll, form the dough into a sausage shape and roll it to a rectangle as wide as the cutter you are using. Discard the last few scraps.

9 Bake the cookies until they are firm and dry looking, 12 to 15 minutes. If your oven gives strong bottom heat, bake the pan of cookies on the lower rack stacked on another pan for insulation.

10 Slide the papers from the pans to racks to cool.

Storage: Keep the cookies between sheets of wax paper in a tin or plastic container with a tight-fitting lid.

Variations: Add ¾ cup blanched almonds, pecans, or honey-roasted peanuts, chopped into ¼-inch pieces, to the dough along with the flour.

essential tips for rolled & sandwich cookies

Rolled Cookies

- Always chill the dough until it's firm. Flattening it to a thin sheet on a piece of plastic wrap before refrigerating it will make it chill more quickly.

- Roll about a third or a quarter of the dough at a time and leave the rest refrigerated; if the dough softens back to its original consistency you won't be able to roll or cut it.

- Before rolling the dough, squeeze and knead it a few times until it has a clay-like consistency but is still cool. If you try to roll the chilled dough directly from the refrigerator it will just break apart.

- Flour under and on the dough with pinches of flour, not handfuls. You can add as many pinches of flour as you like without toughening the dough.

- Roll with gentle pressure; even the chilled dough is relatively soft and it lacks the elasticity of a flaky or puff pastry dough.

- Flour the cutter between cuts and always cut straight down without twisting the cutter.

- Use a wide spatula like a pancake turner to lift the cookies off the work surface and transfer them to the pan.

Sandwich Cookies

- Look over the baked cookies and choose the best-looking ones to be the upper cookie of the sandwiches.

- Invert the others so that the smooth bottom of the cookie is upward and apply the glaze or filling to them.

- If you want to use jam for filling cookies, bring it to a boil and let it reduce to evaporate excess moisture for a couple of minutes or it will soften the cookies.

- Don't overdo the filling or the cookies will turn into a mess. For most cookies, 1/2 teaspoon of filling is the perfect amount.

- When putting the top cookie in place, press gently to make the filling spread to the edge of the bottom cookie.

A   B   C

swiss bull's eyes

The Swiss name for these cookies is *Ochsenaeugli*, or "oxen's eyes." This dough has no eggs in it—it's just a flour-sugar-butter dough that's very fragile after baking. The traditional filling is apricot jam, but use any flavor you like, or even some apricot or prune Danish filling (see page 117). Thanks to my friend Thea Cvijanovich from Berne for this typically Swiss recipe.

Makes about 24 sandwich cookies

COOKIE DOUGH

8 ounces (2 sticks) unsalted butter, softened

1 cup confectioners' sugar, sifted after measuring

Large pinch of salt

2 teaspoons vanilla extract

2⅔ cups all-purpose flour (spoon into a dry-measure cup and level off)

FINISHING

1 cup apricot jam

Confectioners' sugar for sprinkling

2 cookie sheets or jelly-roll pans lined with parchment paper or foil

1   Beat the butter, confectioners' sugar, salt, and vanilla with the paddle attachment of an electric mixer on medium speed until well mixed, about 1 minute. Stop the mixer, add the flour, and beat on the lowest speed. Remove the bowl and use a large rubber spatula to give a final mixing to the dough.

2   Scrape the dough onto a large piece of plastic wrap, fold the wrap over it, and press the dough to about ½ inch thick. Refrigerate for up to 2 days.

3   When you are ready to bake the cookies, set racks in the upper and lower thirds of the oven and preheat to 350°F. Remove the dough from the refrigerator and cut it into thirds. Return two of the pieces to the refrigerator. Place the piece of dough on a floured surface and gently knead it until it is slightly softened and malleable.

4   Flour the dough again and gently roll it out to ³/₁₆ inch thick. Use a 2- to 2½-inch plain cutter to cut cookies, placing them on one of the prepared pans about 3 inches apart in all directions to allow for spreading.

5   Repeat with the next piece of dough, incorporating the scraps from the previous piece. Continue cutting out cookies and adding the scraps. When you have nothing but scraps left to roll, form the dough into a sausage shape and roll it to a rectangle as wide as the cutter. Cut out more cookies and discard the last few scraps.

6   Use a small cutter to make a ½- to ¾-inch hole in the center of half of the cookies. Lift out the cutout pieces of dough and bake them with the cookies if you wish.

7   Bake the cookies until they are firm, dry, and very light golden, 12 to 15 minutes. If your oven gives strong bottom heat, bake the pan of cookies on the lower rack stacked on another pan for insulation.

8   Slide the papers from the pans to racks to cool.

9   Bring the preserves to a boil in a small saucepan over low heat. Strain into a bowl, rinse the pan, and return the jam to the pan. Return to a boil over low heat and cook until thickened, 2 to 3 minutes.

10   Shake a light coat of confectioners' sugar over the cookies with holes in the centers (A). Turn the cookies without holes upside down and spread about ½ teaspoon of the jam on each, immediately covering the jam with one of the cookies with a hole in the center (B and C). After you have sandwiched all the bases, use a ½-teaspoon measure to add more jam to the opening in each cookie.

Storage: These have to be kept in a single layer to avoid marring the confectioners' sugar on them. If you don't serve all the cookies at once, finish off what you need and store the baked bases.

lemon vanilla bean shortbreads

Makes about 24 cookies, depending on the size of the cutter you use

8 ounces (2 sticks) unsalted butter, softened

½ cup sugar

¼ teaspoon salt

2 teaspoons finely grated lemon zest

1 Madagascar Bourbon vanilla bean

2½ cups all-purpose flour (spoon into a dry-measure cup and level off)

2 to 3 cookie sheets or jelly-roll pans lined with parchment paper or foil

A classic Scottish cookie, shortbreads are all about butter. A little bit of lemon zest and the seeds scraped out from the inside of a vanilla bean serve to accentuate the already buttery flavor of these cookies. For a classic shortbread, omit the lemon and vanilla. In both the lemon-vanilla and plain varieties, the delicate caramelized flavor of sugar and butter baked together is predominant and is what makes these simple cookies so good. For best results, do not use any kind of extra high-fat butter to make these or they will be overly fatty, will spread while baking, and will have an unappetizingly greasy texture.

1 Set racks in the upper and lower thirds of the oven and preheat to 325°F.

2 Combine the butter, sugar, salt, and lemon zest in the bowl of an electric mixer fitted with the paddle attachment.

3 Split the vanilla bean lengthwise and scrape out the seeds with the point of a paring knife. Add them to the bowl. Wrap and reserve the remainder of the vanilla bean for another use. (If the vanilla bean is too hard, pulverize a quarter of it with the sugar in a blender, or grate it into the sugar with the tiniest holes of a box grater.)

4 Beat on medium speed until soft and light, about 5 minutes.

5 Remove the bowl from the mixer and use a large rubber spatula to stir in the flour by hand.

6 Scrape the dough to a floured surface and press it into a rough rectangle.

7 Cut off one quarter of the dough, place it on the work surface, and flour on and under it. Gently roll to ¼ inch thick. Use a plain round cutter 2½ to 3 inches in diameter to cut out cookies, placing them on one of the prepared pans about 1 inch apart all around.

8 Incorporate the scraps from the first piece of dough into the next piece before rolling it. Repeat until all the dough and the final scraps have been used.

9 Bake the cookies until they are very pale golden, 20 to 25 minutes. If your oven gives strong bottom heat, bake the pan of cookies on the lower rack stacked on another pan for insulation.

10 Slide the papers from the pans to racks to cool.

Storage: Keep the cookies between sheets of wax paper in a tin or plastic container with a tight-fitting lid. Don't try to store them for more than a few days or the freshness of the butter flavor will be lost.

chocolate raspberry sandwiches

Makes about 24 sandwich cookies, depending on the size of the cutter used

COCOA COOKIE DOUGH

2 cups all-purpose flour (spoon into a dry-measure cup and level off)

⅓ cup alkalized (Dutch process) cocoa powder, sifted through a fine-mesh strainer after measuring

8 ounces (2 sticks) unsalted butter, very soft

½ cup sugar

¼ teaspoon salt

2 teaspoons vanilla extract

RASPBERRY FILLING

¾ cup seedless raspberry jam

2 tablespoons sugar

2 cookie sheets or jelly-roll pans lined with parchment paper or foil

Be sure to use the best cocoa powder you can find for these cookies—I like the Dutch brands Droste, Bensdorp, and Van Houten, but Italian Pernigotti cocoa also has a fine flavor. Thanks for this recipe to my old friend Tim Brennan, who makes them at Cravings, his bakery-café in St. Louis.

1 For the dough, stir the flour and cocoa together and set aside.

2 Combine the butter, sugar, salt, and vanilla in the bowl of an electric mixer. Beat with the paddle on medium speed until lightened, about 5 minutes.

3 Scrape the bowl and beater and restart the mixer on lowest speed. Add the flour mixture in thirds, mixing smooth after each addition.

4 Scrape the dough to a floured surface and squeeze it together into a fat cylinder, then divide it into 4 equal pieces. This dough doesn't need to be chilled before rolling.

5 Set racks in the upper and lower thirds of the oven and preheat to 350°F.

6 Flour one quarter of the dough and gently roll it out to ¼ inch thick. Use a 2- to 2½-inch plain cutter to cut cookies, placing them on one of the prepared pans about 3 inches apart in all directions to allow for spreading.

7 Repeat with the next piece of dough, incorporating the scraps from the previous piece as you knead it. Continue cutting out cookies and repeat adding the scraps with the remaining pieces of dough. When you have nothing but scraps left to roll, form the dough into a sausage shape and roll it to a rectangle as wide as the cutter you are using. Discard the last few scraps.

8 Bake the cookies until they are firm and dry looking, 12 to 15 minutes. If your oven gives strong bottom heat, bake the pan of cookies on the lower rack stacked on another pan for insulation.

9 Slide the papers from the pans to racks to cool.

10 After the cookies have cooled, make the filling by stirring the jam and sugar together in a small saucepan. Bring to a boil over low heat and reduce, stirring occasionally, for 2 minutes.

11 Invert half the cookies so that the flat bottom sides are upward. Top one with a generous ½ measuring teaspoon of the filling and place another cookie on it, flat side down. Repeat with the remaining cookies.

Storage: Keep the cookies between sheets of wax paper in a tin or plastic container with a tight-fitting lid.

ginger lemon sandwich cookies

Makes about 30 sandwich cookies

GINGERSNAP BASES

1½ cups all-purpose flour (spoon into a dry-measure cup and level off)

1½ teaspoons baking soda

¼ teaspoon salt

2 teaspoons ground ginger (see Note)

1 teaspoon ground cinnamon

10 tablespoons (1¼ sticks) unsalted butter, softened

¾ cup sugar

1 large egg, at room temperature

¼ cup molasses

LEMON BUTTER FILLING

6 tablespoons unsalted butter, softened

2 cups confectioners' sugar, sifted after measuring

2 tablespoons lemon juice, strained before measuring

3 cookie sheets or jelly-roll pans lined with parchment or foil

Note: The amount of ginger in the recipe can vary. If your ground ginger is from a freshly opened jar, 2 teaspoons will be enough. If you opened the jar more than a few weeks before baking the cookies, use 3 teaspoons.

This variation on a traditional gingersnap is good on its own or sandwiched with a lemony butter filling as it is here. To add a note of lemon to the cookie bases themselves, grate the zest from a lemon before you squeeze the juice for the filling and add it to the cookie dough. The baking process for gingersnaps is rather odd. The cookie dough spreads and then rises quite a bit, only to fall eventually and become the crisp cookie we recognize as a gingersnap. Sometimes I hasten the process along by opening the oven at the point where the cookies are very risen and lifting the closest side of the pan a couple of inches off the oven rack and then letting it drop back down to encourage the cookies to fall and become crisp.

1 Set racks in the upper and lower thirds of the oven and preheat to 350°F.

2 Mix the flour with the baking soda, salt, and spices; set aside.

3 Combine the butter and sugar in the bowl of an electric mixer fitted with the paddle attachment. Beat on medium speed for 2 minutes, then add the egg. Continue beating until the egg is well absorbed. Use a large rubber spatula to scrape the bowl and beater.

4 On lowest speed, beat in half the flour mixture until it is absorbed. Beat in the molasses and the remaining flour mixture, continuing to beat just until the dough is smooth. Remove the bowl from the mixer and use a large rubber spatula to give a final mixing to the dough.

5 Use a rounded (not heaping) measuring teaspoon to drop small balls of the dough on the prepared pans about 3 inches apart in all directions to allow for spreading.

6 Bake the cookie bases until they have spread and darkened and their surfaces are crackled, 12 to 15 minutes. Halfway through baking, switch the pans from the top rack to the lower one and vice versa, turning the pans back to front at the same time. If your oven gives strong bottom heat, bake the cookies on the lower rack on two pans stacked together.

7 Cool the cookies on the pans on racks; they become crisp as they cool.

8 While the cookies are cooling, prepare the filling. Combine the butter and confectioners' sugar in the bowl of an electric mixer fitted with the paddle attachment. Beat on low speed until smooth, then increase the speed to medium and beat until the filling is fluffy, 3 to 4 additional minutes. Beat in the lemon juice a little at a time, continuing to beat until the filling is soft and smooth.

9 To fill the cookies, flip over half the cooled cookies and spread with 2 teaspoons of the filling. After spreading all the bottoms with the filling, top with another cookie, flat side down, gently pressing them together to adhere.

Storage: Store the cookies between sheets of parchment or wax paper in a tin or plastic container with a tight-fitting lid.

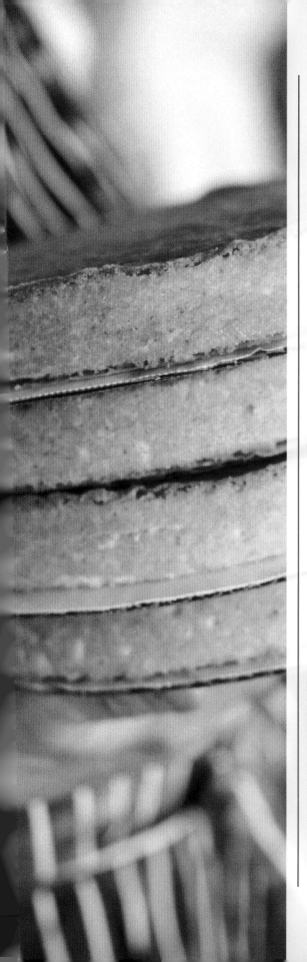

afterword

Much of what we think of as skill in baking depends on accurately executing techniques. In fact, the "essentials" that follow most of the recipes in this book often give the reasons why you're mixing, rolling, or cutting in a specific way that's essential to success. Yet baking is undoubtedly a creative pursuit. If it weren't, we wouldn't be able to enjoy the millions of variations—just think of how many different cheesecakes or brownies exist. The truth is that creativity in baking carries some responsibility with it. You can infinitely vary the flavor of buttercream or the type of fruit you use in a tart, but you really can't do much to alter the way you keep track of the temperatures in your buttercream or how thin you roll your dough. With this in mind, I've added variations where appropriate, though you needn't stop with my suggestions. Take off on your own and remember that creativity in baking, as in all the arts, is governed by experience and a certain degree of restraint. And above all, enjoy the process.

index

acknowledgments

What a pleasure it has been, every step of the way, to work on this, my first effort for Kyle Books. Kyle Cathie welcomed me on board with warmth and grace, and all the hours spent planning and working with my publisher and editor Anja Schmidt have been as enjoyable an experience as I can remember. Of course nothing here would exist without three other important people, my agent, Phyllis Wender, my own freelance editor, Natalie Danford, and Rose Kaplan, who helped test all the recipes. A big thank you to all for your support, kindness, and generosity.

On the production side, thanks are due to designer Dirk Kaufman, photographer Quentin Bacon and his assistant Lauren, prop stylist Roy Finamore, food stylist Liz Duffy, and copy editor Janet McDonald.

At the Institute of Culinary Education in New York, my thanks to owner and president Rick Smilow; career baking program director Andrea Tutunjian; director of purchasing Josh Pappas and all his crew, especially Jaime Olenick; schedule and operations manager Mary Bartolini; and the dozens of other faculty and staff who make it such a pleasure to be there. Thanks also to students Samantha Neal and Ana Borrero who volunteered to help with food preparation for photography, and to the students pictured in the photographs: Joan Ferng, Samantha Neal, Bianca Bianco, Kyle Warendorf, and Justin Wender.

Thanks to friends and colleagues who contributed or inspired recipes: Michael Ayoub, Tim Brennan, Leah Chase, Thea Cvijanovich, Kyra Effren, Maida Heatter, Albert Kumin, Dietmar Muthenthaler, Ann Nurse, Roberto Santibañez, Amy Scherber, Jayne Sutton, Cara Tannenbaum, and Carole Walter. Special thanks to my friend Ciril Hitz, the department chair of the International Baking and Pastry Institute of Johnson & Wales University, for answering my countless questions about bread baking.

And a final thank you to Ron Longe and to all my cooking school friends all over North America for helping to promote the book.